To— Cindy

Love— Chancy Allen

5/16/90

I'M BLACK
& I'M SOBER

I'M BLACK

& I'M SOBER

A Minister's Daughter Tells
Her Story About Fighting the Disease
of Alcoholism – and Winning.

By Chaney Allen

Published by

CompCare®
Publishers

Minneapolis, Minnesota
a Comprehensive Care company

(Ask for our catalog, 800/328-3330, toll free outside Minnesota
or 612/559-4800, Minnesota residents)

This book is dedicated to my oldest brother,
Nelson B. Allen,
who was there when I needed him most.

Acknowledgments

A special thanks to my spouse Maurice for your love and understanding. You make my ups and downs of daily living so much easier. I thank God for you. I also appreciate your support in the promotion of my book this first year.

To my children who saw me at my worst, and still have hearts big enough to say, "We love and respect you, Mother."
Edward L. Mayfield
Vivian Allen
Lynell Allen, Jr.
In Memory
Rev. B.H. Allen, my father
Mrs. Ardellar Allen, my mother
Bradford Allen, Sr., my brother
Bradford Allen, Jr., my nephew
To my brothers
Roy Lee Allen
Lynell Allen, Sr. (Lee)
Henry B. Allen

Katie McClure
Ella B. Johnson
Jessie Stallsworth
Corine Allen
Knoxie Mathis
Dianne Miller
To all my friends, grandchildren, nieces, nephews and all members of my family.

More Acknowledgments

Christian Methodist Church (CME) which bent the sapling while I was young, with my parents' help.

A very, very special thank you to Josephine and Kenneth Swift, authors of O.U.R. series books, for all the endless hours freely spent helping me. May God bless you with your fifteenth book. Your kindness will never be forgotten. I will always remain your grateful friend.

Thanks to Burt Swaim for choosing me to represent the Black woman in his film, *New Beginnings: Women, Alcohol and Recovery.*

Author's Note

Since there are so many alcoholics who still suffer (especially my Black Sisters and Brothers), I had to tell it like it was. I realize that my book is the first autobiography written by a Black alcoholic woman, but we Blacks must start documenting somewhere, sometime, in order to help others. As long as we don't come forward and say we are hurting, society will think we are satisfied being drunks.

Writing this book has been one of the most painful experiences in my life, both mentally and physically. Many things had been buried in my mind for years, but they had to be brought to the surface and I was forced to really face them. Many times I stopped writing because my eyes were blinded with tears, my breath was short, and I had broken out in cold sweats. Some experiences were so humiliating I had to debate with myself whether or not to write them down. *It wasn't easy* for me to bare myself to the world. I felt like I was walking the streets in the nude. But a quitter never wins and a winner never quits.

I kept, as a rule, my Black dialect, because I realize the importance of identification for my people, who need to read material that they can relate to. This is one helpful tool minorities need *now*. Another is alcoholism programs which are open seven days a week with twenty-four hour services. Usually our heavy drinking is done at night and on weekends — when AA and most alcoholism programs are closed. Certain people will not come to the ghetto to help us after the sun goes down. (Some don't come when the sun is shining!) Do you dig, Sisters and Brothers? There are liquor stores on almost every corner in *our* communities, *not theirs*. They are there for profit which goes to other communities. Our people are getting sicker, while they (the owners) are getting richer. We need more programs back in the ghetto to serve the sick alcoholic.

Since audio-visual aids make a great impact, a movie on Black alcoholism is definitely needed and way past due. I have received many letters from readers of the first version of my book, called *I'm Black and I'm Drunk*. There is a great demand for the book to be made into a movie showing a Black recovered alcoholic and our way of life, our patterns and cultures. The movies that have been made have been good and helpful to the understanding of alcoholism but the characters are too rich and too White for we poor Blacks to identify. *We need a Black movie. We drink too!* We need a Black image. Me and two other women have just been featured in a short film on women alcoholics, but we Blacks want the whole thing. *Teen Aged Alcoholic* was great for the young people. But just how many of our Black children can identify with someone who owns horses and stables? If a Black youngster has a horse, he is likely to be plowing with it.

The feedback from Blacks since the first edition has been rewarding. One Brother said to me at the Navy Base here in San Diego, "I started reading your book and didn't put it down until I finished. I just want to say thank you for letting me know what is really wrong with me. I am ashamed to be standing here crying like a baby. I guess you must think I am a very weak man." My answer was, "The shortest verse in the Bible is the most powerful one: *JESUS WEPT.* So who said men are not supposed to cry?"

One Sister wrote me that it had been ten years since she had gone to bed sober. She sat her usual pint of booze and beer chaser on the table and started reading my book. She read all night and had not opened either bottle at 8:00 a.m. when she wrote to me.

I could go on and on because I have so many rewarding letters. Thank God, someone is being helped, which is my main purpose for sharing my experiences. So many people are in need of this book and this information for themselves, or family or friends. I have been really supported by the Black Sisters and Brothers. More and more colleges, too, are using the book to try to better deal with alcoholism.

I am very, very happy and surprised at the unbelievable response and interest shown by many White people. They are anxious to know more about our culture and patterns, so they can better work with Black alcoholics. Many have called long distance for personal advice, and admitted that they are willing and want to help but don't know how. I personally thank each of you for caring.

I have received hundreds of letters from my readers asking me not to change the book by going with a publisher. They were afraid — and I was too — that a publisher would make it all professional and cold and take the heart out of it. First, you will notice there is very little change in the way I've told my story because I want YOU to still be satisfied. Second, my main reason for going with a publisher was to reach as many people as possible. I came to the realization (and I had to be honest with myself) that I was selfish in holding all rights to the book and reaching fewer people. I realized that I couldn't do it alone, again I needed HELP. CompCare Publications and Diane DuCharme came to my rescue. By working together, many lives will be saved, which is my reason for writing this book.

If anyone is helped, I would be more than grateful to hear from you. That will be *my* reward, and I will feel that my book was not in vain.

Chaney L. Allen

Part One
Hunger, God and Growing Up
Peanuts for the Preacher's Kids

Part Two
Glittering Lights to Blackouts
Weekend Drinking

Part Three
Pouring My Own Troubles
Saving Up, Drinking Down

Drinking because I wanted to drink
'Lord, Baby, you are doing just fine'
Filling in the blanks
Getting along bad
It was you or him
Hooked and guilty
Thanksgiving disgrace
Going down slow
Arguments — over nothing and everything
Once I started, there was no stopping
The pastor's daughter — drunk!
Moving from the slums!
No matter what I did, I ended up drunk
Drinking because I *had* to drink
From church to the bootleg house
Unholy spirits at Communion
Getting worse, getting sicker
Drinking to block the guilt
Eleven cents poor to 'nigger-rich'
Getting into trouble at work
Pain and surgery
'Nothing but an ole drunk'
So I lost my job
Not God, but the bottle, is my Master
Out of control and terrified
Now, Lord, I can just live!
As sad as a funeral
Losing my 'cools'
Two female devils
Tranquilizers, sleeping pills and booze
Going down, down
Moving out — and into chronic alcoholism
Nothing to do, with a houseful of booze
Only sorry until the next time

Part Four
The Long Way Back
My Own Skid Row to Sobriety

Part Five
Recovery
Helping Others Like Me

Part One

Hunger, God and Growing Up

Peanuts for the Preacher's Kids

Most everyone was poor and hungry

I was born during the Depression in a little country place in Evergreen, Alabama, but when I was seven months old, my family moved to another rural place — Farmersville, Alabama.

I was about six years old when my family moved about twenty-five miles to Selma, Alabama. This meant we could live in town but Dad was now about thirty-five miles from his rural church.

I remember the day we moved, with all our furniture piled on the truck. Someone said, "It is so high it may catch in one of the telegraph wires!" Now I realize that we must have looked like the Beverly Hillbillies!

There were tin tubs hanging from the side, gardening tools, hoes and rakes. The furniture was typical poor country people's furniture — great big wardrobe, wooden roll-foot beds, iron beds, homemade cotton mattresses that Mom could make up so smooth until they looked like tacked mattresses. There was a flat-top coal and wood cook stove and a potbelly stove with ugly big pipes. The kitchen table was homemade, but it was pretty. Dad had made it out of knotted pine, and I really thought it was beautiful. Mom had many beautiful handmade quilts that she had pieced, and she had some of them spread over furniture to (above all things) protect it from scratches. There were several dressers and a center table that always held an old matching china face bowl and pitcher.

We three younger children were so excited and were too young to be embarrassed. But my three older brothers had gone to school in Selma, and so they rode on the back of the truck with our crude furniture and got off at the edge of town to walk to our new house.

They told Mom and Dad they were ashamed that school mates would see us. They didn't want anyone to see that old "Buick Six," meaning the huge wooden bed on the top of the truck. Our furniture was fine in the country, but it was out of style in town. Mom said, "You better thank the Lord for what we have." But my brothers said, "The Lord could have kept all that junk!"

The neighbors stood and looked as we unpacked. Mom may have been ashamed, but she didn't show it. She was determined to get away from the country and farm. For a long time I had heard her say, "I ain't gonna peep at a mule's ass for the rest of my life for a living!" So we unloaded our furniture and started our life in Selma.

We three little kids were so happy to be living in town. I had only been there a few times in my short life. Lee, the oldest of the three younger kids, made up a little poem that we kept up for years: "Hee Hee Hii Hii Selmii." He opened his mouth wide on the Selmii and wiggled his behind.

We were very poor people because my father was a CME Methodist minister. At that time and until recent years, the "C" stood for Colored. The other two initials stood for Methodist Episcopal. Our denomination got its name "Colored" years ago to distinguish the Colored church from the White Methodist Church. Our forefathers got fed up with sitting in balconies and with being asked to leave or thrown out of the White church. In some cases they were actually pulled off their knees while praying at the altar. We all know what I mean from the history of early American society.

My father was a minister when I was born, and preached for over fifty years before he retired. He had to depend on his congregation for his financial support. The people in town had very little money and the country people had less. In many cases, my father's salary was paid in chickens, peanuts, potatoes, and other things they could raise on their farms. Those beautiful Christian people would have been willing to pay church salary, but they just didn't have it.

Dad had bought a house without any plumbing; we had to pump our water from a pump in the back yard, which had to be thawed when it froze in winter. We didn't have any indoor toilet. The outside toilet was built with a homemade seat that fit over a metal can, just like the big garbage cans used today.

Once a week a man came around to collect those stinking cans. He drove a horse-pulled wagon; and when kids saw him coming, we would all run ahead yelling, "The can man is coming." All the parents would jump up, stop whatever they were doing, and close all the windows and doors because of the stink. We all wondered how he could do this filthy, nasty job, lifting these cans all full of piss and shit, splashing all over his apron and feet — can after can, all day every day! He would take all these cans and dump them in the Alabama River. In later years, the Board of Health made everyone get sewers and toilets to get rid of this filth.

We were never able to afford the whole "bath," but later we did get the water toilet. The back porch was made into the bathroom by adding walls — but no face bowl or tub was in it. We still used the tin tub. The house wasn't even wired. We were using kerosene lamps, and how I hated cleaning the lamp chimneys. We were very, very poor people, all collected in this little house.

We lived at 1709 Voeglin Avenue, right in front of the Southern Railroad track. A turning table operated by two men turned the engine to head it north or south. Even though we were so very poor, we were fortunate because we had heat. The trains banged against each other and pieces of coal, sometimes great big pieces, would fall off. We neighborhood kids took our little buckets in summer and in winter to pick them up. We dumped our precious coal bit by bit into the corners of a little coal house in our back yard. We ended up with tons of coal, which kept us from freezing to death, because there was no money to buy fuel. Picking up coal was quite a social gathering; we laughed and joked and sometimes we set our buckets down and we played games.

Dad and Mom loved each other dearly and had been married since 1911. Although she had birthed ten boys and one girl, only five of the boys reached maturity. These brothers are the only ones I ever knew. Nelson is the oldest. Bradford, the second oldest, died about fifteen years ago. Then came Roy, Lee, myself, and Henry, the baby of the family who is eighteen months younger than I. Dad often spoke of all these natural births with love and respect for Mom.

Like many other Southern Black families, Mom and Dad had six children and no money. Still, they were both very hard-core Christians who believed strongly in God. They raised all of us to truly trust in God and the Lord Saviour and Jesus Christ. My young mind was conditioned to believe that as long as I trusted God, it was alright to be poor, hungry, and not have the essentials of life. All of our suffering was done in the name of the Lord, and it was alright. We would get our pie in the sky in The Sweet Bye and Bye!

At that time, I was going to school hungry — getting up in the morning with no breakfast, going to school all day with no food — coming home to no food all night. Many days when I went to Clark School in Selma I was starving to death. We were all hungry. During the Great Depression, there just weren't any jobs available for Black people. I remember seeing children falling out of their school seats or passing out in the school yard. When the doctor examined them, he found the problem was hunger, not disease. Thank God for President Roosevelt! The school opened up a soup kitchen. Our teacher would announce each morning, "All of you children who didn't eat breakfast, stop in the soup kitchen before class and eat." And almost all of us stopped and ate. Most everyone was poor and hungry — yet my parents kept telling us that Jesus Christ suffered so we down here are going to suffer too. Mentally I accepted this in the name of the Lord.

A good man, a real man, a man of God

Dad was about six feet tall and very thin, very black and very bald. I never knew him to have hair on top of his head. Once I asked him why his head was bare, and he answered jokingly, "I'm a preacher and there couldn't be anything between me and God."

He was always a very strong man, both physically and mentally. He played many roles because he was faced daily with everybody's problems. He talked to couples with domestic problems, with juvenile delinquents and with drunks.

Sometimes he ended up playing probation officer. He went to the jail and pleaded with the sheriff to release a Black person. "I'll get that man to join the church," Dad said. Because the White rural sheriff had some respect for the Black minister, Dad was often successful.

Dad always kept trying to make a few extra dollars to support his family. For ten cents apiece, he cut congregation members' hair. He also hand-cleaned their woolen darned suits with a brush dipped in minspere (something like gas). Then he carefully pressed them with a cloth and a heavy smoothing iron, heated in front of an open fireplace. I still remember going to church on a 105-degree day and seeing him sweat in the heat of that room.

Sometimes Dad would be gone for as long as six weeks at a time at his church and running Revivals. Every week when Dad got his few dollars from the congregation, he walked to the post office to mail the money home instead of spending the train fare. I can remember hearing the postman whistle and call out, "Special Delivery Man." We kids waited like hungry birds; we knew the letter from Dad meant a day to eat. If the week before had been a rainy Sunday when no one went to church, there was no pay, no letter, and no food.

Lynch mobs were another reality of life for Southern Blacks then. Dad preached many funerals for Black men who had been lynch victims. Once while he was burying a man, five of the mob watched from an embankment and made fun of the bereaved family. Some of the bodies had been used for target practice and were only scraps, with the flesh absolutely hanging off the bones. Some had been beaten to death. Others had been castrated, while their females, both adults and teenage girls, were raped.

Only the Lord could have saved Dad the time he rescued Walter Smith, a teenaged church member. Walter was a very good boy who sang in the young people's choir, and was very active in church. Late one afternoon in 1930 Dad was sitting on the parsonage front porch. He heard loud angry voices coming closer and saw about fifteen White men pushing Walter, whose hands were tied behind him. Blood from wounds on his head was running down his face. He was wide-eyed with fear and hysterically crying, "Reverend, help me!"

When the mob crowd got in front of the door, one of the White men told the Black boy, "Tell Preacher Allen goodbye, because you are one nigger he'll never see again."

My Dad, without stopping to worry about his own safety, jumped off the porch and ran into the middle of the lynch mob. The men stood still as though they couldn't believe what they were seeing. By now, Dad said, he was feeling real fears for himself, as well as for Walter. The mob's faces surrounded him like angry devils. His throat was dry, his heart was pounding and perspiration streamed down his face and under his arms.

Dad prayed out loud: "Our Father which are in heaven, the Father of all men both White and Black, look down on all of us gathered here today. Open our hearts and let us love one another as Your Son Jesus taught us to do. Here stands one of Your children condemned to death as Your Son Jesus stood before Pontius Pilate. Have mercy on him. Have mercy on his accusers. Forgive them for they know not what they are doing. These are good God-fearing White people who I know do not want blood on their hands when they face You on Judgment Day. Have mercy on them."

By the time he finished praying, all the mob had taken their hats off and bowed their heads. Not a word was said. Dad walked over to the young man, pulled him to his feet, embraced him and said, "Please God." He slowly turned Walter around to untie his hands. The only thought on his mind was that now the mob had *two* victims instead of one. But he kept on untying the knot.

Mr. Jones, the main accuser, broke the silence and said, "Preacher, you better keep that little Black smart nigger straight or we'll get you both. If he causes any more trouble we are coming looking for you too."

Dad said, "Yes Sir, Boss. God bless all of you. Thank you, thank all of you good White folks. I'll remember you all in my prayers. And I promise this boy will not cause you any more trouble."

The mob headed back toward their part of town. Dad took Walter into the parsonage. They sent up prayers of thanks as Dad dressed Walter's wounds. He left Walter in the parsonage while he walked to his parents' home to share the good news that their son was alive and safe.

That week there was no special delivery letter with money because Dad took his few dollars to buy a one-way ticket north for Walter.

We almost had a lynching in our own family. My

brother Roy had to leave Selma suddenly when he was about fifteen years old. For after-school money he was shining shoes and cleaning up in a barber shop. The White barber hit Roy, and Roy hit him back without thinking. Dad got him out on a train for Cincinnati with a lynch mob on his heels.

Dad hated to play Uncle Tom, to scrape to the White man, but it was a means of survival. He taught us to play whatever roles were necessary to survive. If the White man does a job which he refuses to teach you, peek over his shoulder until you learn. Whatever knowledge you have in your head, no one can take away from you. But always remember that you are a decent human being, no matter what they say to you. You know who you are. Stand straight and look a man in the eye. All of this was drilled into our heads, over and over again, as we were growing up.

Dad didn't allow White insurance collectors at our home because if Mom and I were raped by them, we had no law to protect us. It would be only a "nigger's" word against a White man's word. Dad said that if we were ever hurt, he would die on the spot, but take Mr. Charlie with him. He taught my brothers the same thing: "Fight back until every drop of blood is drained from your body. I would rather see you dead than come home whipped by an unarmed White man." He couldn't stand a sorry-ass man.

Dad was the closest thing to a doctor that many of his poor country people ever saw. And he was often asked for help in the middle of the night. He learned about all the common illnesses when he was just a kid by working for a doctor, cleaning up and going with him on house calls. He asked the doctor questions about what he was doing, and he read all the books that he could understand. He learned what medicine to prescribe for acute indigestion. He made cloth sacks filled with medication for country ladies whose wombs had dropped down from physical overwork. He was Mom's midwife and cut my navel cord. For someone with flu he stirred up a cough syrup, which relieved the chest congestion. His medications worked for these people who were miles from a doctor and who had no money to pay for medical help.

My Dad was a good man, a real man, and a man of God. His congregations always recognized that. Whenever he ran a week's Revival, he was always asked to stay another week. He was very dedicated to the Lord's work. Dad often quoted this Bible verse to us: "When I was a child I spoke as a child, I acted as a child, but now that I am a man, I put away childish things."

Dad believed strongly in family ties. To impress this on us kids, he developed a family ritual which he demonstrated every Sunday at the breakfast table whenever he was home. He would tie six wooden kitchen match sticks together tightly with heavy cord and pass the bundle to each of us six children in turn, asking us to try to break them. It was impossible to break those sticks because they were bound too tight. Then he would untie them, pass one to each of us, and ask us to try again to break them. This time they were easily broken. He'd always explain that if we separated or didn't stick close together, we too would be weakened. Together you stand, divided you fall. Whenever Dad wasn't home on Sunday, Mother demonstrated the togetherness ritual.

When Dad was home, all of us were on our best behavior. He was not mean to his children, but he was firm and positive. We knew his personality, and when he was coming home, we stopped playing games. Dad did not take the foolishness that Mom did. My brothers would send signals to each other as warnings that the "Ole Man" was on his way home or already there. I remember many occasions when the three older brothers got the message to each other by telling friends to pass the word that Reverend Allen was on his way.

Just keep your faith in the Lord

The Bishop of the CME Church had the power to send
Dad and the other ministers to a different church each
year, for no more reason than he *wanted* to. Dad bought
the house in Selma to stop us children from having to
switch to a different school each year, sometimes schools
where the teachers didn't have adequate credentials. He
and Mom accepted the CME minister's way of life for
doing the Lord's work, but they wanted us to have a
decent education. As a child I couldn't understand why
the Bishop who knew a preacher had his house full of kids
would change that preacher so often.

My first and strongest memory of the annual conference happened when I was about seven years old. Even to
my young eyes, the Bishop seemed to be playing God.
Every church was assigned an annual quota of money to
be turned in for the General Fund. One by one the
preachers were called to the front of the meeting to turn in
their reports. But many of the congregations were so poor
that it was impossible for the preacher to raise the money.

I can still see a poor reverend who hadn't met his quota,
wearing an old patched black suit and a cheap, out-of-
shape hat. The holes in his shoes showed as he walked to
the front. There in the Church of God before hundreds of
people and his raggedy wife and children, the Bishop
shamed that man like he was a dog. The minister stood
with bowed head, like a condemned criminal. No matter
how the Bishop hollered, he passively answered, "Yes, sir,
Bishop. No, sir, Bishop."

I looked across the aisle at his family. His kids were too
young to understand, but his wife was crying. Because I
felt sorry for him, I started crying too. I couldn't
understand how any person could stand up on a pulpit
talking about money and let that Dollar blind him from
seeing a raggedy, almost barefoot, human being, with a
wife and children. It was beyond my comprehension then

and still is. Why didn't that Bishop take up a collection to help this preacher and others who were equally as destitute? After all, the Bishop and his family didn't look that bad.

When we left church that day, I asked Mom and Dad, "Didn't you tell me that the Bible says do unto others as you would have them do unto you?"

Dad said, "Certain rules have to be carried out. You are too young to understand now, but you will later. Just keep your faith in the Lord."

We dropped the subject then, but I never have understood, in all these years, why money was more important than the people in the church. I never went to another conference. Even today I don't go to church often, although I believe and trust in the Lord, because it bothers me that organized religion doesn't seem to be absolutely fair.

Blue organdy for Bessie Mae

I'll always remember what a beautiful couple Mom and Dad made. Mom's skin, like Dad's, was real black, and she didn't have a blemish on her face. (I inherited her smooth black complexion.) She had a pretty round face, thin lips, and beautiful hair.

My mother was a very Christian woman with strong feelings about drinking and adultery. She was always home to take care of us, and went only to church or to visit close neighbors. She was afraid to be out alone at night.

Her days were spent washing on a board, boiling clothes in a pot, ironing, cleaning, sewing and cooking, when there were groceries. She could take practically nothing and utilize it. Whenever the big boys wore out a pair of trousers, she cut off the legs and made the younger boys trousers.

She loved my brothers so dearly and enjoyed just

standing on the porch and watching them walk down the street. Yet she lived in fear of their being killed by the White police (there were no Black cops) or by any White man for no reason at all. Every time my brothers left home, she prayed, "Lord, take care of them and bring them home safe." At night her last prayer was, "Thank you, Jesus, for not letting my sons be in the hands of a lynch mob." I hated to see my mother tortured with fear, and her fear projected to me. I felt hatred and fear, plus pity for Mother.

My mother never worked for the White people in their homes. Fear of them was stronger than being very poor and hungry. Many Black girls, some of them only twelve or thirteen years old, told terrible stories of being fondled and raped by White men in the families where they were hired to nurse their children and help around the house. There was no use telling the White police. And what was a Negro's word against a White man's in the South in the 30s? We all knew many Black families with five or six real Black children of their own and a half-White child in the house. The Black husband knew who the father was, but neither he nor his wife could do anything about it. If he beat his wife or the child, he would be killed by Whites or accused of eyeballing or insulting a White woman and be lynched.

But Mom did take in wash from the White families. She walked to pick up the dirty clothes, scrubbed them on a washboard, boiled them in a pot, starched them, and ironed them with the smoothening iron heated on a charcoal furnace. Then she walked back to deliver them. Each bundle took six or seven hours and earned fifty cents for our family.

Although the boys were her pets, Mom and I spent most of our time together, since we were the only females in a house of six men. I learned to take responsibility at a very early age. For example, she taught me to pay bills when I was only nine years old. She told me the truth about sex and never told me the story many of my girl friends heard about babies coming out of a "hollow log." What she actually said was, "Babies come from the same place that you pee from, and the hurt is awful. You'll get a baby by letting little boys play under your dress."

No alcohol or cards were allowed in our home, and everyone in the community knew it. If Mom was sitting on the porch when drunks passed, cursing and swearing, one drunk always said, "Be quiet. Don't you see Mrs. Allen?" They would quiet down, pull off their hats and respectfully say, "Hello, Sister Allen," before they went on their merry way. A drunk was considered to be a very low-class person and was looked down on by everyone in this small Southern town.

It was extremely important to me to show my mother that she had not made a mistake by having a girl. I wanted her to brag about me the way she did about her boys. Things I did like trying to make a doll dress or scrubbing a floor were done for her approval. I wanted her to pet me and tell me how proud she was of me, but she gave the boys most of the affection.

I developed an "I don't care" attitude toward Mom. My dad and brothers took care of me and gave me the things I wanted. When Dad came home, I asked him for anything that I thought Mom would refuse me. I also did the same thing with my brothers. Sometimes I had to be a little tricky to get what I wanted.

One time in school I was picked to say a speech about a doll. I was to hold the doll in my arms and look at it while reciting. Because my doll's dress was old and torn, I picked out a new frilly organdy one which cost twenty-five cents at Kresge's. Mom flatly refused me and said she'd sew one from old material. I cried and cried. She still said, "I'm not spending and wasting a quarter on *no doll dress.*"

Finally I stopped crying and started thinking about how

I could get that dress. Mom thought everything was settled, since I became quiet and didn't show that I was upset. I finished my chores and went out and sat on the front steps while Mom sat in the porch swing. I glanced at her and thought, "Uh huh, you didn't win yet."

What I was waiting for so quietly was for my oldest brother Nelson to come home from his job at the "Bag Mill." I saw him coming two blocks away, and as soon as he got about four houses from ours, I let out a yell so loud that Mom almost turned over in the swing. I broke loose with a brand new flow of tears, jumped off the steps, and ran toward him with my arms open.

He picked me up, hugged me, and said, "What's the matter? Stop crying and tell Big Brother what's wrong." I was crying too hard to talk. He held me in his arms as we reached the porch. "What," he asked Mom, "is wrong with her? What did you do to her?" Mom didn't get a chance to answer.

Between sobs I said, "Mur-Dear won't get me a doll dress, and I have to be on stage in the chapel tomorrow, and I am ashamed of my old doll dress."

Nelson turned on Mom and asked, "Why don't you get it for her? She has pride too, even if she is only seven years old."

By now Mom was very angry with us both, but Nelson was angry with *her* and on my side, just like I knew he'd be. Mom said, "She will *not* get it. There is only one thing she is going to get — and that is a good whipping for acting a fool."

"Whip her for what?" said Nelson. "When you want something, you ask Dad and us boys, so when you didn't get her the dress, she has a *right* to ask me. And I'm going to get it." He turned to me and said, "Come on, Sister." We went to town and bought the dress.

When we got back home, Mom was waiting on the swing with a smile on her face that seemed ready to burst into a laugh any minute. I was so relieved to see she was no longer angry with me. I rushed to her and showed her my new doll dress. She told me, "It is so pretty. Come on and we will try it on Bessie Mae." She had laid my doll on the bed while we were gone and had washed her as clean as a whistle. She helped me dress Bessie in the blue organdy dress with a matching bonnet, socks and shoes. My brother really had me together!

Nelson stood in the doorway and watched us. When we finished, Mom passed him and said, "You boys and your Dad is going to spoil that ole ugly Black gal to *death*. She ain't going to be worth a quarter." He hugged Mom and said, "You and her are both our girls, Mom. I can't stand to see either of you cry for something that I can do." Mom kissed his cheek and walked away.

An extreme fear of dying

My mother was one of the greatest hypochondriacs I've ever known, and she played it to the hilt with all those men in our home. When she wanted things to go her way, she had a "heart attack." She used the same "heart attack" if she didn't want to do something. If someone died, she couldn't go to funerals because it upset her heart. The truth of the matter was she was scared of dead people.

I often heard her say, "The doctor don't want me to be by myself. I may have a heart attack and no one here to help me." She really was afraid to stay in the house alone at night. I don't remember Mom ever staying a night alone in her whole eighty-three years of life. Once when I was about nine years old, she called we three younger children to her bedside because she was dying and told us, "You children love ye one another. Mother won't be with you long. My ole heart has finally given out. I am going on to Jesus." We kids went outside and hugged each other, and cried our eyes out.

The next day Mom was up and doing her housework as if nothing had happened. If Mom heard of someone dying of a disease in Italy, within a few days she went to bed with the same illness. She would be so sick she'd insist on calling the doctor even when there was no money. He'd give her some sugar pills to swallow and call it medicine, and she'd get up until someone else died. I believed she really was sick until I got about eleven years old. I'd see her feel good all day and then get sick about the time the boys came home. It was pathetic because she spent all her life with imaginary illnesses and an extreme fear of dying.

She was a good mother who loved Dad and all her kids. She really didn't mean to hurt me, but as Dad said one day, "Your Mom is jealous, because now there is another lady in the family." I never went to school with uncombed hair and ashen skin. She kept what we had clean. My few dresses were clean, starched stiff and ironed with no cat faces (those cat-whisker marks left by the iron whenever the fabric was too dry).

When I got to be a teenager, some of my girl friends bragged about how late they stayed out, drinking and having sex whenever their mothers weren't at home. And some of their mothers allowed them to stay out late. But not *my* mother. She never allowed me to stay out as late as twelve o'clock. That was a no-no and I didn't want to do it. My brothers played watchdog, too. I was the only girl in the family and I knew they loved me. I wanted them to be proud of me.

'They got to eat in the soup kitchen!'

Regardless how poor and hungry I was, I loved school. I hated when summer came and I had to spend three months out of school. I would go all over the house looking for something to read. There was no money to buy books, so I'd pick up old magazines or anything. But I loved to read. Mom used to tell me, "Keep your eyes out of books all the time before you go crazy."

I had to do something. I played with neighborhood girls

until I tired of them or until it was dark. There was no homework to occupy my time, no TV, no radio, no phone. So, the only entertainment was reading or sitting at the open grate and exchanging stories with the family.

Sometimes we put raw peanuts under the grate and roasted them. Dad often sent us peanuts that were given to him for salary. Many days that was our only food. But Mom said it was alright, because our reward was in Heaven. One night I asked her, "The Bishop eats steaks while we eat peanuts or nothing. Is he going to Heaven too?" Bradford, my second brother, took it up and said, "She is right. Since Dad is working for the Lord and the Bishop eats and knows that Dad has a house full of kids, why don't he give him a church where they can pay a decent salary?" Nelson said it was unfair. Roy said all they cared about was the General Fund budget, and on and on. When we small kids went to bed, they were still debating!

I was always so happy to go back to school, and I studied hard. For Black people at that time, Clark School was a very good public school. It went from first through tenth grades. In Selma in the 1930s, that was as high as any Black public school went.

It was located on Lawrence Street. The main building was two stories and made of red brick. On the first floor were the administrative and principal's offices. There were classrooms on both sides all the way down the long hall. To the left were two drinking fountains, and from the end of the hall were steps that led to the yards. A very short distance away were the girls' toilets. Further left were the ball fields and the carpenter shop in a separate building.

Soup was served in the home economics class in a building farther to the right. Classes were taught in this building. There were stoves so the students could learn cooking, and there were refrigerators that made ice cubes and ran by electricity. Several sewing machines were available to students.

There were stools and a long counter where all we hungry kids ate. Because the stools were limited, we had to stand in line until others finished. The teachers would have us hurry and eat to make room for other kids. I remember the soup was served in thick bowls, and today when I see prison pictures on TV, I'm reminded of the way we gulped down the soup, so needed to help us through another day. Kids are innocent, cruel little things. The more fortunate kids would tease us when they passed. "They got to eat in the soup kitchen! Eat in the soup kitchen!" It was very embarrassing, but hunger overpowered the shame. Many kids were as thankful as I for that soup kitchen at Clark School. In many cases with me, my brothers and many other kids, that was all we had to eat in a twenty-four-hour period. (Just now I am very emotional and the tears are rolling. It is difficult to relive those days.)

I remember when they almost had to close the school and got nurses from the Board of Health to come to the school and give us shots, because many of the children were broken out in festered sores called the *Itch.* Today I have permanent scars on my legs from infected sores. Now I realize that it was caused by the lack of nutrition and vitamins while we kids were starving to death.

Two little Black neighborhood boys, ages 7 and 9, broke in a grocery store and took candy bars. The police caught them just sitting and eating candy. I remember they were sent to reform school for three years and were treated like hardened criminals by mean White guards who were profound nigger-haters.

From first through sixth grades we wore what we wanted. From seventh through tenth grades, the girls wore royal blue uniforms of Indianhead material, which was a heavy fabric. Mom taught me to iron my own uniforms. We used very heavy starch which had to be cooked. If we didn't iron them while they were damp, they had to be sprinkled and rolled tight so the dampness would penetrate the material. Then we would heat the old smoothing iron and go to work. I would sweat and iron. If there were any cat faces, I rubbed a damp cloth over the spot and went back with the iron again. Once the task was completed the cuffs and collars would be twice as stiff with starch as the dress. But they were beautiful.

The boys wore dark trousers, white shirts and dark ties. Their shirts were starched and ironed equally as pretty. When we all were lined up like soldiers in the school yard, it was a beautiful sight to behold! People would stand and lean over the fence that surrounded the school yard just to see how pretty the uniformed kids looked.

I never had an "F" in my life. I always worked to pass. I was not dumb nor smart, just average, but it appeared in some cases that I was smart because I got good grades. But what the teacher did not know was I had spent many hours way into the night, sometimes in the morning, to finish my assignments. A smart student would finish in half the time. But the next day I had it done. I had to.

Joining the Heavenly Band

As I grew up, Mom and Dad insisted that all of us must go to church. We were christened when we were babies and later had to join the church.

If we didn't go on our own, we had to sit on the Mourner's Bench during the Revival meetings. Many young Black children and adults would walk around with sad faces and isolate themselves while they prayed for a great revelation to show them that they had been saved and forgiven for all their sins. Other Black kids wouldn't bother a kid on the Mourner's Bench, mourning and praying. Many on the bench fasted and wouldn't eat until they got religion. And when they got to church and joined the other sinners on the bench, they all sat with bowed heads like condemned criminals.

The minister preached of Hell fire and brimstone, and of how the sinner would burn forever. Often he interrupted his sermon by saying, "Won't you come to Jesus and join the Heavenly Band?" Sometimes a mourner would spring from the bench and head for the minister, which set off a chain reaction. The older people said that "religion spreads from breast to breast." Soon the whole church would be shouting and praising the Lord. The saved sinner's relatives would be screaming, "Thank you, Jesus." Then the mourner sometimes passed out. Then he or she would stand and tell the whole congregation of his or her religious revelation.

Years ago in the country, Revivals were the main event of the year among Black Christians. People started planning months ahead. Some called it THE BIG MEETING. They came from far and near, saying, "Lord, I will be glad when Reverend Allen come and preach! That will be two weeks that he can feed my soul with some good gospel, yes *Lord!*"

They shopped for new clothes or made new cheap print dresses for the Revival. They stored cardboard boxes to put food in to take to the church. Many cakes and pies were baked. Chickens were put into little coops to clean them out, so they could be cooked for the Big Meeting. Some people slaughtered hogs, cows, and goats. It looked like a Robin Hood feast each Sunday during the Revival. Everyone invited you to eat from their box, basket, or small trunk and people were highly insulted if you didn't eat some of their food. That was terrible if one had already eaten or the person was an awful cook. Many times I saw poor Dad try to force an extra bite down or ask to take it home to avoid hurting some nice old ladies' feelings.

Dad was contacted months in advance to run a Revival. His schedule was filled for most of the summer. He was among the Old Country Preachers who preached loud and moved around. Today our ministers lecture, but years ago they demonstrated everything they said with body language. Usually he ran a two-week Revival that started every night about seven o'clock.

The people would start coming as soon as they left their fields and got dressed. Very few people had cars, so they traveled in wagons and on horseback. Many walked for miles. They would tie their shoestrings together, sling them across their shoulder and put the shoes on when they got near the church. They couldn't afford to wear them out walking, because they were only able to get a couple pairs a year.

All the seats in church would be filled, and people would be standing outside looking in the window because the church was so crowded. Sinners who sat on the Mourner's Bench with bowed heads prayed that they would be saved. Dad's sermons were directed at the mourners, but he also reached the congregation who were already saved. We SOULS shout a lot. Every once in a while one of the Sisters would get so HAPPY that the ushers had to hold her! I have seen some ladies actually turn over benches while shouting! They were so filled with the Holy Spirit!

Dad had to leave the pulpit and rescue me one night at a Revival meeting. I was sitting on a bench near the wall, when one of the ladies who weighed about 230 pounds started shouting and waving her arms in and out. Each time she stretched them out, she banged me against the wall. I started screaming and Dad came and got me, while he continued to preach. Later he told me to never sit in an inner seat, but sit where I could get out of the way! Today, I will *still* run from people who shout! I have never forgotten that Sister who beat the Hell out of me when I was a child.

Sometimes, one of the people would spring from the bench and head straight for Dad with outstretched arms. They had found Jesus, were saved and wanted to join the Heavenly Band. They confessed their sins and prayed for forgiveness, now ready to start a new Christian life. Grown men cried like babies when they joined the church.

It was beautiful to see the change in many people who never returned to their old way of life. They no longer gambled or drank. Once some of them found Jesus, they absolutely changed. The sinners still on the Mourner's Bench cried while the minister and other members prayed over them, with hands on top of their sinners' heads.

At one Revival, a minister was preaching about Judgment Day when all Christians would be saved and all sinners would be cast into Hell fire. He said the sun would rise on this awful day and then it would immediately become dark again. Just as he was explaining this disastrous day, the usher turned all the lights out except the small light focused on the minister. People screamed all over the church, and I was terrified! It all seemed so realistic. As it turned out, the Mourning Bench was almost empty that night!

People joined the church either out of Christianity or fear! During Revivals, each night the minister announced the subject of his sermon for the next night. It was just as effective as a series in the movies. One could hardly wait until the next night's meeting. You heard people saying, "Honey, I got to hear that man *preach* that sermon tomorrow night. Good God *Almighty!*"

Good old country Revival meetings had emotion and sincerity. After one of my dad's soul-stirring sermons, everyone left the church crying and saying, "Thank you, Jesus!!" One man was crying and shouting in the road and he said, "You know that damn man *preached* tonight! And that ain't no shit! Yes, My Lord!" We kids repeated his statement for years.

Once I heard a man say, "I walked across Hell on a spider web! I know I am saved." It puzzled me. As usual I asked Mom why "the spider web didn't catch fire in the Hell fire. And how could a thin web hold up a heavy man?" Mom said, "There you go. Asking questions again!" I said, "Well I'll have to stay on the Mourner's Bench until I see something. I haven't seen or heard any voices yet."

I believed in God and wanted to be saved, and forgiven for my sins. I didn't want to burn forever and ever when I died. I didn't want to be burned over and over like a BBQ rib on a grill. How could God be the loving God they told me about, yet burn me for being bad? To me, he sounded as mean as the police. Mom saw I was upset and confused. She asked if I believed there was a God. I answered yes. Then she asked if I was sorry for telling stories (lies). She said, "Being sorry is all it takes for you to be saved, If you really try crossing Hell on a spider web, you would be sure to fall in." She said, "I joined the church when I was nine years old and I ain't seen nothing yet; yet my faith and religion is as strong as many others."

I began to relax, because my young mind was clearing up. The day I joined the church (I was eight years old) the minister's sermon was "As the Eagle Stirs the Nest, God So Stirs the World." He spoke of how smart and wise the eagle was and compared the wisdom of God. I stretched my little hand to the minister and silently vowed to always trust God. As the preacher took my hand he started singing, "I have started for the Kingdom, I have started for the Kingdom. Don't turn back, children. Don't turn back."

I thought to myself, I will never turn back. I am going to be good and do what Mom tells me. I won't tell any more stories and I am going to be good just like Mom and Dad. I am going to make God proud of me.

So, I became a member of St. Paul's Colored Methodist Episcopal Church. I was baptized in the usual Methodist way, by sprinkling. I felt so clean and good inside and bragged to my friends that I had joined church, and was going to join the "Sunbeam Band," a group of kids about my age.

Some kids asked me. "What did you see, Chaney?" I answered, "I didn't see anything, but I believe in God and His Son Jesus who died for me and everyone in the world, good and bad." As I talked I really believed everything I said. One girl said to me, "You're not going to heaven because you was sprinkled and you are a Methodist. I am a Baptist and baptized in a pool like Jesus, so my Mom says we have been washed clean and is sure to go to heaven!" I was getting angry with her. Mom said, "There is going to be as many wet people in Hell as dry ones."

I became a full and faithful church worker, but Mom and Dad didn't smother us with religion. I also did anything ordinary kids did. I played ball, jacks, marbles, sang popular songs, danced, fought, pulled hair, and put my hands on my hips and shook my behind at my current enemy. I was just like any other child in the neighborhood and resented people who said, "Preacher's children are the worst children in the world."

Plenty to do, not much to eat

Mom always woke us up early. One of the boys started a fire if it was cold, and Mom got me up when the room was warm. To conserve fuel we only had fire in one room, where all the family gathered. The other grate in the living room was only lit when company came. In fact, the living room was the only decent furnished room in the house. It had a sofa which opened into a bed, a matching chair, a nice table, a piano, and a wool rug. All of us kids knew to keep out.

If there was no breakfast to cook, then no fire was made in the kitchen stove. The kettle of water would be heated in front of the grate, and we all took turns washing up in the face pan. The face pan and slop jar were the same color (grey).

After we all were cleaned and dressed, the boys went their way and Mom and I started the housework. On school days, naturally I dressed and headed for school. But if it was summer or weekends or holidays, I pitched in to help Mom in making beds, emptying the night pots, sweeping, gathering up dirty clothes, filling the wash tubs. There was plenty to do all morning, and I wasn't allowed to go play until all my chores were finished.

Mom combed and braided my hair, made me take a bath and put on clean clothes. Then I could go out and play. She told me, "If you only have a rag to wear, wash it out at night and wear it clean the next day." If I got dirty making mud cakes and she wanted me to go to the store, I had to come in the house to wash my hands, face and legs and put on my "store dress" that hung behind the door. After I returned from the store, I pulled my clean dress off and put my dirty dress back on to continue making mud cakes and grass dolls with my girl friends.

On days when we had no food, we all still went about our daily chores just the same. Mom prayed, "Lord help us, Your suffering children." Many times she just sat in her chair and rocked while tears slowly ran down her cheeks. Now that I'm a mother I know the pains she was feeling to see her children hungry, as many were during the Great Depression. That is why she was so happy for those fifty cent bundles of wash which helped feed us. But she constantly reminded us that the Lord would make a way.

The days when there was a breakfast, one of the boys made fire in the stove. Mom made buttermilk biscuits, as light as a feather. Fried salt pork (we called it rib meat) and syrup completed the menu.

Many times this was also dinner, when we had meat. My brother Roy refuses to eat syrup and bread today. Dried crouder peas often were the dinner meal. So many peas had been cooked in the house, that the pea pot was actually dyed reddish brown. Peas and cornbread! Dad usually sent syrup, peas, peanuts and sweet potatoes from his charge.

We had a small garden spot which we planted in greens during summer months. But sometimes there was no meat to cook them with. The best eating days were on weekends, when Lee worked at the market and brought meat home that was really scraps or going bad.

Preacher's children

When I was a teenager, Dad was pastoring at a small church named Prosperity CME Church in Orriville, Alabama, about forty miles from Selma. My younger brother Henry and I were excited because we were going to spend our whole summer vacation with Dad. We had always gone to Dad's church for at least two weeks each summer, but never had spent an entire summer. He told us we would be able to ride horses, fish, play ball, and meet other young people. I was really looking forward to the visit.

I was going to movies and church affairs with some boys in Selma, but I was not going steady. So I had no regrets about leaving, and I would only be forty miles away and could take a train home anytime. Mom and Lee said they would join us there within a month. Henry and I packed our few clothes. Mom had made Henry some new shirts and me a few print dresses. I had two nice Sunday dresses and two nice blouses and skirts, one pair of dress shoes and one pair of everyday shoes.

Finally, the Friday came and Mom got a friend to drive us to the train station. Anyone would have thought we were taking a trip around the world. She got on the train's coach for Coloreds with us and kissed us goodbye.

Henry and I both had been given spending change and bought candy and junk when the conductor passed with his tray. We looked out the window admiring the scenery, and laughed at the country people wearing ugly straw hats with their bottom lips full of snuff. We whispered, "Look out there at that old poor Cracker!!" And we laughed some more. It was a long ride.

Today, forty miles is only a skip and jump, but in the 30s riding a cattle train from one small Southern town to another took hours. The train stopped for everything, people, cattle, water, grain, you name it. We were held up fifteen minutes because a cow was on the track and had to be taken off. When the train pulled in at Orriville, we saw our daddy standing with hat in his hand, nose wrinkled in a frown, and sweating on top of his bald head as usual.

Walking together down the one little main street, we saw White people greeting Dad with, "Good morning, Preacher." That was different than the disgusting "Good morning, Uncle," or "Boy," that we were used to hearing in Selma. One of Dad's church members drove us to the parsonage. As we rode, Dad pointed out the houses of some of his members, and they didn't look like shacks. Their farms were beautiful and fertile. I'd never liked living in the country, but that little town didn't seem too bad.

Finally we reached our summer home. It was an old house, but well kept, with paint and a nice clean yard, and a front porch. I think it had two bedrooms and a large kitchen. The dry toilet sat beside the vegetable garden where Dad had planted peas, okra, greens, green beans and melons. Dad enjoyed gardening, a hobby that he, Mom and I had in common.

Dad was a darn good cook. Mom often said, "Your daddy always took care of me and the other kids when I was sick or had a new baby. He never worried the neighbors as many husbands did. He cooked, washed and ironed, cleaned, farmed and preached." That night Dad cooked us a good dinner of fresh green beans cooked with country ham and small white potatoes on top, fried chicken, fresh peach cobbler and cornbread. Henry and I ate like little pigs. Dad said we were going to be sick, but we just enjoyed being full and relaxed.

The next day we got up, washed up and dressed as we

were trained to do. Some of Dad's members started coming in early before breakfast. They were on their way to town to do their weekend shopping. Very few country people passed the preacher's house without stopping to say "hello" and ask if they could pick up something for him in town.

As Henry and I were introduced to each member we immediately stretched out our hands for shaking. We had been taught to shake hands before we even knew our left from right. Mom and Dad told us, "You shake with *this* hand," pointing to our right. I had a permanent scar inside my right elbow, so I was taught to look at the scar to remember the hand to extend to grown-ups! If I met a real old lady or man of the church, I was to shake their hand, plus give them a warm hug and kiss their cheek. My parents taught me that the old mothers and fathers of the church needed and wanted lots of love and attention. I liked making them feel good. Today I still love the feeling of touch, and I still embrace people and greet them with a kiss and smile.

Henry and I spent the first day exploring the small neighborhood of about five or six houses. We walked down the dusty road for a mile, just enjoying the country air and sunshine. I helped Dad prepare dinner although I was not a good cook. It takes *groceries* to learn to cook. He showed me how to make biscuits (which took me years to master), how to pick, clean, cut up and cook greens, fry meats and do some Soul foods.

Sunday morning is always chaos around a preacher's home. We got up real early because the house had to be cleaned, in case members stopped by the parsonage after church. And someone always did. Next, dinner had to be completed and breakfast cooked. We always prepared Sunday dinner before going to church. Then everyone bathed and dressed for Sunday School which began at nine-thirty.

After Sunday School, eleven o'clock service began and

lasted until one o'clock. Usually there was a special meeting immediately after services. Then we went home about two o'clock, had dinner and rested for only about an hour, because often some board or club or choir was giving a fund-raising activity on Sunday afternoon. After this, we attended young people's meetings. Finally, there was night service from about seven to eight o'clock. The preacher's children were expected to attend them all.

This was another reason why Dad and Mom did not like us children living in the parsonage. They realized that sometimes we just didn't feel up to staying in church all day every Sunday. If the minister expected other young people to participate in all the church functions, his children better be there also. In a roundabout way, his wife and children's actions determined whether or not he was respected, and would keep his church. As long as we were at the parsonage, we had to follow this pattern.

Things were different in Selma. If we wanted to go to a movie instead of an afternoon church function, Mom let us. But Dad's members thought it a cardinal sin to go to a show on Sundays. So we adjusted and did what was expected of us.

'Coating'

It wasn't too bad in Orriville, though, because many young people belonged to the CME Church. The Baptist Church was not too far away and a lot of young people attended there also.

Anytime we young girls and boys gathered, we prayed, read, and discussed the Bible and talked of the love and goodness of God. At the same meetings we also wrote on the back of the benches and sneaked little hugs and pinches, which brought on soft squeals and giggles. As much as we all loved God and His church, we loved to go and meet the opposite sex too. Among the older Blacks they called it "coating" and church was the place to meet "nice" girls and boys. (*Coating* was courting!)

I met a tall, thin, boy with high cheekbones and dark brown eyes, who lived a "country mile" from the church. Greg had dark brown skin and beautiful, thick, natural hair which he greased and pressed down with a stocking cap. On the second Sunday I attended church, he approached me. After a long pause, as if he was trying to get up nerve, he asked, "Are you allowed to receive company?" Meaning, can boys come visit? I didn't answer right away because I was doing some fast thinking. Mom allowed me to "court" but I wasn't sure how Dad felt. I was willing to take the risk and answered, "Yes, why?"

He said, "I'd like to come visit you Wednesday night and also take you to the ball game in the school yard Saturday afternoon. I'll bring you home before night."

I told him that he *could* come visit me on Wednesday, but he'd have to ask Dad if I could go to the ball game.

(The nice Negro girls just didn't go and come as they pleased. I had to get permission from my parents, and the boy had to do the asking. It was a trip to see the young men sweating and stuttering nervously while they faced my father, with Dad giving orders about Do's and Don'ts. How well I remember my parents saying, "Bring her back just like you left with her." Which meant no screwing. The poor boy would answer, "Yes Sir, and Yes Mam, I respect Chaney.")

This time Dad said yes. We went to the ball game and joined the other young people, who were quite different outside of church. Now they were relaxed and dressed casual — the boys in sport shirts, sandals, and slacks — the girls in cool dresses made of voile material, socks, and sandals. There were tubs of ice cold soda water, home-made ice cream, cakes, fried chicken and other sandwiches for sale. This Saturday the profits went to the CME Church. The next Saturday would be for the Baptist Church. Greg bought me hot catfish sandwiches and orange soda.

All that summer Greg was my date, coming to see me on Sundays, Wednesdays and Fridays, the usual three times a week for courting nice girls. Sometimes we just sat on the front porch and talked and kissed, or went out to nice parties and church functions. A few times we drove with friends to Selma to movies but didn't go to my house because Mom and Lee had already joined us in Orriville. Soon, I got tired of my summer romance and wanted to get back to Selma with my friends. I wanted to hear all the latest girl talk and get back to the town boys. I was ready for school again. We left Orriville at the end of August.

Nice clean teenage fun

One Saturday, back in Selma, Mom and I were sitting on the front porch when a young man walked up to the house. I recognized him as Bill Morgan, a young member of the Orriville Baptist Church. I had seen him at ball games and had been introduced to him. Mom greeted him, saying the Lord had blessed all of us to be still alive, to see another day and meet again. He had moved in with his sister who lived in Selma, because he had finished the ninth grade of Orriville's Colored school (as far as it went) and was looking for a job. In the three hours he stayed I never guessed I was talking to my future husband.

I found him a very interesting person, and time passed in a hurry as we talked. I liked the way his dark eyes lit up and his sense of humor. I admired his beautiful white, even teeth, his smooth dark skin and neatly cut hair. He was about five feet nine and wore his clothes well. He was not a bad looking Brother. Mom went next door to visit Mrs. Gilliam, a neighbor, and left us alone to talk.

(My parents didn't sit with me when my boy friends came, as many Colored parents did. We young Blacks called it "cock watching," to make sure that the girls didn't get pregnant. Little good it did, because some girls got pregnant anyway. So that is why Mom told me, "I'm not going to try and watch you. I am telling you what is right and wrong, and I trust *you* to do the right thing.")

Before Bill left that night he asked me to go to a movie with him the next evening. I said, "Yes." That was our first real date. After the movie, we ate ice cream at Reed's Drug Store and enjoyed the long walk home. Like most poor Negro boys, he didn't have a car. There were no buses in Selma during this time, so everyone either rode bicycles or walked and thought nothing of it. I introduced Bill to all my friends, and after we had gone to several parties together, my friends started sending invitations addressed to Chaney and Bill. Without realizing it, Bill and I became steadies.I was about fourteen, and this was my first real boyfriend.

He was a very dependable boyfriend who didn't smoke or drink, never stood me up, and treated me with all respect when we were out. He opened doors, pulled out chairs and held my coat. When we danced, he was careful not to put both arms around me or attempt belly-rubbing, which was disrespectful. Bill always tipped his hat to ladies, and never wore his hat in the house. The older Blacks told men, "Our house has a top on it, so you can pull your hat off."

We enjoyed each other's company at parties, picnics, bicycle riding, and barbeques. He attended my school ball games and plays with me. On Sundays we always went to church, sometimes alone to our own churches and sometimes together to each other's churches.

My family learned to love Bill because he was so respectful. He never failed to leave on time; he took me home at the time he promised. We loved hugging, kissing, dancing and just having nice clean teenage fun. For two beautiful years we enjoyed this relationship.

Sparks and curfews

But somewhere during our courtship, the innocent hugs

and kisses turned into heavy necking, with both of us becoming sexually aroused. Bill was becoming more and more demanding. My family training about "no sex before marriage" was stronger than my desires, so instead of feeling relaxed in each other's presence, we were both miserable.

One night we were so aroused that I agreed to go to his friend's house with him. As soon as we walked in, his friend left. Bill put the sexiest song around, "In the Dark" by Lil Green, on the record player. Right away he started showering me with kisses and fondling me, slowly backing me to the bed. We were in love and crazy with desire. I wanted him as much as he wanted me. We fell or stumbled across the bed, still in a tight embrace. I came to my senses like I had been struck by a bolt of lightning when I felt him raise my skirt. I could hear Mom saying, "Don't let boys play under your dress. I didn't want a girl because they get babies before they are married and disgrace the family. Your brothers and Dad will not love you anymore if you ever do that!" I started crying and shaking. He let me go, and without a word we left.

I cried all the way home because I was so mixed up. I loved him and wanted him, but I also loved my family and didn't want to do anything to hurt them either. Finally he said, "Chaney, don't cry. I won't bother you anymore."

When we got to my house, he kissed my cheek and we said goodnight. I didn't sleep but a few hours that night. I laid very still so as not to wake Mom, because I had to think. By the next day, I had made my decision. I wrote Bill a long letter telling him that I loved him, and it was impossible to continue being his girl friend and remain a virgin. I couldn't control my sexual desires any more than he, and I felt it was dangerous for us to be together. I just didn't know what else to do.

When Bill received the letter he came straight to me and said, "This isn't the thing to do. We just don't quit. We aren't angry with each other. I promise not to be demanding anymore." For weeks he kept after me to take him back, but I refused. I returned to my girl friends and once in a while went out with other boys, but got annoyed if they held me too close on the dance floor. My temper was short, and I stayed home a lot. I still loved and wanted Bill.

One night I went to play at Knox School with my girl friends. When we came out, I saw Bill just behind me with another girl, which made me so upset. We looked right at each other and dropped our eyes and heads.

By now he had a porter's job at the A & P supermarket, riding a bicycle to deliver small orders. The next morning he rode up when I was sweeping the yard. For a few minutes we just stared at each other, not saying a word. He broke the silence saying, "Chaney, the girl I was with last night meant nothing to me! She just moved to town, and her aunt asked me to take her to the play since she couldn't go. Why don't we stop this nonsense and pick up where we left off? You know we love each other. Let me come and see you tomorrow?"

"OK," I said in a whisper, and we both smiled.

I was very excited to have my precious Bill back. True to his word, when the necking got too heavy, he either moved to the other end of the couch, or said, "I guess I'd better leave now." Ten o'clock was our curfew for courting time, but sometimes he left earlier.

One evening after Bill and I had been back together for about six months, he cancelled out on taking me to a party. He said he had to work too late. My girl friends and I decided to go to another party across town. Half a block away we heard L.B., the local Black music man, and his record player blasting away. Boys and girls unescorted, were eating sandwiches, drinking unspiked punch and having a ball. I was feeling so young and gay, not a care in the world.

My world crumbled when one of my girl friends said,

"Chaney, come here. Bill just came in the door with Katie." I asked, "Who?" (Katie, who lived a couple of blocks from Bill, had the reputation of being a "pushover." All the "nice" girls and boys talked about her.) "You know, ole pushover Katie." By this time Bill, Katie and I stood face to face. He turned as if to run and grabbed his head with both hands. He turned back to me and said, "Wait, Chaney. I want to talk to you." Katie said, "No, you brought *me.*" He didn't know what to do.

I saw that a scene was about to take place so I just walked away and left the party. I cried all the way home because I was so hurt. Now I realized why Bill could control his sexual desires with me. He was getting sex elsewhere. I was humiliated before my friends. My girl friends walked with me, sharing my hurt and talking about how rotten he was.

Mom was asleep when I got to the house and went to bed. I cried so loud that she woke up and asked what was wrong. I tearfully told her, "I never want to see him again as long as I live." Then another flow of tears started.

When Bill came the next day to talk to me I told him, "You go on back to that girl. Every boy in town has had her." So we broke up again.

I didn't see him with her, but I was told that he was casually seeing her. My brother Bradford told me, "Sister, don't be too hard on him. Sometimes men will mess around with that type of girl, but they really love and respect their real girl friend. Because you caught him doesn't have to mean that he no longer cares for you. After all, you aren't engaged or married to Bill. So when he tries to talk to you again, why don't you?"

I thought a lot about what my brother had said. About a week later Bill stopped by because he "just happened to be in the neighborhood and stopped by to see how you are doing. I miss you, Chaney, and I am so ashamed and sorry about everything. Will you forgive me and give me another chance?"

I asked him to come back that night so we could talk. His face lit up and he said loudly, "Yes! I'll be here with bells on!" We both laughed as he rode off.

We made up again, with the understanding that he'd no longer see Katie, and neither of us would go out with other guys or gals. If he broke his promise he was very careful about it, and I didn't catch him again. For months everything was beautiful and we kept our sexual desires under control. But after all we were both young and human and had been going steady for about two years without completely expressing our love. I was about sixteen years old and Bill about eighteen, and the normal sexual desires returned. We were tortured every time we danced or were alone together. I was so nervous that, many times, I burst into tears. I could see the misery on Bill's face. We continued seeing each other and tried going out with other couples to avoid being alone. But nothing seemed to work.

The turning point came on Thanksgiving night. Mom had gone to spend Thanksgiving with Dad. We'd eaten the good dinner my brothers and I had cooked — chicken and dressing, greens, fried corn, cornbread — and the cake Mom had baked before she left. Bill and I sat around lazily doing nothing, and necked a little as the hours passed. One by one, my brothers dressed and left. Each stopped in the living room and said, "See you kids later. Take care of her until we get back, Bill." Finally we were completely alone in the house. Bill and I settled down on the couch in front of the grate and stared at the flames for awhile. He gently pulled me to him and said, "Come on and give me a *real* hug and kiss." I slid into his arms and we embraced in a long, torn-up, sexy kiss that started sparks flying again. I felt as if I was sinking or floating into another world, but again something clicked in my mind. When Bill pulled me completely on top of him and held me forcefully, I really got scared. I sat up with tears in my eyes, and he stood staring into the fire with his back to me and both hands in his front pockets, trying to conceal his erection.

A wedding on a lunch hour

We set the date for December 24. We decided to marry secretly because I wasn't sure my parents would approve. Also, I was to graduate in June and married girls didn't return to school then. We made plans to meet at the court house to marry when I went Christmas shopping and he was on his lunch hour. We'd tell them that I was eighteen years old, and he was twenty-one. I was excited, because now I would have my man completely. And he would always trust me because he knew that I was a good girl. Our marriage would be perfect.

Everything went as planned. Within fifteen minutes I was Mrs. Chaney Morgan. I remember the "I do" and "I wills" and God knows I meant every word. I thought to myself, "I am going to be like Mom. I'll do everything to make him happy. God help me to be a good wife."

I went on to the ten cent store. I told Bill that I was sick and was going home and to bed because I had awful menstrual cramps. I spent my wedding night in bed with my Mom, where I had slept most of my life.

Bill came to see me that night and brought my Christmas present, a beautiful satin housecoat. It was long — to the floor — and looked like an evening gown. Mom thought the housecoat was beautiful, but felt that it was too intimate and didn't bite her tongue about it although Bill was there to hear the complaining. We looked at each other and smiled. I was beginning to feel guilty because I was keeping a major secret from Mom, something I had never done before.

We had just gone on and gotten married without any plans for living. I had nothing and was still in school, and Bill's salary was exactly five dollars per week.

On December 26, Bill and I went to his sister's house.

She knew our secret, and she and her husband left us alone, claiming they were going to a party and would be gone most of the night. They both liked to drink pretty heavy. At last Bill and I were alone. I finished undressing under the covers. But I was a willing bride and went into my husband's arms to fulfill the fire that we had been smothering for so many months.

Bill was gentle with me, but a girl's first sexual experience is painful. He was surprised to find how little I knew about sex. I didn't even know that women could *have* sex without reaching their climax, and I felt too sore to be touched again for days. When we got home, it was later than we realized, and Mom was waiting. It was a no-no for nice girls to stay out until midnight — only loose-drinking and whore women hung out late hours. We both apologized.

Bill came to see me the next night. He had only been seeing me three times a week but now it was every night. Mom went on to bed and left us alone in the living room as usual. I checked to see if she was asleep. My husband and I sneaked and had sex on the sofa, and the second time was not quite so painful. He assured me that my body would adjust and he was very patient with me. The guy thought I was a lump of "Black Gold."

I couldn't get into bed with Mom when I was dirty, so I went outside and rinsed out my panties which I had used as a towel and hung them on the garden fence. I thought they would be dry enough to go in the dirty clothes bag when I got up. But Mom, always an early riser, woke me asking, "Why are your underclothes hanging outside?" I'll never forget that!! I told her I soiled them because my period wasn't quite finished.

Bill came back that night and made no attempt to leave. I kept talking, and we were still whispering and laughing at eleven o'clock when Mom came in, head rag and all. She said, "Bill, I never like to hurt my children's feelings before company, but it seems that you and Sister have forgotten how to tell time and something is going on. After you leave, I am going to see if I can't take *care* of this young lady."

Bill stood very straight and said, "We are sorry, Mrs. Allen, we didn't want to tell you until after Chaney finished school. We love each other and got married Christmas Eve Day at twelve o'clock at the court house. Don't be angry at her. I don't mean to disrespect your home, but I don't want to leave."

Mom's mouth dropped wide open and she looked from Bill to me. She finally asked, "Is my baby pregnant?"

Bill answered, "No!"

Mom looked so relieved and said, "Well, you children let out the couch and go on to bed, I'll have to think. Lord! What am I going to tell her daddy and the boys!" Mom was saying everything at one time. She was so confused, yet was trying to be fair and say the right thing. She left the room still mumbling and praying, "Lord, give me the strength."

Bill and I felt bad that we just dropped the hammer on Mom without any warning, yet we were glad it was over and he didn't have to leave. We made up the sofa bed and spent our honeymoon there. Bill left early before the nosey neighbors woke up, since they knew nothing of our marriage, and Mom and Dad's home was open for gossip.

Bill and I started living with my family. He agreed to buy food since he worked at the supermarket and got a discount, plus a lot of free food. Mom didn't ask for any rent. To her, he was just another son. The boys silently accepted my marriage.

Mom didn't tell Dad until he came home a couple of weeks later. And he blew his stack. He accused Mom of knowing our plans and helping with our plot. I felt so bad because she was really innocent. She told Dad, "Well, she is going to finish school." Dad said, "If she does, she will be as big as a March rabbit, because Sister is pregnant."

Mom said, "No, she was on her period when she

married and this I do know. She's only been married for
two weeks."

"Well, she is pregnant now," Dad said. He was really
angry at Mom and only stayed home a few days. But he
gave us his blessing and prayed for us before he left. Mom
continued to run the house and I was back in school after
the holidays.

January 21,22, and 23 passed, and my period did not
show. I told Bill that I was scared. Mom was watching me
and asking daily, "Did you see anything yet?" She was
getting on my nerves, and I couldn't concentrate in
school. Many of the kids in school and the neighbors
knew that I was married. But just as my Dad had said, I
really *was* pregnant and started having morning sickness.
I knew by June I'd be too big to remain in school, so I
dropped out. Also, Bill didn't feel comfortable having me
in school with my old boyfriends. I still loved Bill, but
when the honeymoon was over, we had to face reality.
We had no money and had made no plans. We just got
married as many teenagers do.

I don't really know when our troubles started, but Bill
got moodier and moodier. He seemed angry about something. As my stomach grew bigger and bigger, he got
worse. He seemed bored when he came in from work. He
was acting so different from the Bill I knew and fell in love
with. He finally started going to parties alone. I felt lonely
and left out, but at first, I felt no jealousy. I didn't think
he would go near another woman because I thought he
loved me too much, My dream world was shattered when
he started coming home with lipstick on his clothes. His
excuse was that it got on him while he was dancing. I
didn't believe Bill, because I began to notice his eyes
flirting with other women.

After awhile we realized that our marriage wasn't going
right. I couldn't take knowing that Bill was beginning to
run out on me. My mom and dad had been married since
1911, and she often said, "I never had no man except your

dad." To me, that was the greatest thing I could ever think of. That was the life *I* wanted to live. I never wanted but one man in my life and I never wanted but one man to touch my body.

I'd been taught that a woman's body was the most precious thing in the world. Mom said, "God chose Mary to be the mother of His Son, Jesus, because she was a virgin with a clean untouched body. Sex is sacred, so don't share it and throw it around here and there."

With my teaching, I wanted to preserve my body for no man except my husband, this one husband. I couldn't understand that Bill was too young to be settled down. All I could think about was his running around with other women.

Things got worse. He reached the point where he beat me up and slapped me around. When I was seven months pregnant, he jumped on me one night because I got out of bed when my younger brother, very sick with pneumonia, called to me. Mom was gone, and I was taking care of Henry. Bill got real mad and told me I should have asked his permission to go see about my brother. That caused a real hassle. I was so damned mad. I didn't want to wrestle with him.

He kept doing nasty things, like slapping the plate out of my hands at a picnic and saying insulting things in front of his girl friends. He started showing off on me in front of them.

Birthing, with L'il Sister Morris

It took us the nine months I was pregnant to save the ten dollars it would cost to have L'il Sister Morris, the midwife, come to the house to deliver the baby. Every week we put twenty-five cents in a little jar. Many ladies couldn't afford even ten dollars and had to ask for credit. A doctor was out of the question, because he would charge twenty-five dollars.

Part of the midwife's job was to teach the girls having their first babies how to do things like make a baby bassinet out of a cardboard box. We learned to drape the sides with fabric, sew a pillow for a mattress and make a tiny sateen pillow for the baby's head.

L'il Sister also taught us to make newspaper pads to protect our beds during childbirth. We sewed five open sheets of paper together to make each pad, folded them, and put them away until the time came. During childbirth, she would roll the soiled pads up and dispose of the waste coming from the baby's birth.

All poor Blacks had their babies at home. Even those poor Blacks who had doctors never thought of going to a hospital to have a baby. Now I hear everybody making a big deal out of natural childbirth and going to school to be trained how to breathe. All we ever *knew* was natural childbirth, and you just had your baby, although ladies died in childbirth. Only rich White people went to hospitals to have babies. (The rich Blacks — the doctors' and the undertakers' families — who *could* have babies in hospitals didn't associate with us anyway because they were so far out of our class.) We would say, "What for? If she got the baby, she's going to have it!" Those White women didn't need all that attention just to have a baby.

Childbirth, especially with young women, was pretty bad, and many times left them with damaged female organs. I was one of those and it took surgery years later to correct the problems. Now I feel that had I been in a hospital, they would have taken care of me when the baby was born. But that was the way we birthed our young.

On October 13 I went into *hard* labor. L'il Sister came to take care of me and left orders for my mother and husband. They heated towels and put them on my stomach. They held my hand so I could have something to pull on. The midwife went back and forth from me to other ladies having babies at the same time. She'd come to take care of me and see that my bed was all padded and the hot water and towels were there. Then she'd go across town, and see about another girl, then to the next lady to see how she was doing and get her set up before her baby was born. Then she'd come back to see about me.

For three days I suffered, until my brains started getting numb. My whole body got numb trying to have this baby at home, and I went into a convulsion. Everything seemed like a dream to me because I hurt so much. Someone put a spoon into my mouth, thinking I was going to chew my tongue off. I couldn't control the trembling nerves in my jaw and mouth.

The baby wouldn't be born and I remember hearing L'il Sis yell to somebody, "My God, she's choking the baby to death." Later on, I learned that when the baby's head was about out, I tightened up right across the baby's throat. The midwife got up on her knees in the bed and, with both her hands and her thumb, held my vagina open so that that baby could be born. Because money was scarce, I suffered the pains of Hell right at home.

Moonshine — and no roses

Edward, my new son, was a big healthy baby and when he was two weeks old, he looked like he was two months old. After my baby was born, I was nervous and depressed. We'd moved into our own little two-room apartment so I didn't even have Mom's company. I asked Bill to take me out just to keep from thinking and worrying.

Sometimes we went and visited other young married couples. Some of the ladies drank, and most of the men did too. One night, Bill's sister gave a party where we laughed, talked and danced to the radio. They had about two gallon jugs of moonshine, more whiskey than I had ever seen in my life. Everyone was pouring their drinks and having a ball. Finally I was asked, "Sister, do you want a drink?" I had never tasted a drink in my life.

Bill had a glass in his hand and was feeling good; he pushed his glass under my nose and said, "Take a sip. It will make you relax." I almost gagged from the odor of that horrible smelling stuff, and just shook my head. A few minutes later Bill and his sister brought me a tall water glass filled with red soda pop and a slice of lemon. Bill said, "It's spiked, but you won't taste the whiskey." So I took my first drink under the supervision of the man I loved.

Before I finished that sweet drink, I felt a hot glow in my stomach that spread down out my arms, and gave me a light-headed feeling. I just sipped on this one drink for the rest of the night, but the feeling lasted. I wasn't worried about anything, and everything was funny. I hugged Bill very tight as we danced closely. Bill and I rode home on his bike with me on the front rod, and I giggled all the way. I was still feeling the effect of that drink. I hurried and got into bed with my gown still on the chair.

When we went out with other young couples, Bill would be fighting mad if I looked at another man too hard. Yet I saw him make passes at some of the ladies. He had really become embarrassing.

The hostess for one party said, "Chaney, we are inviting our friends and you know that you are always welcome at our house. But to be honest with you, I'd rather your husband didn't come. All the ladies are tired of him making passes." I almost went through the floor I was so ashamed, but I didn't say anything to Bill about this. If I had confronted him, he would only have said, "There you go again! Listening to hearsay!" So I started making excuses to stay away from our friends.

My brother Lee stopped by one day and played with Eddie for a few minutes. Then he looked at me and said, "Sister, I want you to tell Bill to leave my wife alone. If he puts his hands on her again, I'm going to *kill* him. She said he was by there today and ran his hand under her skirt while she was ironing. I came here to have it out with him, but I'm glad he's not home. See if you can talk to him."

I sat there stunned. I got up and changed my baby, warmed his bottle and dusted the furniture. I hated to confront Bill, yet I had to. When he came home, I told him Lee's exact words and he denied it. And he had the nerve to get fired up!

He was still on my case about using birth control. He wanted more children, but I didn't feel he wanted them because of love for me. There is an old saying about wives, "KEEP THEM BAREFOOT AND KEEP THEM PREGNANT AND YOU'LL ALWAYS KNOW WHERE THEY ARE." I felt that was where Bill was coming from. He wanted me to have more children just to keep me at home. He was trying to eat his cake and keep it too. It was alright if *he* did anything he wanted, but he still wanted me to remain a good and true wife to him.

Bit by bit I was losing all respect and love for him. Most nights he was staying out later and later, and he could hardly wait to change clothes before he was ready for the streets again. I was young, but not dumb. As the old saying goes, "You don't have to put your finger in my eye before I know you are pointing at me." Yet I was so hurt and disappointed — all *I* wanted was for us to love and live for each other as we had promised. I didn't want to share him with other women. I wanted his affections, but what I got was nasty talk and yelling. Not being wanted was an awful feeling.

He began flirting openly with other women right in front of me. I saw him at a restaurant with Katie again and he ended up getting angry with *me.* Bill raised the most hell when he got caught. He had a way of making it seem that all others were wrong, not him. Gradually I was losing him and all my feeling for him. Yet I was trying to make our marriage work. I tried talking to him but it didn't do any good. He still found more interest in the streets.

Once I bought him two nice shirts for his birthday, and he insulted me by saying, "I don't want you to buy me a damn thing." So I gave them to Lee. Two days later he saw Lee wearing one, and asked me where they were. When I told him, he got angry, and accused me of giving his things away and told me to go and get his shirts back. My nerves were screaming and my head was in constant pain. Yet I prayed that some miracle could straighten our marriage out.

He was always threatening me. I knew his violent temper and insane actions, and I didn't want to spend my life fighting and arguing, I wanted love and peace. I started making mental plans to leave since things were not getting better. If he would be happier without me, I was willing to bail out. All I wanted was my baby.

A blow-out — and goodbyes

Our unhappy marriage finally came to a head one Wednesday evening. I was slicing bread when he walked in from work. I said, "Hello, honey," and he slapped me. All this built-up misery in me started to come to the surface. All I could see was a monster in front of me, not a husband, not a man. I switched the knife from a slicing position to a stabbing position and stopped slicing bread and started slicing on him. I really intended to cut his throat. It just boiled over and I intended to kill him. My nephew ran to tell my brother Bradford, who came running. It was a great big blow-out and fight.

Later I learned that Bill had gone by his girl friend's house and saw she was with another man. So he came home and took his anger out on me. It was then I decided to leave him and go to Cincinnati, Ohio, to live with my brother Nelson, who had hoboed there about six years earlier. I simply could not take any more. That same night Eddie and I went to Mom's house. Bradford gave me the money for my train ticket. In five days I was packed for

Ohio to start a new life of peace and quiet for me and my child, who was then about nine months old.

We got to the station about ten o'clock in the morning. There was a long line at the ticket window in the COLORED waiting room. We had to wait until the WHITE folks were taken care of first, but I finally got my ticket. A neighbor who worked there arranged help for me from the porter because I had to change trains in Birmingham to get on the train north to Cincinnati.

I went to the bathroom to change my wet, whimpering baby. When I came out, Bill was there with Bradford and Henry. Bill said, "See if your brother can find me a job." I said okay because I didn't want any trouble and turned to talk to my brothers, who were looking so sad. They stood back and let Bill and me talk privately until time to get on the train. White people stood near the front, and the Colored people stood near the end. The conductor called, "All aboard for Birmingham." He pointed we Colored to our coach. My brothers and Bill were allowed to come on the train, and helped me get settled in a seat at the left window. It was time, so I kissed Bill and my brothers goodbye.

The train started slowly, slowly. It picked up speed by the time we passed in front of our house. Mom and Dad and the neighbors stood on the front porch, all waving when they saw me waving my white handkerchief. I saw poor Mom raise her apron to cover her face and I started crying too. I held my baby tight because I needed to feel someone for comfort. I said to him, "Eddie, my God, Mother loves you and needs you. I did get *you* out of my marriage."

Mom had fried chicken for me to eat on the long train ride. The porter took good care of me and the baby. Eddie was restless, so I held him a lot. My feet and legs ached from sitting cramped for hours and hours. After the baby fell asleep on the seat, I covered him and walked through the two Colored coaches. I looked out the back of the train and could see the tracks disappearing behind us. It was an all-night ride from Birmingham to Ohio. At times I looked around the coach at different faces all going in the same direction, but for different reasons. And at times I just sat and stared blankly.

My only amusement was playing a card game called "Whiz" for a couple of hours with three other passengers. They passed around a bottle of whiskey using the cone-shaped paper cups, and a water chaser. I got sick just smelling the stuff and excused myself by saying I was sleepy and had to change my baby.

It was a relief after hours and hours of riding, cramped up on the train, when the conductor finally called out "Everybody off in Cincinnati." We all got up to get our belongings together. I looked out the window as we were crossing the Ohio River, which seemed very large to me compared to the Alabama River. I stopped staring because the water made me dizzy.

Big brother will take care of you

I held my baby tightly and walked up the slope to the waiting room. My two brothers were there waiting! Nelson, the spitting image of my father, stood stretching his neck looking for me. He saw me and held up his hand. I was grinning and so happy to see him and Lee. They both hugged and kissed me at the same time. This was the first time they had seen Eddie and they cracked up over the funny-looking little cap he wore.

Lee took my stub and waited for my bags. When the bags came, they cracked up again. "Where in the hell did you get those damn things?" Nelson said. "You left in a hurry, didn't you!!" We all laughed together.

As we walked through the terminal, I admired its beauty. The Cincinnati terminal was an absolute show-place in the 40s, with beautiful paintings, so large each seemed a story high. The floors were shiny and slick like glass. There were snack bars, alcohol bars, and movies. But most important — there were *no* signs saying WHITE and COLORED when I used the restroom. Everyone sat in the same waiting room. This was the first time in my life I saw *any* form of integration. I had never been out of the South before.

Outside was equally as beautiful! The front was shaped like an arch with colored glass windows. A fountain overflowed with water and formed a small pool at its foot. Small children, both White and Black, played in the water. Beautiful trees and shrubbery lined each side of the street. There was a well-kept park where people were sitting and lying on the grass. Some relaxed under the shade of the trees. Some older people just sat there, enjoying the sunshine and scenery.

As soon as we got one block from Victory Parkway, the whole picture started changing. I saw broken-down shacks that were a mockery to the terminal. We had arrived in the Colored slum part of town. Three and four story apartment houses, all ugly, dull, dirty, grey, were connected or very close together. Nelson told me they were called flats. Once in a while we passed a few brightly painted ones as we drove on to Nelson's and Lee's house.

Theirs was an exact duplicate of the dull, grey flats. Lee's wife greeted me and we hugged and kissed each other. She took my baby and cuddled him while I held her kids in the circle of my arms. Everyone talked at one time. The first thing that caught my eyes was the pickalow (juke box). Rows of shotglasses were lined up on their sink. A couple of tables were set up, as for playing several games of cards. The living room had too many sofas. I had briefly seen a rockola (bootleg) house in Selma, and I dug what was happening here. Nelson was running what was called an "after-hour joint" because people came after the beer gardens closed.

Nelson saw me taking inventory and said, "Making a living isn't easy, Sis. We have to make money any way we can. Selling booze is where I got the money to send back home and finish paying for the house."

I asked how he could be bothered with all those low-class people, and said, "Nelson, what will happen if they all get drunk and start fighting?"

"Don't worry about that," he said. He opened the top dresser drawer and pulled out a gun. "This .38 can take care of all the bad niggers. I live here. You just relax and enjoy yourself. You don't have a thing to worry about. Big brother will take care of you and whatever that is you call a baby!"

Everyone burst out laughing. (He always teased about the babies in the family, but he loved them dearly.)

Nelson asked me very seriously, "Sis, do you want your husband to come to you? I will help you two kids get on your feet." I said no, and he dropped the subject.

They all asked me questions about Selma. How is everything? How is everybody? Are those White folk still raising hell and whipping Negroes' heads? On and on, we talked for hours. Finally I told them I was tired and wanted to go to bed. My baby had already been bathed and was sleeping like the little angel that he was. I got on my knees and said my prayers and stretched out. How good the bed felt after those hours of riding!

The next day, I slept late. When I woke up, my sister-in-law had bathed and fed Eddie along with her kids. It was good to see my sister-in-law again. She and I had known each other in Selma since we were little bitty girls who used to make mud cakes and play with grass dolls.

The mailman brought a letter from my husband which he had written before I left. He warned me not to fool around with any man and threatened to come to Ohio even if we didn't live together. I got real mad all over again. He was passing the buck again and completely ignoring the reason I had left in the first place. I had hurt for such a long time, and he didn't understand my feelings, or a word I had said.

I decided to strike back with something that would hurt *him* for a change. I wrote, "Bill, please leave me alone. I am doing fine here. My brother is a bootlegger and I am going to have a ball in this house. Men come to the house and I will dance and have fun with everyone, everything except go to bed with them. But if I ever find a good man who cares for me, I will do that too. So leave me alone." That did it. I began my new life in Cincinnati, Ohio.

Part Two

Glittering Lights to Blackouts

Weekend Drinking

Just enough to be sociable

Because Alabama didn't have liquor stores at that time, most of the alcohol people drank back there was moonshine and home brew. My only experience with alcohol was the one or two drinks I had had during the time I was with my husband. When I moved in with Nelson, he told me to drink a beer or a few drinks, just enough to be sociable. And I was supposed to laugh and talk with his customers, just enough to make them feel comfortable.

"You can go on and on and have fun — everything except sleeping with these guys." When he gave me orders, I felt just like my father was talking to me. That was okay with me because I still had my own taboos, and didn't believe in throwing sex around. So I just enjoyed myself. It was like going to a party every night — and I always enjoyed partying. If we wanted to dance, all we had to do was drop a nickel in the juke box.

Nelson told me to drink anything I wanted. He said, "Don't ever sit before a customer and say you don't drink. Order a drink, and I can just pour you a shot glass of water and make that sale. The customer can't tell the difference. They'll think it's gin, because it'll be poured from a gin bottle." I went along with his game of deception.

One night I decided to try a watered-down drink but settled for a glass of beer. I sipped on my first taste of beer, and thought it was the nastiest, bitterest stuff I had ever tasted. I wasn't able to finish it the first time, but within a few days I could drink and keep half a glass of beer down.

A few days later I tried something a little bit stronger, orange sloe gin. It was real pretty and tasted sweet. I was almost a drunk after ten days of sipping at my brother's house!! I think that my compulsion to drink started when I started sipping on that first beer. My stomach couldn't take it, but in my head I was saying, "This sure is making me feel relaxed and good." And there was plenty there! It was available all the time and I could have all I wanted.

Here I was — a green Southern young lady who had never done anything but gone to school, church, teenage parties, got married and had a baby. I didn't *know* how people lived on the other side of the track, especially street people or those in the wild drinking world. These people were considered very "low class" and decent ministers' children, especially girls, weren't supposed to associate with them. Ladies just didn't hang around people like that. There I was, thrown into a drinking, bootlegging environment — and I didn't know how to handle it.

Right from the beginning I drank too much. I didn't realize I was playing with alcohol — taking a little beer, a little sloe gin. It tasted good, but I was already building a tolerance to alcohol. Little by little, I began drinking more. It usually made me sick and I would try to lie down. The bed would go 'round and 'round, and I'd get on my hands and knees to hold the bed down to stop spinning and swaying. I'd say to myself, "I'm not going to drink that much. Next time we have company, I'm only going to sip on a glass of beer" — but it never worked out that way.

Finally it took a little more to make me high. Where it used to be one glass of beer to get me high, now it took two full glasses, and where it took one ounce of sloe gin, it took two. Every weekend I drank until I was sick, and it took all the rest of the week to get over my hangover.

I *knew* Nelson made good money. I didn't have to work — he took care of me and my baby. I had nothing to worry about. Everyone respected me and treated me like a queen because I was the house man's sister. There was only one thing wrong — I was learning to drink more each weekend.

The bootlegger: sort of a celebrity

Bootleg houses were very, very popular in the Black neighborhoods for a number of reasons. You could drink, dance, gamble at cards and dice, meet the opposite sex, and just have fun twenty-four hours a day if you wanted to. As long as the house man was making money, he kept the doors open. And if he got too tired, he'd let a member of his family or maybe a good buddy (someone he could trust with his money) take over while he got a few hours sleep before he went back again. I remember Nelson saying, "Man, the joint is hot tonight!" Meaning that he was making money twenty-four hours that day!

The houses were deliberately kept dark, with dark shades and blinds so you wouldn't notice what time it was and would keep on spending money — and so the Law wouldn't notice the house. Some were beautiful places, just like being in a nightclub with booths, tables, and bars. *Everything* was right there. Most of them had transit rooms (bedrooms for prostitutes and lovers) upstairs and they made money right and left in this department also. A person didn't have to go out of the building for anything! Many places sold barbeque ribs and chitlings, and SOULS *love* barbeque ribs, honey. Black bootleggers made money.

The bootlegger was regarded as sort of a celebrity because all the drunks knew where they could get drinks after hours, and run up a tab if they were broke. Nelson, like the others, extended credit to heavy drinkers who looked upon him as a God. They were so grateful they could get their supply of booze even when they didn't have any money.

A bootlegger, like any other money-hungry business-man, often took advantage of the customer once that person was drunk. Sometimes drunks asked for credit and didn't remember exactly how much they had ordered. If they drank four shots, the bootlegger might write them down for five. And if they ordered a half-pint, he added an ounce of water or soda to the booze because they were too drunk to know the difference. Sometimes as much as a half-pint was added to a tab.

Yet, they still looked up to him, because he was supplying them with the booze to support the habit. Sometimes they questioned his honesty and became hos-tile, but they were afraid to get too angry for fear he'd stop their credit. If the bootlegger sold booze by the shot, his profit was extra high. And if he sold half-pints, this was also a great profit. The thick pitchers were considered a half-pint but they were short halves, so he could sell about an extra half-pint from each fifth bottle.

The bootlegger had to be very careful when he bought his supplies. In Ohio, alcohol was sold only in liquor stores, and to buy it you had to fill out a form with your name, address and brand of liquor. All this red tape to get a bottle of booze! It wasn't simple and easy like the states where you just walked in and bought booze off the shelf like a bottle of milk. A bootlegger whose name and address showed up too often caused suspicion and might be checked on by the Law. Police knew that anyone regularly buying that much wasn't drinking it by the cases himself every day — he had to be selling it. This was really bad for business, because sometimes everyone in the house was taken along to jail if it was raided. To avoid suspicion, my brother and other bootleggers would hire someone else to drive them to the liquor store and buy liquor under their own names. Nelson paid many of these people with half-pints of booze.

Another thing that contributed to the Black bootlegger's popularity was that the liquor store closed at ten on Saturday night and did not open again until 11 a.m. on Monday. For people who enjoy drinking, and particularly for the person who was hooked on alcohol, that was unfortunate. Can you imagine any hard-core alcoholic not being able to get a drink for a whole weekend? Most working people had to be on the job by 11 a.m. on Monday, so without booze at home, this person was completely out, unless he went to the bootleg houses.

Also, the beer gardens (called joints or clubs) stopped selling strong drinks at midnight Saturday night. About 11:30, the bartender would yell, "Last call for whiskey and six percent beer!" And one minute after midnight the owner would be in trouble if he was caught selling booze on a Sunday. Brothers and Sisters at the peak of drinking and having fun didn't want to stop drinking and go home at midnight on a Saturday night. So they'd leave the beer gardens and head straight to the after-hours joints where they could ball, Baby, all night long! Many people from Cincinnati went over the river to Newport and Covington, Kentucky, but enough stayed in Cincinnati to support the bootleg houses.

I was beginning to really enjoy my new world. Everyone who came to the house was clean and nice, and very well dressed. Even the known prostitutes who came to my brother's house wore beautiful clothes and diamonds.

Blacks in the "hustling field" dug good clothes and expensive jewelry. They liked to impress their peers — often someone would say, "Joe Blow had on a diamond ring that shined so it lit up the room when he walked in." And, "He was as clean as a M.F. . . . !!" This meant a Black was doing alright for himself! Especially if he was carrying a roll of money big enough to choke an elephant. To top it off, he might drive a fine, big car. These were the Black man's dreams.

When hustling Blacks had good nights on gambling or hit on the numbers (which was booming in Cincinnati and around Newport), they'd go and buy those expensive diamond rings. That's something the Whites may not be able to understand, but anyone who had a good diamond ring, good jewelry and good clothes was never broke. They could always go to the pawn shop to get some money.

Many times you'd see a hustling Black one day with his fingers full of diamond rings and wearing expensive suits, expensive top coats, and all this good stuff. Then you might see him again the next day or two, without a ring on at all! That's because he hit a bad streak, he picked a bad number or lost too much in the poker game or whatever gambling he was doing. Once he hit another lucky streak, he went back to the pawn shop to get his jewelry back.

There was a togetherness among the bootleggers, the gamblers and the prostitutes. Many, many times I saw a person who hit a bad streak and couldn't even buy a bowl of soup walk up to another and say, "You gonna take care of me today? I got busted last night." The other would reach out and say, "Come on." They'd each feed the other one, give him a few bucks to go in his pocket, and look out for him. If he had pawned his last suit, this other Brother would even let him go to his wardrobe and have a good suit so he could make a good impression.

Silver fox for Sister

People like that were beginning to be my models and I was beginning to change, wanting to be like them. The drunks didn't seem too bad to me anymore, because they weren't what would be called skid-row bum types. They were always dressed real nice — *very* well dressed, as a matter of fact. Brothers and Sisters can get it together when they want to. They may not make that much money, but even if it's Mr. Charlie's hand-me-downs, they take it and get it together and make it look good.

My brother bought me clothes, diamonds, anything that I asked him for. He bought me furs too. I will never forget the most *beautiful* silver fox short jacket and great big muff, with a purse and hat to go with it. He kept money at a certain place in the house and told me to go in and help myself to all I wanted. He didn't care what I had, just so I was a nice girl.

One of the things I couldn't do was go to the houses on Sixth Street. That was the first thing my brother let me know when I moved to Cincinnati, "I don't want you on Sixth Street. Anybody who hangs out there is considered low-class people. Guys won't respect any woman who hangs out there and don't you ever fool around with a man who hangs out there — it's rough." So I never went that way.

I did want male companionship, though. John, a man who worked with my brother Lee, constantly came over to the house. He wasn't a heavy drinker and he was very well-mannered. I told him Nelson might not let me go out with him, so he got permission from Nelson himself to take me to a movie. My brother approved but gave strict orders that if anything happened to me, John had better not come back to tell Nelson, "because your ass will belong to me." This first date in Ohio led to many dates with John, and soon we started going steady.

I was drinking a little then, but didn't realize what I was building up with it. I just thought I was drinking to relax, for relief for the moment. I didn't know I was also drinking to escape things that were unpleasant to face, and to get some false courage. Now when John and I went to clubs, I drank the "hard stuff." The taste was pleasant and the effect was fast. I felt it immediately and got drunk on about two gin cocktails and a glass of beer. As I continued to go out, I was able to drink the third drink too.

Jimmy Reed said in his song, "Bright lights and big cities went to my Baby's head." I could really identify with that song, which must have been written just for me! The booze and the atmosphere went together like peaches and cream. I was turned on to the bands, and to all the glamorous people in night clubs. I liked the soft carpeting and the glittering lights. I had never been in them before, so I went hog-wild and pig-crazy.

I enjoyed dressing up in fine dresses with matching bags, shoes, gloves, and hats. Because my hair was only about four inches long, I added a page boy to extend the length, which looked very good under my hat. I was sure I looked as good as the other ladies — and sometimes I was drunk enough that I thought I looked better.

Drinking and visiting clubs continued, with John as my lover and escort. I began to look forward to Friday and getting really high every weekend.

One Friday night, a girl friend and I went to the neighborhood bar to have a few drinks. We only bought the first round because people started sending drinks our way from both our left and right. She refused some of the drinks and drank some of the others. On the other hand, I just kept on drinking until I had had at least six double shots of gin and water. We sat there a few more minutes. We lived in different directions, so we said goodnight and headed for home. All I remember is making it to the first corner.

When I came to my senses, I was rolling down a whole flight of steps at my brother's house. I don't recall walking the other two blocks and I don't recall climbing the steps. When my brothers came to check out the noise, they found me in a heap at the foot of the stairs. My elbows were bloody and I had a busted lip. I had vomited and had also started to urinate. This was my first *blackout* and probably my first real, hard drunk. My brothers picked me up and took me upstairs, took care of my wounds, and put me to bed with a vomiting pot on the floor. I vomited on and off all night. God!! I was sick as a dog for days.

Years later I learned that drinking yourself into a blackout is *not* being a social drinker. I am not saying PASS out — to pass out is to go to sleep, as a person in a coma. A person continues to function in a blackout — you can walk, you can talk, raise hell, fight or have a ball at parties, but the next day you don't remember what happened.

Often I've heard my Black Brothers and Sisters say, "Man, I had to look out the window the next morning to see if my wheels were out there, because I don't remember driving home!" Or the car might be parked with the ass-end four feet from the curb — "I must have hit something because there's a dent in the fender and a different kind of paint!" This brought a whole lot of laughter and everyone acted like it was a joke. But now I can tell you it wasn't funny — it was dangerous. That extra paint and dent in the fender could have been blood from killing a human being.

It is just like having amnesia. I've known of people who committed crimes such as robberies, rape, or even murder while in a blackout and didn't remember one thing about it. When they woke up in jail, they had to be told what they were charged with. According to Dr. Melvin H. Knisley, professor of anatomy at the Medical University of South Carolina, brain damage starts with the first drink. It affects the part of the brain that causes us to think and to make judgments.

A bucketful of Southern hate

No one told me I was on a bus and my destination was alcoholism. As soon as I felt better, I drank again. As I continued to drink every weekend, I needed more and more booze to reach that high peak. John and I would stay straight through the dawn dance. I had a ball but he began to notice how much I was drinking. He'd say, "This is the last drink for us tonight." I wouldn't object, but I didn't want to stop. My brothers also were starting to say, "O.K. Sis, you've had enough . . . no repeat performance of the time before."

I began to feel they were all picking on me and I started to think of a way to get my own apartment. But I had never worked and wasn't trained in any special field. The only thing I could possibly do was domestic work.

Plenty of waitress jobs were advertised in the newspaper but all of them asked for "lightskinned Colored girls." I am very black, which was not considered beautiful in the 40s, so there was no use trying for those jobs. Or I will say, society didn't *see* the beauty.

So I tried a domestic job and lasted only one day. I was on my knees scrubbing Mrs. Charlie's floor when the kitchen phone rang. She rushed to answer it and accidentally touched me with her foot as she picked up the phone. She said, "Hello," to her party and, "I'm sorry, Chaney," to me. I assume the party on the phone asked what happened because she said, "Oh, nothing . . . I just accidentally stumbled on my maid."

When she said that, I went wild! I suppose all the built-up Southern hate came out and I took it out on her. I told her to clean her own damned floors. I went so far as dumping the whole pail of water all over the floor, sink, table . . . and I walked out. I never went back to collect my pay. When I got home to my brother, still raving mad and crying, he just laughed and collected his bet from my brother Lee. He said, "I told you she wouldn't last one week!" He poured me a drink and finally I was laughing too.

In trouble with drinking

My brother told me to stay home, and he'd take care of me and my son. I remained cool for a short time. World

War II was getting into full bloom by this time.

Jobs and pay were increasing and I read in the paper that a youth training school was opening. Ladies now were being trained to do defense work during the war. I walked about fifteen blocks to inquire, filled out an application and was enrolled about two weeks later. God, I was so happy! My first attempt to earn my own money! It paid a beautiful salary of $25 a month while training. There I was taught how to use high-power machines, like the ones used in sheet metal work and welding. I learned fast and was very interested in the work.

I'll never forget how I sat and waited on my paycheck each month so I could go shopping for skirts and blouses, which I bought with my own hard-earned money!

Many young people were in training with me. When we left school about 9:00 p.m., we'd stop to have drinks. Although none of us was twenty-one, old enough to purchase alcohol, there were always one or two in the crowd who looked older and bought it. Sometimes we bought beer, which we kept in the bag so the police wouldn't know, and drank while we walked home.

We planned our fun for each weekend. Whether it was visiting the beer gardens or partying at someone's house, drinking was always involved. Some of the young people were social drinkers who only drank a couple of beers or shots. But several, me included, usually drank too much. I'd get sick and have to call my brother to come to take me home. John got on me for running with a wild crowd, and my brother was still nagging. I didn't see anything wrong with young people having a little fun and didn't realize that several of us were in trouble with our drinking.

As John and my brothers kept on me about drinking so much, I started hiding an extra bottle in my closet so they wouldn't know. I'd drink one drink in their presence, then sneak into my room and have another, or add something to the drink in my hand. I really had them fooled, sneaking drinks. I guess social drinkers don't really care that much about alcohol because they can drink it or leave it alone, even if they are in a room full of free booze. But as I was sneaking drinks, alcohol was becoming to have a very special meaning, playing a major part in my life.

I continued drinking and running with the young people from training school. My personality and moral values began to change. I was good at jokes and toasts and expecially loved telling a very profane one called "The Signifying Monkey" which was very popular with Black people.

"The Monkey told the lion one fine sunny day,
There's a burly M.F. down the way!
Now I *know* that you two don't get along!
But every time I see that clown, he sure has got a song!
I don't know how to tell you what I have to say,
But he's *talking about your Mama,* in a hell of a way!
The Lion got mad and went in a rage,
Like a young punk blowing his gauge!
He knocked down coconuts, and pulled up trees,
And brought giraffes to their bending knees!
He finally found Mr. Elephant lying in the shade of a palm tree
And said, "Get up you big M.F. it's gonna be you and me!!"
The Elephant looked at him out of the corner of his eyes
And said, "You better go on, small fry, and play with someone your size!"
The Lion led off with a hell of a pass,
But missed Mr. Elephant and got knocked on his ass.
The Elephant broke his jaw and messed up his face,
And knocked his assbone plumb out of place!
Mr. Lion finally crawled off, more dead than alive —
Again, from the top of a tree Mr. Monkey began to Signify.
Ah Ha! Mr. Lion, you done caught hell!!
Mr. Elephant done beat your ass to a fare-you-*well!*

When you left here the jungle rung,
And here you come back, damn near hung!
Call yourself KING OF THE JUNGLE, ain't you a *bitch!!*
Your face looks like you caught the Seven Years Itch!!
The Monkey got so excited and he jumped up and down,
But his feet slipped and his ass hit the ground.
Like a bolt of lightning or a streak of white heat,
Mr. Lion was on him with all four feet.
The Monkey looked up with tears in his eyes
And said, "Please Mr. Lion, I apologize!"
Mr. Lion said, "It's no use pleading and crying.
Today, I am going to put a stop to your Jungle
Signifying!"

I would emphasize each word of profanity, which brought on hysterical laughter from my audience. It is a long toast that takes about twenty minutes to tell, and I could hold a whole room full of drinkers spellbound while telling it. Many times I was asked to parties or asked to tell that toast in the beer gardens. Everyone would applaud and start sending drinks to our table from all directions, which made me feel like a celebrity. Before, I never used curse words and detested anyone who did. And here I was, publicly using the worst profane words, and thinking nothing of it. I was with the crowd, and did what they did.

John hated those people and did not want me with them. I knew that he and my brothers didn't approve of my drinking or the toasts, so I started telling more lies. I'd tell John I was going to a shower — girls only. Or I had to work late, or was going to visit one of the girls who was sick. *Any lie* to get away from him spying on me and trying to run my life. Of course, we began to argue constantly. He'd say, "Who do you think you are fooling?"

I'd say, "I'm not trying to fool anyone — can't I have a little fun with my friends without you nagging? I have a right to visit the *sick* and they had drinks there. I only had a couple and we got to talking and time just passed." I was really beginning to believe my own lies. So I continued with the crowd, drinking and going to dances or anyplace else where there was a fun crowd.

John and I continued to argue and then broke up.

Hurting the ones I loved most

One Saturday night the crowd had all gone to the Cotton Club, where we stayed on through the dawn dance, feeling high, and still didn't want to go home. We walked back to the Elks Club, about four blocks away on Eighth Street. Because it was a private club, it stayed open around the clock. We went in like a noisy army troop, pulled about four tables together and continued to ball.

I was feeling good and high, but not really drunk the whole night. I knew I looked nice, and my outfit was expensive. I had on my silver fox fur jacket with matching muff and hat, a grey tailored suit, red blouse, shoes and gloves.

That night I felt very free because now I didn't have John breathing down my neck. I continued to drink and play the juke box. One by one, everybody started to leave until about four of us girls were left at the table. As people left, the waitress moved the empty tables away. Now I realize we four were really getting in trouble with booze and didn't know it. We sat there and whispered about everybody, giggling and having fun.

A good-looking, well-dressed man came over to our table, pulled up a chair without being invited, and started talking. Earlier I had noticed him sitting at another table with two girls because he had sleepy looking eyes and a beautiful gold crown with a diamond set right in the middle of it on one of his front teeth. I had never seen such beauty in a man's mouth before. He was a real sharp cat.

As he talked, his eyes were constantly traveling from

my head to my feet. He started talking directly to me. "Where did you get your beautiful furs? I've been noticing you since you came in and admiring your outfit. You must have a good husband looking out for you."

We talked for about half an hour and then I told him and the girls I was leaving. He offered to drive me home, but I said no. He followed me out and as I turned right to head home, he violently pulled me in the opposite direction. I said, "What's the matter with you? Take your hands off me. I'm not going any damn place with you."

He flipped open a switchblade knife and held it to my side, and pushed me in front of him. I was terrified. Although I was pretty high when I walked out of the Elks, this scene brought me to my senses real fast. He told me he was taking me to the hotel where he kept all his other whores. "I know you're lying about a brother buying your clothes. I know damn well you're working on your own. I want you to pull those furs off as soon as we get to the hotel because I have a girl who's going to meet a heavy cat, and she needs to make a good impression."

I thought I had to be dreaming! Here was a strange man who never had seen me before, talking to me and counting me as one of his girls. I looked around hoping to see someone who could help me but no one was in sight. Everything flashed through my mind, but he still held a firm grip on my arm and the knife to my side.

He walked me up to the corner and made a right turn in front of Stowe School. I saw a car coming. When I saw that there were four black men in it, I screamed, "Please help me," at the top of my voice, and kept screaming. The car stopped, and the men got out and came over to investigate. The pimp's whole facial expression changed, and he calmly told the men, "That's alright. Everything's okay! This is my wife, and she's been out all night long away from our children. I'm sick of her pulling this shit on me. And I'm taking care of her, so just go on."

I kept trying to tell them it wasn't true, but he really

was a very good actor and convinced them that I was a no-good wife who'd been out from her husband and kids all night long. So they got back in the car and drove away and left me. I felt a stinging in my side, and I saw the knife had penetrated through all my clothes. When I glanced down, there was blood. God, was I scared and I was still praying. Steps at Stowe School led from the sidewalk into the basement classrooms. He pushed me down the steps and said, "Later on, I'll take those furs, but right now, I'm going to get some pussy. If you don't want me to empty your guts, you better do as I say." He started pulling at my clothes trying to raise my skirt, while pushing me down at the same time. Because I knew there was no use struggling with him and I didn't know how badly I was cut, I tried not to show panic.

I calmly told him, "You're right. I'm living alone, and you're an attractive man. Why go through all this shit? Why don't you just come on and walk me home to my apartment and we can spend some time together?"

He toned down, and accepted my proposition, but he still held the knife on me. From time to time as we walked, I could feel the point of his knife as he shoved a little to reinforce his sincerity. I prayed every step of the way, "Please God, let my brother be at home. Don't let my brother be upstairs!" Maybe a policeman would pass. I knew that things at home might be pretty quiet at that hour. Nelson might be at his girl friend's house and Lee might be asleep upstairs, so he wouldn't hear me even if I got into my room. This man could still kill me and no one would know.

When we reached the house, I unlocked the front door and my heart stopped. There was not a soul in sight, not a sound in the house. The man came in and said, "Okay, let's get the show on the road." He closed the door. I remember saying, "Wait here while I go to the bathroom." We were standing in the living room, and he asked, "Where's the bedroom?"

I pointed to a door that really led to a hall. The bathroom actually led through to the bedroom and then to the kitchen. From the kitchen I'd be able to escape outside. That's where my mind was — if I could just get through, I could get out. I got as far as the bedroom, and, Oh God, thank you, there was Nelson stretched out across my bed, sleeping like a baby. Oh what a beautiful, sweet, lovely Black man! I was never so glad to see anyone in my life.

I moved around the bed to quietly wake him. As I glanced into the kitchen, I saw John sitting there sipping on a beer! I held my finger to my mouth to try to get John to come and be quiet. When he came, I woke Nelson. I shushed him and told them there was a man in the front who said he was going to rape me and rob me or maybe kill me. I pulled my coat back to show them where he had held the knife to me all the way home. Blood had soaked all the way through my clothing and was running down my skirt.

When they saw this, all hell broke loose. Nelson grabbed his gun and John picked up the meat cleaver. They went crazy. Just then, the man called out, "Well . . . don't take forever, bitch, I'm tired of waiting."

My brother ran out the back door, made it in a split second to the front and kicked the door open. He threw a half-brick at the man and shot at him a couple of times. The pimp started hollering and running toward the bedroom. By the time he got to the back, John was standing there saying, "No, M.F., you don't come this way!"

I saw they were definitely going to kill him and started to scream. I kept thinking they would both go to the electric chair. All this kept flashing — I knew the man had put me through hell, but I became hysterical. I could just see somebody dead lying there. They were more upset about my screaming because they let him run out the door. Nelson and John tried to quiet me down and put me in bed. I felt full of remorse and guilt. Within my mind I knew that if I had been home, all this wouldn't have happened. I was so glad it was all over. But it wasn't

A week later on a Sunday morning, two policemen knocked on the door and asked if my "husband" was home. I told them he was in Detroit. The policemen said, "We're here to arrest your husband for cutting with intent to kill last night at the Elks Club."

At first I thought they were really talking about my husband, but my mind just opened, saying, "Oh my God, no." Their description fit Nelson to a "t." They said he was real tall, thin, and real black. I knew it must be Nelson, but I denied knowing him. I was scared to death because he wasn't home, and I didn't know what to say. As I stood there with the police, my mind kept saying, "O.K., somebody else *is* suffering for what you did."

I was hurting the people that I loved most. Both those guys could have been in jail for murder. Nelson had been asking around that week until he found out who my attacker was and that he was not only a pimp but a drug addict. I was told that Nelson walked into the Elks and saw him picking on another lady. When Nelson called his name, the man turned around, and Nelson just started to cut on him.

They told me Nelson went hysterical and stood on a table to announce that any S.O.B. who put his hand on his sister better be prepared to die or to kill him. He just went crazy.

The pimp ran outside the door, half cut to death, and collapsed on the sidewalk. For weeks he was in the hospital, hovering between life and death. No one knew if he'd die or not.

The police started coming to the house regularly, looking for Nelson and asking questions. To avoid prosecution Nelson had to leave town and go to New York.

Nelson was gone. He had to give up his bootleg

business and everything else. In another way he really was paying for my stupidity, although, thank God, it wasn't the electric chair. He *wasn't* arrested but he was paying for my being out there in the streets, drinking all night.

My attacker lived and later told the Elks bartender to tell me and my brother that he had dropped all charges. He said he knew he was wrong and was sorry for his actions. He told them he was just tripping on drugs and didn't know what he was doing. But about a year later, this same man was sent to prison for raping and assaulting a girl in Terminal Park, so he was a very sick man.

I called Nelson and told him all charges had been dropped, so he could come back home if he wanted. He was happy that he was no longer wanted by the police, but he chose to stay in New York in his new *legal* business, a combination grocery and liquor store. He invited me to come live with him. I liked Cincinnati and wanted to stay there.

Trapped in a hole

Lee and his family moved with Eddie and me into an apartment. We no longer sold booze, which meant there wasn't very much income without the bootleg profits. Lee washed dishes and was general porter at a restaurant, and his wife was now going to the youth training school with me. She didn't run with the gang much because she had a husband to go home to, and because she could either take booze or leave it alone. Lee's salary was now about $25 a week since the war had come on in full bloom and caused everyone to get raises. Both Lee's wife and I were making our little $25 a month salaries for training. We were able to manage since the apartment rent was only $14 a month.

We lived in a one-bedroom apartment with no hot water and no bathroom on the first floor of a three-story building. All three floors shared one toilet in the back

yard, a type of toilet that flushed itself when you got off
the stool. And stayed filthy. I'll never forget how I used to
go out there with buckets of hot water and scrub to try to
clean it and the next day find it filthy again. Oh, I hated
that.

It's funny now to remember — how we would sit there
on the steps waiting for the toilet until the other person
came out. And how we stood out in the yard, gossiping
and talking, with everybody holding their own rolls of
toilet paper. This was typical housing in the poor Black
slums. Most Blacks lived this way, and the landlord didn't
give a damn — he just collected the rent from these rat-
and roach-infested dumps.

We washed our clothes in the kitchen in a tin tub with a
washboard and hung them in the yard to dry. Each family
had special wash days assigned for the clotheslines. If it
rained or snowed, we stretched lines all over the apartment and turned up the heat in the kitchen so that the
clothes could dry. There were no laundromats at that
time. The same tin tub was also our bathtub. It was class,
Baby, when we went to a hardware store and bought a tin
tub shaped like a bath tub. Wow!

We had only one single bowl, an ugly kitchen sink, for
everything in this slum apartment. There we had to brush
our teeth, wash our dishes, and dump out the bath and
mop water. It wasn't sanitary to put dishes in this sink, so
we washed them in a dish pan, set them in a dish rack on
the drainboard, and scalded them with a kettle of hot
water. We all managed to live in the little apartment by
using day beds and studio couches for sleeping room.

And if any of us poor Blacks complained to the
landlord about fixing up the place, he got very nasty. "If
you don't like it, move. I can always rent to someone
else." This blew our minds, but he was telling the truth.
He could.

This may sound like it happened a hundred years ago,
but Blacks lived like this right there in Ohio in the 40s.

And many of my Black Sisters and Brothers are *still* living like this, right here in *America the Beautiful.*

We shopped for cheap food at the Sixth Street Market each Saturday, so at least we weren't hungry. Blacks started getting refrigerators during World War II when they became popular. Like most other poor Blacks then, we just had an ice box, and we bought ice daily from the iceman. The icebox didn't preserve the meat well enough to load up on it because it would spoil. We also bought coal from the iceman.

Rats as big as kittens ran around that dumpy apartment. We had to nail tin over the places where the rats had absolutely cut holes in the floor. A lady who lived in back of us had hot flashes and said that she always slept with her feet out from under the covers. One morning about two o'clock, her husband had to rush her to the hospital because a great big rat came while she had her feet hanging out and bit her on the big toe. It was all bloody, a severe bite, and she had to have several shots. After it was over her husband said, "Now, you'll keep your damn feet under the covers!" We laughed because it was sort of a joke, a woman going around with her big toe all bandaged and swollen up because she had her toes hanging out from under the covers! But still, rat bites were serious, and I was scared to death. They could bite my baby and other kids. I dreamt of how rats might chew his lips off or bite him in the face.

Another thing that made me sick about this dump and our living conditions was the pots we had to use because there was no bathroom. One morning the kids woke up and were playing in the bedroom before we had emptied the night pots, which we had all urinated in during the night. All at once, we heard little Vivian scream, "Momma, Daddy! Come here. The baby done fell in the *tea pot* and he can't get out!"

We all ran to see what the hell was happening and there was my baby with his head down in this darn pot, positively drowning in everyone's piss. Oh my God, it made me sick! He couldn't turn the pot over and he couldn't get out! You can imagine how I felt. My brother rushed him to the hospital and I was too upset to go. I was just sick to think of the filth that poor little thing had swallowed and how sick he was.

Later we put in a gas stove and gas heat. We had to have it installed and pay for running in the gas lines ourselves, because the landlord absolutely refused to do so. When he came to collect the rent he saw we had nice gas heaters and that we had painted up and papered the walls. (We really went to work to try to fix the place up real nice.) Believe it or not, the next month that bastard raised our rent four dollars! Brother Lee was so damned mad he went down there to his office and threatened to kick that man's ass. He raised hell, he clowned, he said everything, but, again, this landlord said, "Pay, or move."

So we had to pay the additional four dollars a month to stay in this trap. If we moved, he could just collect more rent from the next person who moved into it. And if we moved, it would probably only be to another dump with filth, nailholed walls and no gas heat — we'd be harming ourselves more than anything else. So we, as many other poor Blacks, were trapped.

But I was still trying to find a way out. I still wanted my own apartment. Too many of us were crowded into a one-bedroom apartment. There was Lee, his wife, their two kids, my son, and me. I never did like too many people living with me. My mother used to say, "Every rat should have his own hole."

A way out

Mother and Dad invited me to come on and live with them, but I didn't want that. When I left the South, I'd said I wasn't going back. I remember telling my sister-in-law, "I'll stay here in Cincinnati and pick shit with the birds before I ever go back to the South to live. Never, never will I move back there. Things will *never* get tough enough for me to go back." I was used to things being tough and at least I didn't have to listen to people discussing a lynch party. And I never did go back, except to bury my brother, Brad.

But I did want to move out of that apartment. My mind was really set on Laurel Homes, which were apartments something like government projects but so very nice compared to the dump that we were living in. But it took money to get there and I couldn't make those rent payments and live out of $25 a month! It was the old saying, "Money talks and shit walks." Meaning if you don't have any money, keep on walking! So, I had to keep on walking! I kept "walking" to the youth school to learn whatever I could, which was all I could do right then.

While my sister-in-law and I were in school a lady who lived right next door kept a lookout for the kids. After several months, a nice lady who lived on the third floor told us the kids were *not* exactly being cared for. She said, "Your babysitter is taking those kids to joints, and drinking too much around them, and everything like that."

Regardless of my own drinking, I didn't like this. I still wanted Eddie to be taken care of properly. Now that the war was coming on, Lee was afraid he would be drafted, so we had to think a little bit ahead. If Lee *was* drafted, it would be too much to leave those children in the hands of an unreliable babysitter. We also knew that we would have to make a living if he were gone. Until we graduated from Youth School, neither of us was really trained to do anything.

My sister-in-law and I wrote our parents in Selma, Alabama, and asked if they could keep our children until we finished school. Both parents agreed. Mom took my son, and my sister-in-law's mother took her son and daughter while we worked.

Now that I knew that my child was well cared for, I studied harder to learn everything I could in this youth training school, but I was still drinking and playing this role. We were still balling, and John was still dropping in to see me sometimes.

I remember the very, very tough head lady at the school who we all called "Red Head." If she happened to show up when anyone was playing around, she'd expel everyone, including the supervisors. So I was scared stiff when I was called into her office. I had worked so hard to learn, was getting good grades and had almost finished my six months of training.

For a full minute, which seemed like hours, she didn't say a word. She just stared at me and then picked up my records which were in a brown folder in front of her.

Then she asked, "How would you like to go to another school? This will be a *promotion*. The supervisor says you are doing an outstanding job, and he feels you could make it. It's a defense-training school and if you pass all the written practical work, you'll get a job at Wright Aeronautical Plant!"

My heart did about a hundred flip flops!! I knew a few people who had gotten jobs at Wright's. (The war was really all-out now, and defense plants were opening everywhere!) My head was just spinning, thinking of the difference between $25 a month and $35 or $40 a week. But I caught myself trying to cop out by saying, "I haven't even finished high school, I don't know what bus to ride."

Red Head saw I was uncertain and confused. She said, "Just go to this address at 8:30 Monday morning." She wrote the address on her card and told me who I was to see.

Oh, I walked out of that office with mixed emotions; I felt sad, scared and happy. All that weekend I was too nervous and anxious to get drunk. Instead, I prayed to help me to keep my nerves quiet.

It seemed like a year, but finally Monday came, and I rode to Fountain Square which was in the center of town and the main place to get on buses going in all directions. I arrived at the building, and asked for the man whose name Red Head had given me. He asked me to wait with what seemed like a multitude of people, sitting on benches and chairs.

My heart fell again. There were so many competitors. My feelings only worsened as I sat and listened to the conversations. Some were talking about their previous work experience. Some talked of the high school education they had finished. Some spoke of when they attended college. And here I was, a tenth grade dropout with just a little training at the youth school! It really didn't give me very much confidence in myself.

Finally we were all ushered to a large room set up as a regular school room with desks. We were given applications to fill out. Were you ever arrested? What race? Your grandmother's maiden name? And so on. What's your height? A chart showed about how much you were *supposed* to weigh if you were a certain height. I'm 5'5", and I should have been at least about 125 pounds, but I doubt that I weighed 110 pounds. And then there was math, but, thank God, some of the problems were just like the ones we had in youth training school.

Another page asked what should be done for safety in a shop. Then there were the little blocks which tested how fast we could move our hands. Fortunately, at the training school we often passed break time by playing with those things. Sometimes we'd bet a beer to see who could finish first. So I passed that test also.

When I finished all the tests, they told me to go home and wait until I received a letter telling me if I had qualified for the training. God, that was a ten-day sweat! Watch the mail box! I was jumpy and nervous. I actually dreamed of getting my first weekly check of $35. I needed and wanted that job.

After all that torture, at last the letter came and I was scared to open it. My hands shook and sweat ran down on me. I almost got sick to my stomach. Finally I pulled my bottle out of my closet and made a couple of drinks. As the first drink took effect, I felt I could face the worst. I ripped open the envelope with my finger. The first thing that caught my eyes was, "You are to report for training Monday," and on and on and on. I ran all over the house, hollering and telling everyone! I was so excited and so thankful. "Thank God, thank You Jesus! Thank you! Thank you!"

Iron monsters and Amazons

Wright's training was really rough. When I walked into that place, I saw larger machines than I had ever seen before. The machines at the youth center were just toys compared to these. I would be trained to operate an I.D. Grinder, which ground the inside of barrels which went on airplane motors. I was taught how to read a micrometer, a small gauge rubbed inside the barrel to check whether it was smooth enough. This micrometer was broken down into minute parts of an inch. And everything had to be right.

I had some drinks during my six weeks of training but I was so busy studying and so anxious to pass that I really didn't have time for the crowd. After they tried to get me to go out with them for a couple of weekends and I refused, they let me slide. I worked religiously and when my six weeks were up, I had made it! I passed! I was to report the following Monday with my birth certificate!

When I got to the plant I had to be examined by a doctor there for blood pressure, heart, and so forth. I was underweight. You never saw a Sister put on more of a *show* when they said I might be rejected because I was so skinny! You see, the machines were so huge — the barrels were heavy and had to be held with a puller that swung them in and out of the machine. It was quite possible, being so skinny, that I would tire easily and not reach my quota. I guess the doctors and nurses were tired of me acting a fool, or felt sorry for me, because they laughed and patted me on the back and said, "Go on to work."

When I got to the assembly line, there were *rows* of I.D. Grinders standing like iron monsters. Rows! Huge things! Wouldn't you know that *my* machine was between two great big, healthy ladies! I remember thinking, "Chaney, you've got to do your thing to keep up with these Amazons. I can do it. I'll show these mothers that I can work. I've got to do it or go back to Mrs. Charlie's floors."

So I squared my shoulders, took a deep breath and dug in. Put the hook on the first barrel. Insert it, clamp it in my machine, press the button, and oh, that beautiful sound — singggggg, grind, stop! Examine with my "Mic," push the button, singggggg, grind, stop, examine with my "Mic," over and over and over again, barrel after barrel. And when the first day was up, I was only eight barrels behind those ladies who had been working weeks before I got there!

I was tired and my shoulders ached, but I was determined, regardless of how skinny I was. I was always skinny, like my dad who stood over six feet tall and was thin as a rail, but no man outworked him. And I was just as determined as Dad was to do whatever I had to do. So I finished work that day, went home, took a bath, rubbed down with alcohol, got up the next morning, went back the next day and over and over again ground barrel after barrel. The second day I ended doing five less barrels than the Amazons.

When the week was over, I was right even with the two ladies on each side of me! The next week I worked even harder. I wanted to do *more* barrels than they could, and I did. My supervisor was reporting to the main office about my progress, and I wanted to make a good showing.

I can't put into words how I felt when that first check for two weeks' work came. I kept staring at it and saying, "Seventy dollars!" I had never had that much money before — just for myself. I had to cash it! I remember telling one of my friends, "I wish I could frame this and keep it for the rest of my life." I sent some home to Mom for my baby and went and bought a few things. I felt like I was rich!

Soon I stopped running with the crowd from the youth center. I was still drinking, but now it was with the people from Wright's who were not like the youngsters at the youth center. And I didn't want John to bother me at all anymore. I'd found these new people who were very much more adult and went different places. We would get off at midnight, go to the beer gardens and stay there until we went to an after-hour bootleg place. We'd stay there and ball 'til day, then go home and rest so we'd still be able to make work at four o'clock in the afternoon. I was digging every minute of it and feeling grown-up.

I had written Mother to tell her about my good job and ask her to keep the baby while I made this money. She was happy because now she could start saving some money too. My dream of moving out of the slum was still very strong and I was beginning to make plans. Each paycheck I had a certain amount deducted to buy War Bonds. I'd given up all hope of ever getting an apartment in the Laurel Homes because the waiting list was so long. It would be almost impossible for me to get in because people who had lived in Cincinnati longer and servicemen's wives were the first to be considered. You had to know the right people or you never would make it. I decided to continue saving money by buying bonds to maybe buy a small, cheap home whenever the war ended. As much as I disliked that ugly apartment, I was still fortunate because *any* form of housing was scarce during World War II.

From - Sister

To - Dad,

These photographs of me and my family (shown here and on the
following pages) bring back different times in my life — some good
and proud times, like my own and my children's graduations; some
bad times, like the ones when I was drinking. But I always enjoyed
dressing up in fine dresses, with matching bags, shoes, gloves and
hats. For years I kept on snowing myself with the phony idea that
alcoholics don't dress well or look good. So obviously I wasn't an
alcoholic!

My parents, the Rev. and Mrs. B.H. Allen, photographed in the early 40s (above) and sometime in the 50s (below), were married in 1911 and had a long and loving marriage. Of their eleven children, six reached maturity. Dad served the Lord as a CME minister for over 50 years. He used to say jokingly about his bald head, "I'm a preacher and there couldn't be anything between me and God."

Lee (above) and I were always a close brother and sister. None of us ever forgot Dad's lessons about keeping strong family ties, which he illustrated for us children by passing around a bound-up bundle of wooden matches during Sunday breakfasts.

My brother, Nelson, dressed as quite the dandy when he was running his "after hour" place. (A bootlegger was sort of a celebrity.) Nelson took care of me and my baby when we moved north to Cincinnati from Selma. He was always there when I needed him.

My brother, Henry (right), tap danced for a U.S.O. program. Both Henry and Lee lived with us off and on in Ohio. Even grown up, we all stuck together and helped each other out. Not pictured are my brother, Bradford, now dead, and my brother, Roy.

When I visited my children in San Diego in 1968, our reunion called for a celebration — and some clowning around (above). Lee and Mom and I all moved to California a couple of years later.

My children, Eddie, Vivian and Spike, posed in their Easter outfits when the boys were ten years old and Vivian was twelve. My kids knew that all I could give them was a high school education, but they all went on to school and college on their own. They never gave me any trouble. I'm so proud of them. Here we are (below) in Mexican sombreros during my trip west to visit them in 1968, the last year I drank.

Eddie, valedictorian of his high school class, went to college, then joined Spike in the Marines before continuing in college. He is now president of the San Diego Chapter of Operation PUSH (People United to Save Humanity) and works with a program to screen for sickle cell anemia. He has a black belt in judo.

Spike was handsome in his U.S. Marines uniform. He and Eddie both were stationed at Camp Pendleton in San Diego. After graduating from high school with honors, besides being a great athlete, Spike, too, went on to college after the service. He now is an engineer for the Post Office.

I saw that Vivian took some practical nursing courses in high school, before she was married. She has since gone on to further studies and has specialized in psychiatric nursing. All three of my children now live in the San Diego area.

This gold formal was the dress I wore on my LAST drunk weekend in 1968. (Afterwards I balled it up and threw it in the garbage.) I even wore my mink stole, which proved I couldn't be a "common drunk!"

Some weekends my head was as blurred as this picture! I learned to cover up my blackout periods, by letting others fill in what I had said or done. Then I would chime in like a deacon in the Amen Corner.

At my graduation from high school in Cincinnati, I felt as though I'd earned a Ph.D.! My elation showed in this photograph, which was the best picture I ever made.

Part Three

Pouring My Own Troubles

Saving Up, Drinking Down

Drinking because I wanted to drink

Alcohol was beginning to play a major part in my life — I was depending on the bottle. There didn't have to be any particular problem now (I used to drink to "try to get my nerves together"); I was just drinking because I wanted to drink. Every weekend that's all I would be looking forward to — doing some serious drinking. And how I could hide a bottle and how I could be devious and how I could drink all I wanted, without having anyone breathing down my neck and picking on me. (That's the way, usually, an alcoholic starts thinking.) But I figured I could stop when I got ready — at this point I just wasn't "ready!"

Instead of wanting a hot cup of coffee right away when I got up in the morning, I felt an urgent need for the first drink. Saturday mornings when I'd wake up I *really* wanted that drink because I was beginning to feel nervous — *highly* nervous — and shaky-like. I'd say, I need me a drink. I'd take a glass of water into the bedroom, then sneak me a drink out of the closet and use water for a chaser. Of course, that toned me down. I could come out and laugh and talk with everybody but that drink was the only thing toning me down.

I didn't understand what was happening to me when I would get drunk at night. Why did I feel so shitty the next morning? I felt so guilty.

While working at Wright's, I met Ray. After a few

weeks of going out and drinking real heavy, we were invited to a private party of four couples at a small suburban place called Mt. Auburn, about six blocks from where Ray lived. When he'd invited me to the party, he asked, "Would you like to bring a change of clothes? The party is Saturday night, and we can take in a movie Sunday." He didn't have to twist my arm — there was really an understanding between us.

The host and hostess had everything in order. They had the latest records, and the combination (record player) was stacked. A platter of fried chicken was in the middle of the dining room table. Next to the chicken was a large relish plate, potato salad, lettuce and tomatoes in a bowl of ice. There was a fruit cake which had been soaked for weeks in bourbon, scotch, rum and three kinds of wines. A cooler held iced beer, along with different kinds of pop. Everything was perfect for a night of fun.

It was plain to see the other three couples were well on their way by the time we arrived. Of course, Ray and I had a few drinks before we got there, too. Everyone greeted us warmly and loudly. Ray's first words were "Let me have some steam." Meaning a drink. The host replied, "Pour your own troubles, M.F.!" The hostess put my bag in the bedroom and the party went on. We danced and fixed plates of food. We all necked and told jokes and toasts, each trying to top the other. As usual, I wound up the toasts with The Signifying Monkey.

I was pouring more whiskey into each cocktail and getting higher by the hour. Everyone was dancing (or just standing and swaying). To add to the slow music, the lights had been turned off, leaving only a dim stream from the bedroom to light up the living room. The combination played down to its last record and was repeating Ella Johnson's song, "Please Mr. Johnson Don't Play Them Blues So Sad." The lady was doing her thing with this sexy tune that had the whole Black race turned on.

Someone brought us back to reality by saying, "Hey

Ray, you all can go home or to a room any time you get ready!" (Meaning a couple was really worked up sexually.) We all burst out laughing again and made it back to the bar for more drinks.

I made myself a double, double whiskey and Coke. I knew that we would be leaving soon and I had to drink enough to face having sex with Ray. I was grateful for alcohol to help me over rough spots. I didn't get drunk, but neither of us was feeling any pain. We were both as high as we needed to be. We finished our drinks, said goodnight and left for Ray's room.

He lived in a rooming house, on the second floor rear, overlooking a slope with pretty green grass and trees. For about six dollars he had a nice clean room and the use of the kitchen. When we walked in, I saw a radio, a very nice bedroom suite, and a beautiful white bedspread which covered the bed. He showed me the bathroom which he shared with three other roomers and gave me towels to shower with. When I came out he had neatly folded the spread and turned the covers back, revealing clean white linen. A fifth of gin and one of whiskey stood on the dresser. He brought up ice and glasses from the kitchen, seeming so cool, as if he had a lot of practice at this. And all at once it really dawned on me that this was not my teenaged Bill and not my young John, but now I was dealing with a full-grown experienced man who was years my senior! So I poured another drink.

He was back within a few minutes as he promised. (As we ladies know, it doesn't take men long to shower — especially when they're going to get a new piece!!) He stood for a split second and smiled that crooked smile as he looked at me.

Slowly he walked to the dresser, picked up his drink, tasted it and added some more whiskey. He sat on the bed facing me, took another gulp from his glass and beckoned, "Come on and sit next to me." I obeyed.

We changed the radio station and heard our song

played again ("Please Mr. Johnson Don't Play Them Blues So Sad — Because Night Before Last I Lost the Best Man I Ever Had"). The music and his nearness relaxed me and the fire returned to both our bodies. I was no longer afraid, not even when he turned the light out and maneuvered me to the bed. Slowly he unbuttoned my robe. Soon we both stood nude but continued to try at dancing until the bed became a magnet which automatically drew us into it.

I wasn't as smart in life or sex as he, but I was sure the feelings were mutual because after we made love we became steadies and really dug each other. He constantly visited me on my line at the I.D. Grinders. We'd exchange the little sexy remarks that were uttered during our lovemaking, which made no sense to the listeners but *we* understood.

'Lord, Baby, you are doing just fine'

My mind was still on my living conditions in the slums. The bonds I had deducted from each paycheck were piling up, getting closer to what I needed for the down payment on my little dream house. I never told Ray nor anyone else of my plans. But sometimes things have a way of working themselves out.

One pay day Ray came to my line and asked, "Do you have any cash on you?"

"Yes, about twenty dollars," I said.

"Good, let me have it. I'm going out with the boys for a while tonight." As he was talking, he was signing his paycheck. "Here, cash my check when you cash yours and take whatever you need out of it." He left his check on my table and went back to his line.

From then on, each pay day he gave me whatever I asked, just as if I wasn't working. Also, he was an extremely snappy dresser and each time he bought a new suit he had one made for me too. As a result I spent very little of my own money. I sent Mom money for babysitting and mailed big boxes of clothes to her which I bought for her and my baby.

Mom and I wrote each other weekly. Finally when she was visiting me, I told her my plans to move when the war was over. "Look Mom," I said, "how many bonds I have! I'm going to get me a little house. I don't want my baby raised in this environment. He'll be a delinquent before he's ten years old." She said, "Lord, Baby, you are doing just fine. I didn't even think you'd hold a job since you never worked before." I gave all my bonds to her for safekeeping and each month thereafter mailed them to her.

I was able to snow Mom about my drinking the week that she visited me. I raised up off the booze. I knew she'd raise hell and tell Dad, so I did as a popular song of the day suggested, "Please Be Careful If You Can't Be Good." I didn't take a single drink the whole week Mom was with me. And that was the only reason she didn't see me drunk. Ray and I took Mom to the terminal so she could get her train back to Alabama.

As soon as she left I said, "Come on, let's get something to drink. I have been about to die!"

Ray smiled, "I'm ahead of you! Here." He pulled out a pint bottle from his inside coat pocket.

We stopped at the terminal sandwich counter and bought two Cokes with plenty of ice. I poured a good stiff first sip, feeling that warm glow that goes with the first drink. My stomach felt warm, my upper arms and feet tingled, and slowly my head began to feel light. The second drink I didn't sip — I gulped it. I needed to really feel my booze.

I told Ray, "Pour me a little more. I've got a whole week's drinking to catch up on."

"That isn't all you've got to catch up on, Baby!" He pulled me to him and of course I got the message.

We continued to attend parties with our drinking

friends where he usually drank too much — to the extent
that he became aggressive. His actions were mostly passed
off by others as "Aw, don't pay him any attention, he's
drunk." But to be honest, I wasn't too far behind him. The
only difference was it just took more to get him drunk
that it did me. My Mom's observation was coming true
because when Ray became upset, it was usually because
some man was dancing or talking with me — yet he was
always in any woman's face. Also, he had been spending
more time out with the boys during the last year. It
bothered me, because he made it plain that he preferred I
stay home when he was out. I'd get drunk and say, "If you
want me home, you better stay with me. You know,
what's fair for the goose is fair for the gander." He'd say,
"Chaney, if you ever think of anyone else, I'll break your
damn neck. You've got to bring ass to get ass." We argued
on and on. But he still went out.

My brother Lee was stationed in New Jersey and asked
my sister-in-law to join him there. I'll never forget how
she and I packed and cried. She didn't want to leave me in
Cincinnati alone, yet her place was with her husband. I
had only been living in Ohio for about two and a half
years — now both my brothers were gone and here I was
on this Saturday night. She was saying, "Goodbye, Sister,
take care of yourself. Ray, you see about her." We
watched her train pull away from the terminal. That night
her leaving was my reason for getting drunk again. I was
drinking whiskey and club soda. I drank and cried, and,
as all drunks do, repeated myself. "She is just like a sister
to me. If I had anything, it was hers, and if she had
anything, it was mine. Did I ever tell you, Ray, about the
time when we were little and I wanted to be grown and
put on Mom's big bloomers and pinned them up with a
safety pin?" (You can't stop a drunk from talking.) So I
continued, "Well, me and my sister-in-law ran into some
girls and we got to fighting, and they won the fight and,
above all, I lost Mom's big bloomers. Those girls held

them up while I ran home bare-assed!"

On and on, I talked and drank while Ray half-listened. When I came to the next morning, my head felt like it was being attacked from four sides with huge sledge hammers. My stomach was turning upside down. I tried to say something and started vomiting before I got out of bed. Ray tried to fix some food for me, but just smelling it made me sick. I spent all day that Sunday in and out of bed.

Monday came and it was time for work. I was still very weak and nervous, but I managed to go anyway. I told my supervisor that I didn't feel well, but I didn't tell him why. Ray came on my line several times with coffee or milk, since he knew that I couldn't eat yet. I was never so glad to see a workday end. I went straight home and crawled into bed.

Ray said, "Go to sleep. I'll be back in about an hour." I must have slept for a couple of hours when a noise woke me. It was Ray, who had returned to my apartment with all his belongings. He said, "I just gave up my room and I'm moving here, because you can't take care of yourself." I didn't say anything except, "Find somewhere to put your things," and went back to sleep.

The next day, Tuesday, when I woke up I felt hungry and stronger. I ate like a starved pig. "You're trying to get the wrinkles out of your guts, huh?" We both laughed. I said, "I'll never hang one like *that* again!" I helped him arrange his things until time for us to leave for work.

Filling in the blanks

We agreed to meet our friends on Track Five after work, at a place called Kitty Kat. Before I got there I told Ray, "I'll have a beer tonight and that's all. I can't go through the same shit as last weekend." We joined our tables of friends and immediately one of the guys called, "Give these two dry Negroes something to get the dust out of their throats." I ordered a beer and Ray ordered a double double whiskey. So we were partying again. I sipped on my beer. Half had been poured into my glass from the bottle that sat on the table. By the time I finished the first glass I was already feeling it, so the remaining beer was soon gone. We had all night to party and I had already finished my portion. I asked Ray, "Just order me a shot of whiskey, and that's all I want."

The taste of the strong drink hit the spot. I was beginning to liven up. To add to the mood, the jukebox was playing: *I'm drifting and drifting like a ship out on the sea, I ain't got no body in this world to care for me.* The booze and sad song preyed on my emotions and brought on a flood of tears. Of course, I got pity and sympathy from Ray and all our friends. Everyone knew how close my sister-in-law and I were, and they felt sorry for me. So they all helped me by saying, "Take another drink to help you forget your troubles." A couple of the ladies and one of the guys joined me on my crying jag. (It's so easy for an alcoholic to cry in his beer.) So I was off and running again.

Ray was so busy throwing drinks down the hatch that he forgot to notice how many drinks I was consuming. At 1:00 a.m. everyone suggested we go over the river to finish partying. So we all finished our drinks, piled into cars and headed for Newport. As we rode, we were still singing, "I'm drifting and drifting." And that is all I remember, so help me.

The next morning I woke up about nine o'clock and laid there trying to mentally put the pieces together. But nothing registered. Did we go over the river? Where? When? What happened? What time did we get home? Absolutely nothing entered my mind. My head hurt again and I felt sick but not as bad as last weekend.

Finally I heard Ray waking me up. He called, "Wake up you rich, lucky devil, you!" He kept talking as we headed for the coffee pot, "The Sportsman Club was really jumping last night, wasn't it?" "Yes," I answered; now at least I knew where we were. "You surprised the hell out of the gang! Even the dealer was shocked when you won. He was laughing his head off." (Ray didn't realize he was piecing some parts of the night together.) So I laughed with him.

Ray said, "I think when you bought two fifths, that was good enough. At least you shared with them, and did you hear Ellen when she said, 'Don't be so cheap.' You really told her off when you said, 'I am neither cheap nor charitable. Fifty dollars goes home with me!' " Ray laughed harder.

So I joked my way out of the not-knowing by pretending to know. I didn't understand that I had been in a major blackout for hours, four hours at least, since Ray said it was 5:30 when we got home. He spoke of me undressing and rolling my hair, but I didn't remember. I couldn't remember one word I had said, nor who I talked to. My friends didn't know that I was in a blackout, and I didn't know. Yet Ray was telling me things I had said and done.

Later when I talked to friends they also repeated things I had said and done. Like the man who had the nerve to stop me on my way to the restroom and say, "I'll give you twenty dollars to go to a room with me." I retorted, "I'll give you twenty-five dollars to stay out of my damn face."

I had danced and the people had formed a ring around me, because I loved dancing and was a good dancer. My partner was a local celebrity (anyone who could follow him had to be good) and all the other couples let him and his partner have the floor. We put on a show jitter-bugging to the "One O'clock Jump." So help me, I still don't remember dancing at all.

Now I knew that something was wrong. Regardless of everyone else thinking I was acting normal, I was confused and scared. I had acted like a person with amnesia. I couldn't remember. As I continued to drink and the blackouts frequently occurred, I just *never started talking* of the last night's actions. I always waited until others talked, and then I would chime in like a deacon in the Amen Corner! I learned to let others fill in. I was now taking another major step into alcoholism. I was definitely becoming devious and learning to manipulate others. I was acting a lie. It never occurred to me to stop drinking so that the blackouts would stop also. Instead I continued to drink and continued to find ways to cover up and fool others. I didn't realize that *I was the fool.*

I only liked going out on weekends, but Ray chose no special time to go out with the boys. Many times he'd come home drunk or the boys would bring him home, and he'd do a lot of "off the wall" talk (things that made no sense). The next day he knew nothing about what happened. I often told him, "You need to raise up off drinking. If ever I get as bad as you, I'll stop." I'd go on and on after him about drinking too much. I saw all wrong with his drinking and actions, but didn't see it in myself. Yet I was equally as bad. I tore my butt just as much on the weekend as anyone who drank daily.

Now I had reached the point where I was getting drunk every Friday and Saturday night and all day Sunday. I'd stop on Sunday evenings to straighten up for work on Mondays. Often I blacked out one of those nights but, as I said before, I had learned how to cover up and no one knew that I couldn't remember. So I continued to drink more and more. The few drinks no longer got me high enough. I was consuming at least a half-pint of whiskey, plus a lost count of beer.

Getting along bad

Ray was often showing up with lipstick on his collar and face after he'd been out with the *boys* and I'd ask, "Who do you think you are fooling?" He'd say, "But I'm not

doing anything, Baby. I want you to know that you are
starting this shit! I told you, Chaney, don't you ever think
of messing around with anyone else. You really don't
know me, but I have a reputation of kicking my woman's
ass from Birmingham, Alabama to New York City!"

We were getting into some very heated arguments,
which usually goes with two drunks. We were out one
night when a lady came to our table and said, "Mr. Ray,
come here. I would like to speak to you." I was not drunk,
but was well on my way. It was obvious that he knew her,
and there was something going on between them. I never
gave him a chance to answer, and snorted, "He's not
going anywhere. Whatever you have to talk about, it
better be said right here."

She said, "If I wanted to talk to you, I would have
called your name!" So she and I verbally attacked each
other. She cursed me and called me a bitch. As I said, I
hadn't used profanity before I started with the booze and
wild crowds. But gradually I'd changed from saying,
"Lord have mercy" to "Well, I'll be damned" and on to
hard core profanity. So I called *her* another bitch. Finally
the manager came and made all three of us leave. She was
angry at both me and Ray because he did not come with
her.

He and I argued all the way home and into the night. I
told him, "I knew you were lying about being out with the
boys, yet if I look at anyone, you raise hell all night!"

"Aw, Chaney, that woman is crazy and just wanted to
start trouble."

But now I definitely knew he was cheating on me. He
still bought me anything I wanted. And I was still able to
save most of my paycheck and do more for Mom and my
son. But my feelings concerning cheating were the same.
The same resentments I'd felt for Bill returned. We started
getting along bad, and I no longer trusted him.

A few weeks later we had a party at my apartment for
all our friends and others from our departments. We had

plenty of food, whiskey, gin, rum, beer and wine. By the time guests started arriving, we both were well on our way to being high. I'd worked and mopped most of the afternoon. Everything was in order, the apartment was shiny clean, the booze was on the table along with the food. The combination was stacked with the latest records. I had bathed and dressed and was doing my last-minute checking with a drink in my hand. Ray was dressed and holding a drink also.

We greeted our first guests and the party was on its way for the whole of Saturday night. Everyone was having a real good time jitterbugging, and some were in the bedroom playing cards. I moved from one to the other, making people feel welcome. Ray was making sure that they didn't drink his share. I had an extra bottle hidden, so I wasn't too drunk since I couldn't run out.

About 3:00 a.m. he said, "I want to talk to you in the back yard." He looked very angry, and I didn't know why. I excused myself from the people I was talking to and went with him. He said, "I don't want you talking to Sam anymore. That S.O.B. has been in your face all night."

I said, "I haven't talked to him any more than anybody else."

"You are a damn liar, Chaney."

"You are another liar. I don't have to do what you do!" (I was drunk enough to really get worked up.) "You are screwing every woman that says yes and you are the one who has been showing your thirty-two's (teeth) in every bitch's face all night. I am sick of you, with your whorish ass, anyway!"

I turned to go back into the house. He pulled me around and slapped me silly. I screamed and some of the people came out. I was crying and told Ray, "I want your ass out my apartment tonight. If you close your eyes here, so help me, I'll kill you!" He made another attempt to hit me, but the guys restrained him. So the party was over, everyone left one by one.

His friends helped him pack while he poured drinks by the glassful. By the time he was all ready to leave, he was stumbling and leaning drunk. He stood in the door and said, "Well goodbye. I am sorry it had to end like this." I said, "Just go on, you drunk S.O.B. I'll be ready for you if you ever hit me again."

I slammed the door after him and his friends, locked it, and sat there steaming mad. Finally I got up and started cleaning the mess that always follows a party. I poured a good drink and gulped it. I made myself another to sip on while I worked; I was so resentful and plain mad. When I got mad, I worked like wildfire — banging glasses, washing dishes, cleaning the floor and stopping to sip. I was mentally planning how to get even. I thought, "I'll fix him. I am going to Ben's Pawn Shop and get me a spring switchblade knife and if he hits me again I am going to empty his damn guts." The drinks made me more evil.

Even if I didn't drink I was a typical SISTER, and when we are messed over too much we usually figure a way to get even. We just don't fancy taking an ass-whipping for our men's gratifications. When we get tired of being screwed over, we will fight back any way we can. Rosa Parker, who started the Montgomery Boycott by refusing to stand up in the bus showed a perfect and dynamite feeling of the true Black female's strength.

I finished cleaning and was very drunk when I went to bed. The next day was Sunday, and I slept late. About noon, Ray showed up at my door, all hung over. "Can I come in?" he asked. I didn't answer but I opened the door. He looked at my swollen jaw and tears came into his eyes, "I am sorry, Chaney. My friends told me what happened. What was we arguing about? I don't remember nothing that happened. Can I come home?" So we spent the rest of the afternoon drinking and making up. But I didn't let him move back in.

It was you or him

Monday morning I did go and buy a knife, just as I had
planned on doing. Although we made up, I wanted to
have the knife, just in case. I didn't stop to think that
maybe he didn't know what he had done, just as many
times I didn't remember what I had said or done. All I was
thinking was, "Look what he did to ME."

So we continued together, and so did the drunken
parties. One night I was at his room when an out-of-town
visitor came to see him. He introduced him to me, and I
made drinks for the three of us. Ray said, "I think we'll
walk down on Track Five for a few minutes and have a
few snorts (drinks)."

I said, "O.K., you guys go on and enjoy yourselves. I
may go to the Kitty Kat later on and gossip with the
girls." So they left. About an hour later, after four drinks,
I dressed and walked the couple blocks to the Kitty Kat. I
sat at the bar so that I could stare in the mirror. I loved
sitting there, admiring myself, as most sick alcoholics do!!
I could be anybody or anything (mentally) that I wanted
to (when I was drunk). I looked in the bar mirror and
thought, "I look just like Lena Horne! No, more like Ethel
Waters or Mahalia Jackson!" In reality I am plain and
always was, but whenever I dressed up I was sure that I
was the center of attraction. Every eye in the joint must be
upon me only! I didn't know that all drunks feel the same
way. I sat there and paid no attention to anyone except
for a little kidding with the barmaid and the bartender.
We knew each other because I was there often. Tonight I
was feeling alright with the world and as high as I needed
to be, but not really drunk. I had just ordered a double,
double whiskey and soda, paid for it and taken a couple
sips.

The next thing I knew, Ray was there, slapping me off
the bar stool. I landed on the floor in the middle of the
aisle. I felt my face and knew there was blood on it. He

had broken my glasses on my face and my eye was cut. I held my hand over one thinking, "My *God*, he has put my eye out!" I don't know if I felt fear, shock or what. His out-of-town visitor held him and said, "Don't do that, Ray! She isn't doing anything."

"You ain't got a damn thing to do with my business, M.F. Just carry yourself back where you came from! This is my woman and I'll whip her ass when I get ready!"

By now I was on my feet and my senses were returning. My mind did a flashback on something my mother had said: "If ever a man beat you once and you take it, be prepared to be his whipping boy for the rest of your life." The bartender came up from behind the bar and handed me my purse. He said, "Here is your purse. You and Ray get out of here and don't come back. This is twice you all done raised hell in here." I was fighting mad. Ray had no right to hit me and show off in front of his friend. The bartender had no right to throw me out and talk to me like I was dirt. Ray said, "When I get outside I am really going to beat her ass!"

I walked out ahead of him, so damn mad. I intended to never associate with him ever anymore. This was for good! I was going to have him arrested to putting my eye out. I wiped blood away and I could see. The blood had it blinded.

As I started crossing the street someone screamed, "Look out, Chaney! There he comes!!" Quick as a flash, I opened my purse and got my hand on my knife, hit the spring on my switchblade, and as he raised his hand to give me a backhand lick, I hit my target once, twice, three times, in the chest until he collapsed. I was getting ready to straddle him and cut his damn throat.

The man said, "Don't, Chaney! He's already down."

"I told him to stop hitting me. Turn me loose and let me kill that no-good bastard." I was hysterical. "He don't give a damn if he put my eye out or not. He'll never walk around with two eyes and I don't have but one."

But the guy held me fast.

We went to General Hospital and the doctor worked for hours to get the shattered glass out of my eyebrow and eyelid. Ray's friend took him to Christ Hospital where he stayed for three weeks in critical condition. He told the police that he didn't know who hurt him or why.

When I left the hospital, I went home to an empty house. I sat there in the dark asking myself, "Why did he hit me? *What is* wrong with him?? He must be losing his mind! I wasn't doing anything!" And I prayed, "Please, God, don't let him die. If he doesn't die, he will kill me next time he sees me. I can't ask Nelson to come back. Lee can't leave the Army. I don't want Mom and Dad to know I was out drinking and fighting."

Although I had fought in self-defense I still felt guilty about cutting Ray. I was losing my mind. I got up, found my bottle and sat back down in the dark. I took a sip from the bottle and weakened it with saliva. I had never drunk whiskey without a chaser before, and it was so hot that it gagged me. But I didn't have the energy to go to the kitchen for water and a glass. I had to think.

I decided to call New York to talk to someone. "Nelson, this is Sis." I was crying so hard that he said, "Hold it and tell me what's wrong." Finally I did tell him what had happened. He said, "Don't feel too bad about it. It was you or him. If he had *you* in the hospital, I would have come there and we would hang up until one of us ended up either in the hospital or in Hell. Listen, Lee's wife is here with me now. He's leaving for overseas so I'll send her to be with you in a couple of days." Bless his heart!

My sister-in-law came, and we both went to the hospital to see Ray. He was not angry because he, again, had no idea what happened or why. The poor guy had been experiencing blackouts and became violent, yet he had no recollection of what happened. Neither of us knew just how sick we both were. No one believed him when he said, "I don't remember what happened." But I did believe him, because the same thing was happening with me. Yet I didn't feel sorry for *myself*, and raise up off the booze.

Ray lived and recuperated, but I was afraid of him, not knowing when he would beat on me again. He still said, "I better not see you with anyone else." So I stayed home more often to avoid him. I no longer went to visit with him on his line and he didn't come on mine. I prayed and thanked God for not letting Ray die. I made a promise to God that I would never pick up another weapon to hurt a human being as long as I lived.

Hooked and guilty

I didn't want to hurt anyone. And I didn't want to go to jail. (If he had died, I might have been on my way to the electric chair. During the 40s it seemed that a poor Black went to the chair every week and I could have been one.) After that, I went out with girl friends, to places where he was not likely to go. But I was still drinking more and more, experiencing blackouts most of the weekends. I shopped, cooked, laughed, talked with people and knew nothing about it. All during the week I'd torture myself trying to put the pieces together. I was really hooked on drug alcohol and didn't know it. (No one had told me that there were *week-end* alcoholics.)

I tried to stay in close touch with Mom and my son. Once I wrote her to watch him closely because I dreamed that he fell into a deep hole and he called me to get him out and I couldn't. In the dream he finally sank out of sight. I watched that mailbox daily until she wrote that he was alright! I wasn't sure if I dreamed this or did it *really* happen? I was having trouble separating fantasy from reality.

Mom wrote me that she now had Lee's kids also. He had won custody of his girl and boy and asked her to keep them and he would send an allotment for their support. She asked if I could find another soldier suit for his son, because he cried every time my son wore his. So I went shopping and sent it to my little nephew.

Mom wrote that she had received the box and was so happy that I was doing so well and living a "good life." I felt very guilty when I received her letter. I couldn't tell her that I was so drunk that I wouldn't know God if he walked in my front door and introduced himself. And I no longer went to church. I didn't even know where the CME Church was! Because of my religious background I suffered a double guilt. One was the natural guilt that goes with alcoholism, which I didn't understand at that time. The second guilt was that I knew I should go to church. I'd hear the church bells ring on Sunday morning, and the sound was physical and mental torture to my nerves and to my very soul.

"Here I am a minister's daughter, raised to be decent, to serve God and do his work. My father is now standing in the pulpit preaching to hundreds of people this morning. He is doing the work of God and dedicating his life to save souls, and here I am, his only daughter, too drunk to get my head off the pillow." I'd talk to myself this way until I had to have another drink, enough to drown out the shame. I had to drink to pass church time. I was sick.

Thanksgiving disgrace

Thanksgiving Day I had four bottles of booze in the table bar, all set up just in case someone stopped in for a drink before work at four o'clock. I cleaned my apartment early, took my bath and slipped on my good robe. I fixed me a drink and sipped on it. Every sound I heard I hoped was someone to stop by. I was feeling so lonely and didn't want to spend Thanksgiving by myself. No one showed up by the time I finished the drink. So I fixed another and by the time I finished the second drink, I no longer felt sorry for myself. Instead, I didn't care if anyone wanted to come see me or not. To hell with them! I didn't need anybody anyway! Didn't I work every day? And take care of myself? I went and fixed another drink and another. Finally I lost count and just drank. I was high but not drunk, and I had to get dressed for work. My rider was coming in about forty-five minutes. Well, it didn't take me long to put on makeup, comb my hair and put on the crepe dress that was already laid out on the bed.

I was dressed when my rider came for me. I asked them, "Would you like a taste before we leave?" They all came in for a quick drink. Quite often we drank at work if we wanted to and many took bottles with them. I never liked drinking during the week, however, this was Thanksgiving. So we all had a drink together before the thirty-five or forty-five minute drive from my place to Lockland. I was very high because I had been drinking for hours.

When we got to work and all of us got out of the car, I could hardly stand up. I was really and truly drunk. That booze had burst like a cannon in the car with the heat turned up. My riders all said, "Chaney, you are too drunk, you can't go in. You know the guards won't let you pass. They will take your badge and then you'll have to go to personnel office before you can come back to work — you may even get fired." I said, "I am not drunk, I can do my work as good as anybody else. I'm going to work."

Finally they gave up on me and I stumbled on as far as the guard's desk. Drunks just will not keep their damn mouths *shut*, so I said, "Happy Thanksgiving, guards!" One said, "Lady, you've been celebrating. Sorry, but you can't come in — you are *drunk.*" The guards had to put me out of the plant as I was holding up the line of hundreds of other employees.

So there I stood, backed up against a wire fence. I couldn't get into the locked car because my rider was in the plant and I was about fifteen miles from home. Buses ran about once an hour (it was cold in November in Ohio). I was blocked from every angle. I stumbled back to the guard's desk and asked, "Could I come in and use the bathroom?" He said, "Lady, if I let you in, I will lose my job. So will you please go on home and sleep it off." Back I went and took my place at the wire fence again. There I was, right at the main entrance where everyone passed me. I wanted to go to the bathroom, and I crossed my legs, trying every which way to hold my water. Finally, like an over-filled balloon, I just couldn't control myself. I stood there and pee ran like the '37 Flood. And to make myself more conspicuous, I started crying at the top of my voice. It was cold, and I had to ride home as pissy as a pole cat!! That wet crepe dress had shrunk up to my waistline! It was rough until I got back home and cleaned up.

Later I met the gang when they got off work. My God, I was really going insane. I had to get out of my apartment. I couldn't stand the loneliness, the walls were closing in on me. I was not too drunk to know that I had disgraced myself at work. When I got home again it was daybreak. I paid the cab and went straight to bed. Lord, I had to report to personnel before going to work on the line!

In the morning I managed to pull myself up by the time my rider picked me up. As soon as I got in the car everyone started asking, "Why didn't you stay in the car? Why did you talk to the guards? Why? Why?" I shouted, "Why don't you all just kiss my ass!" They all started laughing and that stopped the interrogation.

Sheepishly I entered the small room and confronted the man in the personnel department. The secretary had told him who I was so he said, "Hello, Chaney, have a seat." I only nodded. I couldn't speak with a lump in my throat. The tears were flooding again. The man in personnel talked to me for a long time. "You are endangering your life and the lives of others when you operate a machine while drinking. Remember the lady that got her hair caught in the machine? And the man who was actually chopped up? Well, you see what could have happened if the guards had allowed you to go in?"

Meekly, I said, "I'm glad they didn't let me in. I don't want to hurt anybody."

"Since this is your first time and you have a very good work record, I am giving you a week's suspension without pay. Should you come in drunk again, you will be fired."

I walked out of his office ashamed, but grateful that I still had a job. I vowed that nothing anymore would cause me to take a drink during the week. Only on weekends for me! I don't care what holiday comes! I balled that entire week since I didn't have to worry about going to work. By the Sunday before my return to work I was so sick that I took medicine to clean me out for the following Monday.

I went to personnel and they returned my badge. So I was back on the I.D. line with my machine. I started to think people were talking about me. Later on in the day I knew they were. They'd be whispering and when I got near, they'd jump apart and call, "Hi, Chaney," with chicken-shit grins on their faces. So I thought, "To hell with them! They drink too! Who do they think they are? I'll stay away from all the S.O.B.'s."

I sat during the break alone, and ate my lunch alone. On the afternoon break I sat alone again. An older man we all called "Rev" came and sat on the table next to me and said, "Chaney, you are always so friendly! So, what is wrong? You're not saying anything."

I said (with tears running again), "They are all talking about me, so I'll just leave all those gossiping Negroes alone. I don't need them anyway."

He sat quietly for a few minutes and said something that today I still remember, "Chaney, you are young and have a long life ahead of you. You are the one who makes your own reputation. I know what happened. If you had done something nice, everyone would be talking about that too! What you did was *not* nice nor respectful so you are causing people to say nasty things about you. Why don't you stop pouting like a little girl, square your

shoulders, face them and don't let that happen again." As
he walked away he said, "Remember what I told you! *You
make your own reputation.*"

I went to one of the ladies, smiled and asked her for a
match. She said, "Sure, Chaney. Here, I have an extra
book." By the weekend we all was back together again
and back on Track Five drinking together.

'Going Down Slow'

If Ray heard about me making an ass out of myself, he
never said anything. As a matter of fact, we completely
drifted apart. I didn't see him until years later (and he was
still drinking and so was I). I continued drinking with my
girl friends and co-workers until World War II ended in
1945. Wright's plant closed immediately, as did others all
over the United States. I signed up for compensation and
sat back collecting my weekly check. Now that I was no
longer working, I had friends come in and we played
cards and drank draft beer bought in gallon jugs. I wasn't
too much of a beer drinker, so I still did my real drinking
on the weekends. Two girls who lived upstairs were my
running pals and we went out together most of the time. I
wasn't really interested in a steady boyfriend although I
did go out sometimes with a couple of guys to movies or
over the river to drink. I seemed to have lost interest in
becoming involved with any man.

I continued going out more and more with girl friends
and getting drunk every weekend. One day Bill wrote me
that he was now stationed at Fort Knox, Kentucky. He
asked if he could come on the weekend to see me. I wrote
him back and told him to come on. I drank all evening.
When I met him at the terminal that night, I was very
drunk. We continued drinking and soon I started crying
about how he had treated me. I got so drunk that I finally
went to bed. The next day I woke up and saw I had wet
the bed! I almost died from embarrassment. Here I had
not seen him for years and I had become a pissy drunk.

He came to see me several weekends but we couldn't make it because he tried to attack my girl friend. He was the same ole woman chaser.

My brother Lee had become extremely nervous in the Army and received a medical discharge. He didn't come back to Cincinnati but went to Mom, Dad and the children. Dad was still pastoring in Leeds, Alabama. Mom wrote me that Lee was very sick and so thin. She said Dad was taking him to the Veterans Administration and to the doctor every week, but if he didn't improve, he would have to be hospitalized. When I read her letter, I became very upset. I loved my brother; we had always been so close. I told my girl friend, "It seems that everything happens to Lee. He was beat up by the police when he was small. He has the responsibility of two kids. Now that damn old war has made him sick." This was on a Friday so I had a good reason to get drunk. (Alcoholics find anything a reason to get drunk, from the death of Aunt Fanny to a flat tire, or just for the hell of it.)

I really did hang one on that Friday night, Saturday and Sunday, sitting at the table in the Kitty Kat. I kept the juke box going playing the song "Going Down Slow." I don't remember who wrote the song, but I remember the words — "I have had my fun if I don't get well no more, I have had my fun if I don't get well no more, I have had my fun if I don't get well no more. My health is failing and I'm going down slow. Please write my mother, tell her the shape I'm in. Please write my mother, tell her the shape I'm in. Tell her to pray for me, forgive me for my sins."

I played the record and cried in my drinks for the whole three days. My girl friends stayed close to me for two reasons. First, we were drinking buddies and they sympathized with me. Second, I was paying for the drinks. (As long as a drunk is buying booze, there is plenty of friendship, and the receivers will stay close by and go along with whatever the buyer wants. So naturally they

stuck with me.) By Sunday night I was so sick I couldn't
drink another drop. I hadn't eaten for the three days and
was vomiting foam from beer mixed with whiskey and
soda. I was so sick. For the first time I gagged so hard that
my knees collapsed, my heart pounded so awful loud, my
stomach cramped. Finally only water and yellow stuff
that tasted bitter came up.

I gave up and my girl friend put me to bed because I was
shaking all over. She stayed with me all night, fixed me
hot tea and toast the next morning, which was Monday,
and then she went home. I was in and out of bed all day.
About eight o'clock that night she knocked on my door
and called me to open the door. She said, "I met a couple
of guys at a neighborhood restaurant, and they are
outside in the car. They want to go out, so come and get
dressed and we can go out for a few drinks."

I said, "I don't want to go out. I don't want to be
bothered." "Come on, I really dig the guy I am with, but I
don't want to go out with two strange guys alone."

I asked, "Who the hell are they anyway?" She went out
and brought them in and introduced them to me as Steve
and Troy. Steve was the extra man. They weren't bad
looking guys, and I was civil toward them, but I was
about as interested in this man as teats on a bull! I had my
hair in rollers, no makeup and was wearing an unattrac-
tive, faded chenille robe. And as I said earlier, I am plain.
Hung over, I looked awful. I am very black, yet darker
rings had formed under my eyes almost to my cheekbones. I'm sure Steve didn't like what he saw. But he did
ask, "Are you going out with us? We're just going to the
Shuffle Inn to get a couple of pitchers of booze."

My girl friend put records on the combination while I
took a spot bath in the face pan and applied some heavy
makeup to hide the rings under my eyes. I combed my
hair, adding a page-boy fall which made my hair four
inches longer, and hurriedly put on a light blue tailored
suit with matching hat and jewelry. I wore navy shoes,

bag, blouse and gloves, along with my tan camel-haired coat. I returned to the living room feeling fine because the couple of drinks had stimulated me. Steve asked, "Where is the lady that said she was going with us?" My girl friend said smiling, "That's her." The two guys looked at each other and cracked up laughing. They positively didn't recognize me.

I wasn't feeling too much like drinking "heavy" so the pitchers of whiskey were really enough. Steve asked after a few drinks, "Would you like if I bought a bottle and we went to a room for awhile?"

I replied, "I am not selling anything, and I don't sleep with any man the first time I meet him." The subject of sex was dropped. Sexually, I had reached the point where I was absolutely disgusted with men. It seemed that mistreatment was all I was getting, no matter how nice I was to them. For months I had found my companionship in the bottle. I was thinking, "If I just drink and don't get involved in no affairs, I won't have to report to any man, no more arguing and fighting. Equally important, I won't be worried about becoming pregnant. I can just stay alone and drink and have fun." The more I drank, the less I desired sex. I was becoming more frigid after each drinking bout. I was hooked and so sick from the drug alcohol that there had been a sexual decline which was not normal for a young woman. But I didn't know at that time that I was helping the abnormality by poisoning my body with booze.

When Steve propositioned me about sex, I deliberately gave him a smart answer. I intended to put not only *him* in his place, but all men. I was sick of them! All men were no good — only looking for a new piece of trim! Within a few months, he'd start chasing other women and mistreat me also.

Even though I was turned off, we had a nice time together. They took us home after about three hours. Steve asked, "Can I come and see you again?"

I told him, "I am going to stay home this coming Saturday night. I joined church, and I'm going to start attending church on Sunday."

He asked, "What church do you belong to?"

"Philip Temple CME on Carlisle Avenue."

He laughed. "That is my church also," he answered. So we both laughed.

He called daily and by Friday I was really looking forward to his arrival. I dressed carefully in my grey tailored suit with red accessories, silver-grey fox muff and hat. When he and his friend arrived, we all went to the Cotton Club and later to an after-hours house where we drank all night long. Like all of us, he could really drink. Steve and I had a good understanding, and he did not approach me about sex all night. We both just drank. Misery loves company so we were just two people out on the town, trying to drink it dry. I remember stumbling into someone's table and upsetting their drinks. Steve had to pay for them to avoid a fight. The house man said, "Why don't you take your lady home and let her sleep it off?" I knew I was tearing my butt again.

I had a memory blackout about midnight that night. When I woke up, we were in bed in my apartment. It was 9:30 a.m. Sunday. I knew that we had had sex because there were towels as evidence and I was wearing my prettiest gown. So I must have prepared for a sexual ritual — but I didn't remember. Now again I had to pretend to know what had happened.

We talked for a while and he said, "Well, we're not getting to church today. I'm going home for a while." He lived with his parents only a few blocks from my apartment. Although he was grown, they didn't like him staying out and coming home in the morning. Steve had never been married, but he had a three-year-old daughter living in the West End. He mentioned another daughter he might have fathered in Mississippi, although he wasn't sure she was his child.

Arguments — over nothing and everything

Steve and I became steadies, and started going everywhere together. He worked at his brother's restaurant and I found a job making salads at a big restaurant downtown. As we all know, employment dropped just after World War II. Even so, my idea of moving from the slums had not changed. Mom still kept all my bonds and I had about 600 dollars in the bank. I just hadn't seen the house I wanted and now that I could get it, I wasn't worried. Furthermore, it took time on my weekends to look for a house, and I was never sober enough to do so — either drunk or too hung over.

Steve and I soon started having the usual drunken arguments about nothing and everything. He came to my apartment one night when I was in bed. When I went to open the front door, he was immediately hanging on the back door. I went to the back and he was at the front. I asked, "What the hell is the matter with you? Make up your mind which door you want to come in! Are you crazy?"

He said, "Hell no, I ain't crazy. If you got some S.O.B. in there, I'll catch him trying to get out of one of those doors!!" This led us into a big argument. I wasn't doing anything, but he had been out drinking and his whiskey told him that I had another man in my apartment.

One night after we both were as drunk as skunks, he asked me to fix him something to eat. "You fix me some food, Sis; I bought it, at least you can cook me something to eat." I went into the kitchen at eleven o'clock at night and staggered around for an hour, frying pork chops, steaming cabbage and making hot corncakes. I fixed it nice on a platter and took it to the bed where he was resting. I called, "Steve, here is your food. Steve!" He raised up and said, "I was asleep, so don't call me anymore."

"Well, you said you wanted food! Here it is, so you

better come on and eat it."

He hollered, "You better go on."

I sat the food down on the dresser, went to the cabinet, poured a big drink, and sat there at the table fuming. I finished the drink fast and poured another, resenting the hell out of that sleeping bastard. I was very drunk after I downed the second slug of whiskey. I went back to the bed and called, "Steve, wake up and eat your food."

He sat up in bed and said, "Damn it, I told you not to call me anymore." I took that platter in my left hand and with my right hand I grabbed a handful of cabbage and threw it right between his eyes. Then another and another until the platter was empty. He sat back and looked like something from outer space, peeping through cabbage dripping from the top of his head.

The walls, the bed, the floor were all a greasy, nasty mess. We both settled down and spent all night cleaning up that mess. Eventually, I had to get rid of the mattress and paint the room because of the stink. We continued to go steady regardless of the misunderstanding!

Once I started, there was no stopping

Lee wrote that he was returning to Cincinnati and wanted me to meet him the next week. I was so happy to see him looking well again. We hugged each other and were so glad to be brother and sister, back together again! I soon noticed, though, that he was not the same. He was very nervous and paced a lot, only half listening when I talked to him. But, at least, the war had left him alive!

He met Steve and they liked each other. Soon we had drinks to celebrate his homecoming. Lee was not a heavy drinker — he immediately noticed I was drinking to the extent of getting drunk and told me so, in no uncertain words. "What in the hell is the matter with you?" I said, "Oh, I just got overjoyed because you are home." So he dropped the tongue-lashing.

As time passed, he saw I came home absolutely drunk every weekend. I hadn't been around my family since I had started hard drinking. Now that he was here, I could no longer hide. Lee bawled me out every weekend, yet I couldn't stop getting drunk, no matter how I promised. (I tried, God, how I tried, to just have a few drinks! But so help me, once I started there was no stopping.) Steve and I both drank regularly, and would laugh at how my brother and his family raised hell about us drinking and staying out all hours.

There was a man in the neighborhood who no one cared to be bothered with. Sometimes he visited the lady next door. One day I sat down on the steps to talk to her and the man stopped by with a fifth of whiskey. She went in and got three glasses and a Coke and we sat there drinking and talking. I didn't see any harm done. When my brother came home and saw me sitting with this man, he really went ape. "I don't ever want to see you in the presence of that ole wino. He lies on every woman who says hello to him. In fact, I am going to write Mom and Dad and see if they can come here and get you straightened out." He said, "Look at you, drunk now, and it is just Friday afternoon. You'll be drunk again all weekend as soon as Steve gets here."

True to his word, I was in a blackout the whole weekend. Today I do not know where Steve and I went and I don't know what happened Friday through Sunday. I felt so remorseful facing my brother. I couldn't say anything because I didn't know what to say anymore. If Steve and I stayed at a room to sleep it off, I caught hell for staying out. And if I went home drunk, I still caught hell and I simply could not stay sober. So I was always in a mental chaos. I was always afraid of something or nothing. I couldn't find peace of mind, day or night, drunk or sober.

To add to my problems, my younger brother Henry wrote that he was being discharged from the Army and

was coming to me also. He didn't want to go back to
Selma. He drank pretty heavy too, but it was different
with a man. (He said, "I love you, Sis, but I don't want a
drunk for a sister. It looks bad and it is bad to see a
woman drunk. Even when I am drunk, I don't want my
woman drunk.")

One Friday morning I was on my way downtown to
talk to a real estate agent. I stopped on Track Five to have
a cold beer and talk for a few minutes with the barmaid. I
saw an old friend from the crowd at Wright's Plant who
asked about Ray and others. Finally he said, "Well, Sis, I
better be on my way. I'm going to the newspaper office to
run an ad. You know my father passed away, and I'm
putting the house up for sale." I asked. "Are you talking
about the house where your sister lives? Where she had all
of us come to a party?" "Yes." he replied. So we started
negotiating that day.

Within thirty days the deal was closed although we had
to wait thirty more days until the people moved out. We
were all up in the air about moving! Moving from the
slums!! All my friends thought I had lost my mind to be
moving about fourteen miles out of town with no car.

The pastor's daughter — drunk!

About the same time, I received a special delivery letter
that Dad was real sick with pneumonia and was not
responding to treatments. I called Leeds, Alabama, and
Mom started crying, "Your Dad is so sick, I am almost
crazy with worry." Lee and Henry saw me to the terminal
and I took the all-night ride to Birmingham.

I had a bottle with me and drank all night, between
naps. About an hour before we reached Birmingham, I
really started to drink heavy because I had to face a
problem. I didn't know how sick Dad was, or if he had
passed away — so I had to drink to fortify myself for
whatever was ahead.

I vaguely remember seeing the man who met me at the station, but I *did* see the shock on his face. After all, I was his pastor's daughter coming home drunk to see her sick father! I had a memory blackout during the ride from Birmingham to Leeds, snapping back when the man said, "O.K., we are here and your mother is standing waiting." As soon as I saw her, we both started crying. She was too upset to notice how drunk I was.

My son Eddie and Lee's two kids Spike and Vivian ran to me and we all hugged and kissed — my boy and I holding on to each other for dear life! I said, "What a big boy you are." He asked, "Are you going to take me with you to Cincinnati?"

"I sure am! And Spike too!" Which I did.

Mom and I immediately went to the hospital to see Dad, although he wasn't aware we were there. Dad was sick for a couple of weeks.

I stayed until he was out of danger and home from the hospital. I stayed sober during my two weeks' stay because there was no way the minister's daughter could go and purchase a bottle. Leeds was a small place with a very few stores and everyone there knew who I was. It didn't bother me as much through the week but those two weekends were hell! My glands secreted on Friday and Saturday, and my mind stayed on the joints in Ohio. I could picture myself drinking a cold beer and a double, double whiskey.

Returning home with the boys, I bought a bottle from some stranger who charged me twice the regular price. As soon as I settled the boys down for the night, I started on my first drink. Oh, that glow after two weeks of thirst! Then the second drink and the third. When I got to sleep, I was drunk again and slept all night. My brothers met us at the terminal and the boys dashed for Lee. It had been months since they had seen each other. A few minutes after we arrived at the apartment my son Ed yelled, "I don't like this place. We don't have any grass to play on and no yard. Where are we going to play ball?" I told him, "We'll have a place where you can play in a few weeks!"

The school was only one block away, so I enrolled them the next day and told the teacher they would be there only a couple of weeks. But we were held up for two more months because there were some problems with the people moving out of our house.

Now I really was having problems — someone had to see to the *children*. I *had* to spend some time with Steve, and I *had* to get drunk and listen to my brothers nag. I soon learned to bathe and get the kids to bed and then leave. One of my brothers usually stayed if I was going out. (I stayed when he went out.) And I would make it home before the kids woke up. But many days I was too sick to make breakfast, and Lee or Henry had to cook.

Moving from the slums!

The day finally came! We loaded our belongings on the truck! I said to my brothers, "Well, God answered my prayers. We are moving from the slums." The kids sat on the back and talked the helper's ears off all the way to Rossmoyne, Ohio. As soon as the truck stopped, those kids were a sight to see. Without any warning they jumped off and started running like wild horses up the dirt street! Down and up and down, again and again, until they were exhausted! We all just stood there and watched them run. Those kids were so happy to have room to play that it was worth every cent invested in the place!

We soon had the place all fixed up. The kids had a good school within walking distance, although the school was predominantly White. There were only about eleven Black families in the neighborhood who were early settlers. None of us had any racial problems. I heard several White policemen say, "We don't even realize that those Colored people are in the neighborhood until someone is sick or gets hurt. They are such nice and quiet people." So the children felt very secure and happy in their new surroundings.

I had found a way to protect myself while drinking on the weekends. The apartment we had moved from had two rooms, which I sublet for the rental fee. I still had a room for myself so I could go back into town and drink. (Also I didn't want my kids to see me drunk. And definitely I couldn't afford to let them see Steve and me sleeping together and not married.)

My brother Henry decided to go back in the Service, which left only Lee and myself to care for the children. We worked out a system. I would go and spend the weekend in town and when I returned home on Sunday, he would go stay a few days.

Once when Steve's car broke down, I had to take the bus and transfer three times. I had been drunk Friday, Saturday, and all Sunday afternoon. I was far from sober when I started home, but I did manage to transfer downtown and took the Deer Park bus to the end of the city line. It was a long ride and by the time we got there, I had gone to sleep. The bus driver had to wake me and almost drag me from the bus over to a little building where people sat and waited for the bus going to the suburban areas. It was very warm in there and I got sick and started vomiting all over the floor and my skirt. I heard people saying, "She is *drunk!*" My God, I was so sick, and nobody cared! Through my foggy mind and eyes, I could see the disgust in their faces. I wanted to go to the bathroom, but there was none. Finally, the bus came and I pulled myself on. I was so dirty, my coat belt had dragged in my vomit, my face was smeared. I sat in the back and opened a window and made it to my bus stop. It was dark, and as soon as I got off, I used the shadow of a tree for a bathroom.

I slipped into the house so the kids and Lee wouldn't see me in this condition.

No matter what I did, I ended up drunk

That night was only the beginning of my drunken bus rides home. Many times Lee would say, "You be home about six o'clock because I have to take the 5:30 bus to town." Now if I failed to get home, the children would be alone. So I had to make it, no matter how drunk I was. God knows I never wanted to neglect my children, yet I couldn't stay sober. I tried using will power and I tried eating before going out, as someone told me to do. I'd eat all those greasy Soul pigsfeet, slaw and cornbread and still get drunk! Plus I'd get sick and throw up, usually before making it to the bathroom. Someone told me that taking a few spoons of mineral oil to coat my stomach would prevent me from getting drunk. So I tried that too, only to learn that mineral oil went right though me with no pains and left a greasy ring on the back of my skirt. I really did everything anyone ever told me might turn me into a "successful drinker"! No matter what I did, I always ended up drunk. I envied the woman who could drink and still act like a lady. (Later I learned that if one's body is allergic to alcohol it doesn't matter what you try. And it doesn't matter if you drink a cheap bottle of wine, beer, or top-shelf Scotch, the end result is that you get drunk and sick if you are an alcoholic.)

I met a few Blacks in the neighborhood and it didn't take but a very few weeks before the boozers started dropping in or inviting me to their homes. In the drinking world, people seem to find each other. There were many grapes on our lot and I started making wine that everyone enjoyed. Soon we were all friends and drank together on the weekends that I stayed home.

One man named Jay made it very plain that he was interested in being more than "just a friend." I was nice to him, but let him know that I was going steady, with no intention of becoming serious with anyone else. Jay never cared for Steve the first day they met; he said, "Sis, I don't feel that he is strong enough for you. He seems more like one of the children. He seems to depend on you. It makes me wonder what will happen if you ever have to depend on him."

"Oh, he is O.K.! And we love each other." So the subject was dropped.

One Saturday night we were all drinking in the kitchen when a lady asked, "Sis, which one of these boys are yours?"

I put my hand on my son's head, answered, "This one," and he went downstairs to play. I never thought about it until my little nephew Spike burst into tears, ran in the bathroom and locked the door. I ran after him and heard him crying his heart out.

I asked, "Spike, what's the matter, Baby?" He wouldn't answer. I asked again.

"Go away Sis, you don't love me and you don't want me. You said Ed was your son but you didn't say I was."

I thought, "Oh my God, what have I done to this five-year-old child." I went back to the kitchen and asked my guests to leave so that I could think of a solution. I was really thinking and went back to the closed door and sat on the floor with a drink in my hand.

I called, "Spike, listen." His sobbing quieted. "I don't want you to tell Ed, but come on out and go to the store with me. I'll buy you a big ice cream cone and a whole box of animal cookies all by yourself. But it will be our secret. Do you promise not to tell?"

He slowly opened the door and peeked his little teary-eyed head out. I dropped my whiskey glass, grabbed him and we hugged each other, only this time *my* tears were running. From that day on he became my son in words, feelings, love and deeds — and I always said, "my sons" or "my boys."

Each time I shopped for them they both wanted the same suit. One would be very happy and the other in tears. So I got rid of all their clothes and went shopping again and bought everything identical.

I wanted to be a good mother but I couldn't leave the bottle alone. Sometimes I would get confused trying to play the role of mother, sister, and drunk. Now that we had the house, all my savings were gone.

My brother Lee was not improving but seemed to be getting sicker. He was becoming very moody and would sit for hours alone, staring. He was short-tempered with the kids, who were confused over his change. I went to the Veterans Administration and talked with the doctor about his nervousness. The doctor asked me to bring him to the VA Hospital because Lee was much sicker than I imagined. I was told that he'd have to be hospitalized for extensive treatments. I prayed, "My God, will my troubles never end?" His total income for supporting himself, his son and his daughter was exactly $41.40 a month from his VA pension. I only had eighty dollars a month allotment from Bill. Henry paid the $32.20 a month house payment to the building loan, which gave us an income of exactly $121.40 a month.

The doctor had said it would be sixty to ninety days before he could process the necessary papers to get Lee into the VA Hospital. In the meantime, he would receive outpatient treatment. I made sure that he took his medication when I was sober and at home.

I started job-hunting because we needed more money for just daily living. I found a job downtown washing dishes in a cafeteria. My take-home pay was $17.50 a week, plus my meals. Financially I was back in a bind again, with less than $200 a month for food, heat, phone, clothes, doctor bills, etc., but I kept trying to manage. I'd come home from work and can vegetables and fruits grown in the yard. Many meals included leftovers gathered at the dishwasher.

One day when I came in from work the children were crying. They said Daddyo (Lee) was sick and crying too. I went in and found him shaking all over with sweat pouring off him. I knew that he wouldn't be able to wait sixty more days, so I called Mother and asked her to come right away. By the time she came, Lee was worse. He hardly recognized Mom.

I was so upset that I went downstairs and poured a big drink to quiet my nerves. Before the night was over, poor Mom had had two bad experiences: her sick son *and* seeing her drunken daughter. She moaned, "Lord have mercy, my daughter is drunk." She was shocked and hurt, but she saw repeat performances many times afterwards during that stay with us.

Because I had no car I traveled by bus to the VA for weeks, going through all the red tape to get Lee into the hospital. Finally they admitted him. In the meantime, the children had to be cared for. The VA wanted to place Spike and Vivian in a home since Lee was no longer able to care for them.

A wonderful attorney turned out to be a true friend who helped guide me in the right direction. I felt so helpless, lonely, and lost. When I got to the attorney's office the next morning, I had swollen red eyes and was shaking all over so badly that the secretary gave me two aspirins and coffee. They didn't know that I was so hung over. That morning I'd swallowed Listerine after brushing my teeth, using the old chewing gum trick to camouflage the alcohol on my breath. (Later I learned that I wasn't fooling them at all!)

The attorney said, "The courts are looking at your income and you just can't support the kids with eighty dollars a month plus $17.50 a week.

On the day of the hearing I was hung over as usual. I dressed the three children and we all took the bus downtown to the VA office. We went into a small room where a man talked with the children. "Are you happy with your aunt? How would you like to stay somewhere else and you would have other children to play with?"

All the kids came to me and held on for dear life, crying

and pleading. I had tears streaming down my face as I stooped down and gathered all three children in my arms. I looked at every face in that room and asked, "Will you please let me keep them and *try* to work things out? These children need me. Please let me try and help them. Please."

The kids held on and wouldn't let me go, so finally they agreed to let me take them home on a trial custody for six months. The VA would check periodically to see how the children were. They explained that if the kids didn't have adequate care they would be taken before or after the six months.

We were four happy people when we left that place! We celebrated — we had hot dogs and Coke. The children went to the movies, which cost ten cents apiece. And I went across the street to the bar and drank until the movie was over. They were three exhausted kids when we took the long bus ride home. I was very high, almost drunk, but I managed to transfer and get them home. I told them to wake me up a few blocks before our bus stop. As soon as I got off, I made it to my usual tree to urinate. It was getting harder for me to control my water. Also, the pains in my side and back and hips seemed to be getting worse. I had never completely stopped hurting on and off since my son was born.

I put the children to bed and kissed them goodnight. Vivian slept with me and when I checked on her to say goodnight, she reached up and hugged my neck so hard it was painful. I turned out all the lights and went downstairs and poured a drink. I sat there and asked myself, "Now where do you go from *here?*"

We made every effort to manage. We ate fresh vegetables from our garden. Meats were scarce but we just divided the amounts evenly. The children came home for lunch and ate homemade jelly and preserves with margarine and bread. I made canned milk and kept it in the refrigerator. I was able to bring scraps home from the dishwasher. (If people were served three pieces of chicken and only ate two pieces, I'd take the extra piece and tell the boss it was for my dog.) I didn't tell anyone of the struggle I was having, not even my parents.

Drinking because I HAD to drink

For Spike and Ed's sixth year birthday party I had no money for ice cream and cake. I had only fifty cents to my name, which bought three cans of sardines, one dime box of crackers, a five-cent package of Kool-Aid, and five cents worth of cookies. I brought my party supplies home with me and made it sound exciting! "Look what Sis brought you! Get the table ready and let's all have a party!"

They tore into the bag and with eyes stretched, asked, "We get a whole can of sardines apiece?"

"Sure, it's your birthday, isn't it?"

"Wow!" They scrambled and everyone was busy setting the table, putting sugar in the Kool-Aid, getting forks. They were three happy children and anyone would have thought there was a table set for kings. Today they often mention that party!

While the kids ate, I drank beer and homemade wine. It was near pay day and I was broke. As tough as things were financially, I still bought a bottle out of the $17.50 a week. If I had a five-dollar bill for groceries, I still had to figure out a way to feed us *and* get the bottle — because I was so hooked on alcohol. I was drinking because I *had* to drink.

The boys were doing very well in school and spent hours at the kitchen table doing homework. But Vivian was doing poorly in school and had to be forced to study. She just didn't seem interested. I started noticing little trinkets that I didn't buy in her drawer. I'd ask, "Where did you get this scarf?" She'd answer, "I found it."

One time it was a couple of candy bars which she said a

girl friend bought for her. After her friend said she hadn't bought them, I gave Vivian a spanking for lying and made her confess that she took them from the store. Several more times she picked up things and each time I punished her.

One day I was sitting at the table drinking whiskey and Coke. Vivian sat with me and said, "Sis, I don't want you to be mad at me. I'm sorry, I don't know why I bother things. I don't mean to, I just do it." She came around the table and laid her head in my lap. As that child climbed the stairs, she seemed to be carrying the weight of the world on her shoulders.

I poured another drink and said out loud, "Lord, what can I do?" and sat there for a half hour or more.

Somewhere in my mind I decided to call General Hospital. I really didn't know what to say but I asked the receptionist, "Could you tell me who I can talk to concerning my child who has recently started picking up things?" I told the lady the whole story of what had been happening. She set an appointment for Vivian and me to come in the next day. She talked with Vivian alone and then called me in. She said, "Vivian is a very confused child who is scared to death."

I asked, "But why? My kids have nothing to be afraid of. I whip them, but not severely."

"No, that's not what I mean. She has been handled by too many people. First she was with her parents, then to her maternal grandmother, then to your mother and father, next she saw her dad sick and taken from her. She just told me that they may take her from you at the end of six months. She feels insecure. Don't just love her, but tell her and *show* her. I am going to call the VA and your attorney and see if we all can keep her with you."

She did call and the worker came out and saw the kids were healthy and very happy with me. They allowed me to keep them. After that, I often said, "I love you, Vivian, you're my little daughter now! And don't you forget that we ladies have to stick together." So my nephew became my son, and my niece became my daughter.

I continued to work and asked my next door neighbor to keep an eye on the children. I would get them ready for school and then take the bus into town. They would come home three hours before me. We had a good wire fence around the house and a dog named Blackie which the kids had raised on a baby bottle since he was two days old. I gave the kids strict orders not to leave the yard and not to allow other kids in when I was not home. If they disobeyed, I gave them a spanking. After a few spankings they really got the message and I had no more trouble in that department. I felt, as my parents did, "A good ass whipping is like a good prayer. It changes things." They really weren't bad children.

From church to the bootleg house

I was a drunk. Although I saw my children went to Sunday School, I lived in constant fear of the VA and Bill finding out about my drinking. I knew of mothers who were branded as unfit mothers and had lost their kids because of drinking. So I tried harder to be a good mother to my kids and felt guilty drinking and getting drunk in their presence.

Our church was in town. I had to stay home Friday and Saturday because I no longer had a brother with me. We'd get up early Sunday morning, have breakfast, and then I would dress the children. After Sunday School they went to the movie with sack lunches and money to buy pop and candy. They looked forward to the Sundays and were very happy. As soon as I got out of church, I headed straight for the bootleg house, about four doors from my church. I'd stand around and talk until everyone had left — then Steve and I would duck in and drink all Sunday evening until time to pick the kids up. To this day, I don't know why I didn't forget to pick my kids up.

Steve was the passing-out type and would go to sleep, while I danced or talked, with my drunken mouth running like a bell clapper! We both knew better than to go to my downtown room and lie down, for fear of not waking up. My kids had no one else to care for them. Sundays became very special to me — I would try to justify my actions by saying, "At least I went to church today! Some people don't go at all." I knew I should stop living that drinking life but I couldn't. I prayed to God to help me, but I still picked up the drinks. I was always ashamed for people to see me drunk.

I decided to become more active in church (maybe if I did more for God he would do more for me). So I attended choir rehearsal and sang in the choir. My uniform was a white dress that represented pureness and how clean I was of sin, etc. I was also a Stewardess in the church — quite an honor in the CME Church and I really felt honored. I prayed, "God make me worthy and make me better." But I still got drunk. As soon as I left church I went to my room and pulled the uniform off, redressed, went to another bootleg house and got drunk. My God, I was not getting better but worse! The bootleg house, near my downtown room, attracted a different class of people than I had been associating with.

Unholy spirits at Communion

There was the time that I had been drunk all Friday night, all day Saturday until four o'clock Sunday morning. I still got up, bathed and made it to church because I had to get there now that I was a Stewardess. I woke up with the shakes, took two aspirin for a splitting headache, and drank black coffee. My stomach was quivering and I felt sick. But I had to go to church. I had promised to be there. I had promised to uphold the rules and do my duties as a Stewardess. So I went on to church.

We had prepared the bread and wine for sacrament

(Holy Communion). There were many of the tiny glasses, all filled. Two other ladies and I had the job of refilling them when empty. It takes a steady hand to spot those tiny glasses. I poured about five or six and started having muscle spasms. My hands shook and shook. I tried to grip the "wine" bottle (grape juice) hoping that it would steady me, but to no avail. As I tried to spot another small glass, I shook worse. The shakes were spreading all over my body. My head was shaking, my knees shook and sweat started running from my arm pits to my waist. I spilled Jesus' blood all over the altar and broke out in tears. We SOULS shout in our church, so the ushers ran to me with fans and smelling salts because everyone thought I felt the *Holy Spirit* and was happy and shouting! But I knew I was feeling the *Gordon Gin Spirit!* I went home and prayed again, "God forgive me. You gave your son Jesus to save me, and I can't stay sober one Sunday to serve the bread and wine. Forgive me and help me." (That bread and wine was, and still is, very sacred according to my religious background and belief, which was why this was one of the worst things that could happen to me.) To make me feel even more guilty, one of the church members called and said, "Child, you really had the *Spirit* yesterday! I hope you didn't have any special problem pressing you because you don't usually get *happy* in church."

Getting worse, getting sicker

Steve and I went to the ball game one day.

Thousands of people were present. It was about the time Jackie Robinson had finally been accepted. We took a pint of whiskey and bought beer at Crosley Field. Because we spied a member of our church a few rows behinds us, we sneaked and poured our whiskey. It was hot and soon a few drinks with beer chasers had me drunk — I didn't know how drunk I was until I stood up to go, and Steve pulled me down in my seat hard. I asked,

"What is the matter with you?" He replied, "Sit down until Mr. Jones leaves. You done peed clear through your clothes!" I sat there and started crying. I never even *felt* the urge! What was happening to me? It had only been two or three weeks since I had made a fool of myself in church. Now, again, in view of a church member! I thought I must be losing my mind. I MUST CUT DOWN. I tried and even told Steve, "From now on, I am only going to drink two shots and two beers. Don't you give me any more, even if I ask for it." So now everything was settled.

The next weekend when we went out, he followed my suggestion. I became so upset when he didn't give me any more that I locked my arm in the steering wheel while he was driving and tried to wreck the car. I actually intended to kill us both and told him so. No matter what happened, every weekend I ran right back into that brick wall. I was getting worse, getting sicker.

Drinking to block the guilt

Some people from my drinking crowd, including Jay, called and said they were coming over one Saturday afternoon. I asked, "Jay, will you bring me a pint?" I just wanted a pint of security. So he brought it, along with plenty more from the other people. We partied until late that night and Jay spent the night with me. I felt guilty because I had cheated on Steve, but Jay was no stranger. It wasn't really serious — just one of those drunken things. But I felt cheap.

Sunday came again and the kids were off to Sunday School. I got dressed to join them. Being that it was Sunday, no liquor could be sold. I was many miles from church and couldn't very well come all the way back home for my pint, so I put it in my purse and took it to church with me (praying that I would not get sick and someone find my bottle — or suppose I dropped my purse and the bottle broke in church?) I knew that I was being wicked and a deceitful hypocrite. God just might strike me dead. "What's done in the dark shall come to light." I stayed terrified all through that church service and was so glad when they said, "Amen!"

My eyes had been scanning the crowd. I looked and thought there is Sister So-and-So! She is always gossiping. What if she knew I had a bottle right here under her nose? There is Brother So-and-So! He probably would like a little snort! Oh yes, I was sick!

As soon as church let out, I told Steve, "Come on and let's go to your car and have a taste." We drove a few blocks away and killed the pint, then went over the river to sit in the lot to finish getting drunk. As soon as I drank enough, I could block out my guilt and made a joke of the matter. I was just like Santa Claus, always a ho!ho!ho!, but I felt miserable inside. As soon as I sobered up and had to face reality, the remorse and guilt set in again. Me taking whiskey to *church!* What would my Dad say? What would Mom say? I knew Mom would give me one of her backhand licks. I promised myself that I would never do that again. And I didn't take another bottle to church any more. I kept trying to live like I was brought up, but as soon as I took one drink all promises and resolutions failed.

I was tired of washing dishes for nothing so I enrolled in cosmetology school. I'd always liked working with hair and decided to become a beautician. I had to do 1,040 hours of training and practice before going to the State Board. I felt that my side, back, and hips would stop hurting if I could stop lifting those heavy dish racks. When I was drunk I didn't feel pain, but when sober sometimes it was pretty bad. Each menstrual cycle I was flooding more, and longer.

Trying to learn that trade wasn't easy for me. It was very hard to concentrate. I went five days a week and was supposed to study on weekends (which I spent drinking). I had no money in the beginning and once I gave up my job, there was even less. I bought my three white uniforms, which I kept starched and ironed, at the Goodwill. The day finally came when I went to Columbus, Ohio, and faced the State Board of Cosmetology. I PASSED! I was so happy and so proud. No more dishwashing! No more bussing dishes! I felt proud to say, "I am a Beautician." I worked long, hard hours in a shop at Seventh and Mounds Street. I took time to build customers, so I was growing in my work.

We had been wearing very short dresses, and *overnight* dresses dropped to the calf. I had beautiful clothes left from the war and couldn't use them (and I was caught at a time when I had no money). Only another woman knows what it is to have a wardrobe completely wiped out overnight! I wore my short dresses as long as I could, along with purchasing a grey plaid suit and a navy taffeta dress — all I had while trying to get off the ground as a beautician.

I heard one of the operators talking about me one day. She said, "I am tired of seeing Chaney wear that blue dress. I feel like asking her to take it off." I pretended not to hear. It really hurt because I couldn't do any better. I slowly bought a few things for myself, but not too many. Clothes money was spent on the children. I was determined that they would not be hungry. Maybe they wouldn't eat steaks, but they were going to eat, no matter what. As my customers increased, more of my time was consumed. Sometimes my first customer would be at eight-thirty in the morning and the last would be at eight-thirty at night. On Saturdays and before holidays I worked until ten or ten-thirty at night.

Eleven-cents poor to 'nigger rich'

I was afraid my boys would become delinquents, and my daughter was becoming a big girl who might become pregnant. So I packed up my tools and went home. I started making a few dollars doing hair in my kitchen for the neighbors. Financially things were rough, and I could hardly see a way out. One morning I woke up and had exactly eleven cents to my name, one cup of grits, two bread ends plus one slice of bread, and a piece of margarine about an inch thick. I fed all of this to the kids and told them to stay in the yard.

I was forced to go job-hunting. Very few Blacks lived in the neighborhood, so I was sure I could get a day's cleaning in some White woman's house — only I would have to ask for advance payment so I could feed my kids. I walked to several places in Deer Park, but to no avail. Then I walked the opposite direction and stopped several places where I left my name and phone number.

Since I was so close, I decided to go on to the Post Office. (At that time we had to pick up mail. There was no delivery.) I went in and chatted a few minutes with the lady behind the counter who gave me my mail. There was a check addressed to me from the U.S. Treasury Department, but it wasn't time for my allotment. As soon as I got outside I tore the envelope open and saw it was for five hundred dollars!! I hurried home and called my attorney to ask if he knew anything about it. He said, "Yes, Chaney, that is the result of your trying so hard to get a raise for your brother! I've been pushing it and told them how you've struggled to keep the children together. You are to take that check and get the children's school clothes and whatever else you need." He added, "Get something for yourself too; you really deserve it. You should receive two or three more checks in the near future, but don't cash them. Bring them to me and we have to open a bank account in your and your brother's names."

That day we did have steak! And we talked about our shopping spree. I paid electric and phone bills. As we SOULS say, I was "nigger rich." It had been many moons since I had five *hundred* dollars.

True, within a week another check came for about $1,500 and then one for $2,000 and so on. My brother was getting retroactive pay for three years. He was a one hundred percent disabled American Veteran and the authorities had goofed when they allowed him only forty percent disability. My attorney said the kids would be allowed a certain amount monthly for their support. I got down on my knees and thanked God.

The very next week a lady called from the grocery store and asked, "Do you still want a job?" I said, "Yes." She said, "Well, call my sister and go to the dry cleaner in Deer Park to talk to her. She's looking for help."

I thanked her and decided to walk the five blocks to talk to her. When her husband interviewed me, he asked, "Did you ever work at a dry cleaner?"

"No, I didn't." (I thought, "Well, here goes this gig.")

He said, "I'll be able to train you. My trouble has been finding *experienced* spotters. I am willing to teach you the trade if you promise to stick with me. Report to work Monday morning."

I was so happy to have a job close to home! Also, it had made me sick to think of cleaning Mrs. Charlie's house or nursing her kids while leaving mine at home alone. Financially, things got much better. The owner and his wife were wonderful people to work for, and I really liked my work there.

Getting into trouble at work

So I was in my world. I worked there for years and enjoyed my work. Many Mondays I showed up hung over; it was pathetic, but I usually made it. I'd lie and say it was something I ate, but I'm not sure that I was fooling anyone except myself because I was so awful sick every Monday. By that time, I had been drinking hard and heavy for almost *ten* years!!

During the holidays we were loaded with work and were working long hard hours. My brother was home from the hospital for a visit. Mom came to be with us for Christmas. My back, side, and hips ached like a toothache, off and on. I told Mom, "I've been standing too much and lifting too many heavy clothes. But the rush will soon be over and then I can slow down and will feel better."

"Why don't you wear a girdle for support?" she asked.

"Mom, as skinny as I am, I don't have anything to tie down. I won't have any butt at all if I wear a girdle! I've got to have a little hump in the back to show." We all cracked up.

The supervisor bought beer for the help and opened a Christmas bottle. Everyone was feeling high as a kite when we left that evening. One of the ladies and I decided to go into town for a few hours and have a few drinks. I couldn't stop drinking once I started so at 2:00 a.m. when the bartender called "lights out," I was still in the bar. From there I went to the bootleg house down the street from my room, and at five o'clock I was still dancing and running my mouth. I was supposed to be at work at 7:30 a.m. and was miles away and drunk, very drunk. I tried to think of a good lie to tell the boss. At seven o'clock I called to explain why I couldn't make it. Evidently, the minute I dialed, I had a memory blackout. I don't remember today a word I said or the balance of that Saturday or the next day. Steve said I stayed on my feet and acted quite normal. Of course, he was drunk also — so the blind can't lead the blind.

I didn't call Mom and she was angry with me when I got home and she saw that I was still inebriated. My boss was angry with me and said, "Chaney, you tried to lie to me, but I know you were drunk! You just kept saying the same thing, over and over. You can do as you please on your time off, but if you want your job, I expect you at work." I couldn't defend myself. I was guilty and didn't even know what I had said.

I was getting into trouble at work. I was getting sicker but trying to be careful not to drink if I had to work the next day. Now that Mom was with the kids, I spent more weekends drinking downtown. I'd take my church clothes with me on Saturday evenings, and Steve and I would spend the weekend at the room. I still kept my private sex life away from the kids and never let them know that Steve stayed there all night with me. He and the kids got along great, but we both respected them and refused to shack up in their presence. I told him, "My kids will never throw it back in my face that they saw me sleeping with any man. They may do that and I wouldn't be able to say a word if I had done the same thing." So I was able to keep them from knowing.

Pain and surgery

One night without any warning I started hurting while sitting on the side of the bed talking to Steve. I felt as if I was having labor pains, only there was no let-up and I doubled up and fell across the bed. My whole body was contracting. I started screaming out loud, not knowing what was wrong with me. Booze was not causing this much hurt! Steve got excited and called the lady upstairs. When she came down, they rushed me to the hospital. The doctor gave me a pain shot and examined me on the table. When they smelled the booze, the doctor probably felt I was just another drunk. He gave me a few pills with strict orders to see my family doctor the next day.

When I left the hospital I felt better, so I slept for a few hours, got up and took the two pain pills, and continued to drink whiskey and Cokes. It was Sunday and I didn't go to church but continued to ball in my room, next door, upstairs, and down at the bootleg house. I slept for a few hours because I had to take the bus home.

I was dressing so slowly that Steve asked, "You don't feel good, do you?"

"No, I don't, my side and stomach still hurt a little."

"Well, you be sure and go to the doctor tomorrow. Come on and I'll ride downtown with you to get your bus home," he said. His car wasn't running. He rode with me, and I took the express bus to Galbraith and Deer Park.

When I got about halfway home, everything started to look fuzzy and pains began, just like the beginning of labor. I thought this was the hangover. When I rang the bell to get off the bus, I had to pull myself up by the back of the seat. I staggered to the door and made one step down. My God, it felt as if I was giving birth again! As I stepped to the street, I looked down and saw blood was running down my legs into my shoes. I made it to the street, right in front of my house, and collapsed. My brother put me on the couch and I started to throw up. My fingers and toes were curling. Mom cried, "Lord, my child is having a stroke!" The whole house was in a turmoil, calling the ambulance, trying to clean up vomit and blood and stop Mom from screaming. My three kids were crying.

I passed out, and ended up having surgery at Jewish Hospital for an infected left tube and ovary which the surgeon said should have been removed years ago. I am sure that the excessive drinking contributed to my illness. I am not qualified to speak from a medical point of view, but hundreds of alcoholic ladies have been hospitalized because of flooding. I've known many who've had to be packed to stop the bleeding. As soon as they are better and go and drink again, the same thing occurs again.

While I was in the hospital, Bill had the divorce papers served. I had thirty days to contest. I was too sick to contest, plus I had no intention of going back to him. He had asked me to send his mother part of his military allotment, but that meant taking food out of my child's mouth. He also had asked if me and the baby would join him at camp but I couldn't leave the other two kids. It was just over with us. I had lost all feelings for him. When we got the divorce he wrote that he no longer wanted to support his son. His supervisor, or whoever handled the pay, wrote me and told me what he said. Also, Bill had told him that I drank heavy and he was ashamed of me.

I waited until I got about drunk and answered that officer's letter: "Dear Sir, you tell Bill Morgan that this boy is his and was born in wedlock. He saw him birthed in this world. Tell him if he doesn't want to take care of his son, I will take care of him myself. And I will never ask him for a damn dime as long as I live. P.S. Tell him to kiss _____ _____. Mrs. Morgan." And I never have asked him for any child support.

I did tell my son what his father had said. I told him, "I want you to know and remember to never kiss anyone's behind that don't want to be bothered with you!"

Now that I was divorced, Steve and I started talking of marriage. The kids were growing up, and what I was trying so hard to keep hidden was known to my kids, although they had not seen. I told Steve, "We have to marry so I will be protected. With a man it is quite different." One Saturday morning we went and got married. We celebrated with the usual drunken crowd.

'Nothing but an ole drunk'

Every weekend I was getting drunk. Mother was very upset because no matter what she said, I still got drunk. Even if I was home on weekends, I couldn't stop until I was *absolutely* drunk. When I had guests in, I always got drunker than anyone else.

Mom burst out in tears one Sunday evening when I came home staggering, with vomit all down my front. She was so embarrassed before the neighbors and made me hurry into the house before the kids saw me. I was too drunk to care so I cleaned up and went to bed, glad to escape her tongue-lashing.

The next morning she said, "You are a disgrace to the

family. I wish to God you had been born dead. You are nothing but an ole drunk and everybody out here is talking about you. And if Steve had any respect for you he wouldn't be wallowing in that hole downtown with you. When he gets ready for a *wife,* he is going to drop you like a hot potato."

I didn't tell her we were married so she continued, "I know how to straighten you out. You just wait and see. Why can't you be a respectful lady? I never had but one man in my life and that is your father."

She had hit a sore spot and it hurt. I envied her for living like I wanted to live. I half-mumbled, "You don't know what's good 'till you try something different. Variety is the spice of life." I landed flat on the floor with a busted lip from Mom's backhand lick. She didn't even turn around, but she hit her target. I sat there and cried like a baby. I was so sick and hung over, so ashamed of coming home like that — and so mentally confused. All I wanted was for someone to put out a hand and help me.

I went on to work with a fat lip. By Wednesday I felt better. When Friday came, I promised to really control my drinks that weekend. I promised to come home right after church. I got home that Monday instead, and Mom gave me the silent treatment. Steve and I overslept, and I had goofed again. The next weekend I did the same thing, plus I didn't work that Monday. When Steve and I drove past the house to turn and park in front of my door, my father was on the front porch! My heart stopped. I knew that mother had him come to straighten me out. I said to Steve, "I am really in trouble now!"

"No, you are not. Where is the marriage license? We'll show him!" And we did show them the license. They both were happy for us. Steve liked it out in the country, so we stayed in Rossmoyne for a year. He worked at the blacktop company, and I continued at the dry cleaner until we saved a down payment on a home, a real nice three-bedroom, two-story brick house in Walnut Hills.

The drinking continued and we argued every weekend when we got our heads bad. The kids took our arguments as a joke. They'd say, "He is winning this one, but wait until ole Sis comes in with her dig!"

I had Steve try to get his little girl to live with us. She could be a companion for my daughter, but he couldn't get the kid since he never married the mother and she had full custody. But I saw that the child support was sent and also bought clothes for his kid.

Now I had a good husband, a nice home, and some custom-made furniture! But, so help me, I *still* could not stay sober. Steve and I bought whiskey and beer and pop. We'd put the bottles in an ice cooler in the trunk, and every weekend we went downtown. Sometimes we just sat in the car and drank in front of the bar. But most of the time we enjoyed having *saloon arthritis*. (That was, we got *stiff* in every joint.) I don't know why we didn't get killed or jailed as drunk as were in that moving vehicle.

Many times we kept a crowd in our house, with the records playing all night. Or we would be at someone's house balling around the clock. I always worked my butt off during the week, housecleaning, cooking, washing and ironing so that I would be free to drink on the weekends. We had a big, upright freezer, so I would cook and freeze the food. The kids had plenty of home-cooked food, their clothes were all clean and the house was clean.

Steve and I both were working and the Veterans Administration sent the two kids checks every month, so I cannot say that I was drinking because of any financial problems. I drank because I was hooked on alcohol, period!

My children now were all in their early teens and going through adolescent changes. Sometimes they could be impossible and had to be corrected. They were at the age "where they were beginning to smell themselves" and become little mannish boys or fast gals! I knew the kids were growing up, and had to be corrected when they were wrong and made mistakes.

The only problem was I didn't like Steve's cursing at them when he corrected them. I never told him about this in their presence, but many times in the privacy of our room, I said, "I think you talked too harsh to them. After all they are children. You shouldn't talk to them like they are grown."

He said, "Well, I will not say a damn thing to them. I'll just let you raise your kids and stay the hell out of it."

We had many serious arguments about this. I was so upset one day after his cursing spree that I said to myself, "When my kids grow up I am going to leave his butt! I am sick of his acting a fool." But I wanted my children to have the security of a home and school, and a good normal social life.

Mom was still in Rossmoyne because Nelson got very sick in New York and moved back to Ohio. Dad told Mom to stay to take care of him. So Nelson and Steve's family joined us on some weekends. We all had a ball, and I always ended up drunk.

One night I was so drunk I went to bed in my clothes. My husband's nephew came into the room and called, "Wake up and take your eyeglasses off before you break them." I replied, "I can't! I've got to see how to sleep, honey!" He and everyone else cracked up and teased me about that for years.

One Monday morning when I woke up the bed was soaked in blood. My God, I was flooding again. I was rushed again to the doctor and had to go back to the hospital for another operation. This time I had a tumor that had to be removed. One month later I was drunk again. It was cold and I dressed to go to a party in a beautiful two-piece blue dress and no coat. I was half drunk all the time I was dressing, and by the time I finished, I was too high to feel the cold. I had had major surgery only six weeks ago but I went to the party and later to a joint. I was drinking at every stop and was so drunk that I don't remember getting home. From the exposure I took pneumonia and almost died. I almost killed myself chasing a bottle of booze!

So I lost my job

When I'd recuperated, my boss told me, "I have hired someone else. The lady is big and strong and said that she could do both your job and press too." So I lost my job. My salary was needed to pay part of our household expenses. I started to fill out applications at hospitals, hotels, and the Board of Education food handlers department. For months I heard nothing.

My brother Henry had sent me some money which I had banked for him. I used his money to pay a couple of house payments and had planned I would replace it as soon as I started working. Unfortunately, he came home before I could replace his money. I said, "I hit a bad spot and used your money. I will either borrow it and pay you now or you can live in the attic apartment rent free until the money has been repaid." This arrangement was fine with him and with Steve and me. Henry shared the kitchen and bath with us. Now he and his girl friend were added to the drinking crowd, and we kept on partying. My brothers all knew that I was a drunk and nothing anyone said could stop me. (God knows I wanted to, but I couldn't stop.)

Henry and his girl friend drank heavy also and would have some loud arguments. Steve and I raised hell too, but after all, it was our home. So, as soon as my brother had been repaid his money, I asked him to move. He said, "O.K., but I think you are being nasty." As my grandmother had said, "Every rat should have his own hole." Finally he got over his anger and joined us on weekend parties again.

I received a letter asking me to come to the Board of Education for an interview for a food handler's job. I went on a Monday and filled out papers. There were many questions such as where had I worked and how many jobs had I held for the last ten years. Had I been arrested? I answered "no" and thought, "Thank you, God, for being so good to me, a sinner. It is not *my goodness* that has kept me out of jail or the electric chair." After all the red tape, I was hired as a salad maker at Withrow High School. About 5,000 kids were fed daily, so the work was hard, steady and fast, but I enjoyed it. I loved working with the kids, and the faster I worked during lunch hour, the better I liked it. Many of the children called me mother.

The head cook had been with the Board of Education for many years and got a promotion. The lady who replaced her was a wonderful Christian lady. I liked teasing her, and sneaking crispy ham and bacon skins from her. I called her my Big Sister. Whenever I walked into the kitchen and said, "Here is your little sister," she'd ask, "What do you want now?" She and everyone would break out laughing because they knew I was food hunting. They all said they hated me because I could eat all day and gain no weight. I really liked all of them.

My supervisor and I got along well. Her only complaint was that I talked too much. (I can't whisper because I have a heavy voice that many people says sounds like Pearl Bailey. When I think I am talking low, it resounds all over.)

None of those ladies knew about my serious drinking problem. I worked as normal as they during the week, and they didn't see me in my drunken stupors on weekends, since we didn't visit each others' homes and didn't go to the same places. They didn't know that every Monday I was hung over and as sick as a dog. Many times I'd go to the bathroom, quietly throw up and wash my face in cold water, praying that the day would hurry and end. There was very little to be thrown up because I hadn't eaten since 1:30 p.m. Friday.

The odor of the food would make me so sick that I could hardly get a few spoons of soup down for a couple of days. Usually I said, "I ate something on the weekend that made me sick. I have an upset stomach." When I think about it today, I don't understand why no one noticed that I only had an upset stomach on Mondays and after holidays. Drunk or sober, I liked people, and always kept up so much fun and bullshit that they hardly knew if I was serious or not. One of the ladies who was a good friend would laugh so hard at something funny I said that she would pee on herself and have to run to the bathroom. Drunk or sober, I've always had a sense of humor — and still do.

Those ladies at work didn't know that I envied them chatting on Monday mornings about the nice places they had gone on the weekends. Some had spent all day at church, some visited the sick at hospitals, or spent a day at Coney Island. Some had gone on family picnics. They spent their weekends doing just the things of a normal life, and I spent my weekends in some smoke-filled bars. I wanted to be like them again. Once I *had* lived like them and wanted to again, but couldn't detach myself from the bottle and the drunken life.

Many times I'd say that I had gone to a birthday party or wedding and had so much fun there. One of the ladies told me, "I just envy you and your husband. You have such good times together. You always seem to do so many things together."

"Yes, we do enjoy the same things."

But the truth was we both "shared" *drinking*. Steve drank heavily also but wasn't hooked as I was. Many times I have known him to take a shot before going to work, and a couple after work. A pint would last him all week. But if ever I took a drink it was "goodbye and bottoms up!" I would not stop until I drank the whole thing. We got paid every two weeks and if money was short sometimes, we would buy some pale dry sherry at the grocery store. I could only drink the white wine, because any sweet drink made me sick immediately. Where once I could drink the sweet sloe gin, my system had changed and I could no longer stomach it.

Next door to us lived a bootlegger who helped accommodate my alcoholism. We soon made friends, and I ran a tab if money was low. Now I had become one of the same type people who looked up to my brother Nelson for their booze. *I* was now looking up to the lady next door for credit. I knew the score — I knew I was being cheated with the thick pitchers and a few extra drinks added to the tab, but I *had* to drink until pay day. She knew I was working and would pay. Some of the people who drank there were loud and vulgar, but I had to have my drinks. So I joined in the noise. Also, because I was just next door, I could easily see about the children. If I got too drunk, I just went home and went to bed. It was perfect for an alcoholic like me.

My children continued to grow up, and the years were really passing. My daughter grew into a beautiful young lady who never drank or smoked. I never had any problems with her being fast or staying out late with a fast crowd. I taught her about sex, and she was well prepared for her first menstrual period. It always took a few drinks for me to get the nerve for serious talks, but at least we talked. I told her, "Vivian, girls are not supposed to have sex with boys, but if you will do so, please use these and be sure the boy puts them on right. I can't have any extra babies to raise." (The pill wasn't popular then.)

Steve told her, "I am going to tell you, if you come up with a baby, you are going to get the hell out of my house. And if Sis doesn't like it she can go too."

The boys were about fourteen when they made the great discovery that their penis was made for more than just to pee! They were very different than their sister. They had gone cock crazy, chasing every little pushover girl they heard of. I had to get half drunk to talk to them.

First I gave them a book to read which explained the biological changes in their bodies. Next I just talked to them from the nitty gritty. "You boys think you are being smart by having sex with a girl because she is easy. But I want you to know that is dangerous. You may get germs and be very sick with a discharge. Or the girl may get pregnant and say you are the father of her child. You might know she's having other boys, but you'll have to marry her, and have a whore for a wife. Or you may have to support a child that isn't yours until it is eighteen years old. So the easy girl isn't always the best girl." Both the boys looked at each other and cracked up.

Steve didn't sit and talk to the boys about sex. I had to deal with these things both with Vivian and the boys. But my booze always gave me courage and strength to face unpleasant situations. The kids and I talked openly about sex, and shared jokes. I felt that if I allowed them to talk, I'd know what was on their minds. I always tried to be a good and fair mother, but the bottle kept interfering. Their friends saw me drunk. I'd prepare food and be nice to their friends, but many times I couldn't remember what I had cooked or what their guests looked like. My kids didn't realize that I usually was operating in a complete blackout. For years I did the same thing, every weekend.

Not God, but the bottle, is my Master

Time didn't stand still, and the kids kept growing. Vivian was interested in nursing so I saw that she learned practical nursing while in high school. She was prepared to take care of herself. Finally she met her dream boy, and they told us they were going to be married. I really liked the young man, who was from a good family. They planned a church wedding, with her cousin and girl friends helping make all the wedding plans.

I cried all the night before her wedding day. That was a good excuse for me to get drunk — after all I was losing my little girl. On her wedding day I woke up with a hangover and a splitting headache. I took a couple of aspirins, only to throw them up, which set off a spasm of gagging and dry heaves. I bathed my face in cold water and painfully went about the million things to be done — the finishing touches in the house, the food and drinks, etc. I had to have a drink because I was shaking. And a short time later a second. I was off and running again. I was drunk by the time to go to church, but I stopped at a bar and bought a couple of drinks. I forgot the boys' shirts, and someone had to go back for them. And I had forgotten to call the florist, letting him know the specific time to bring the flowers. My daughter knew I was drunk, but as I said before, she would never hurt my feelings. She helped me do the last minute things at church, and then she went in the dressing room and her bridesmaids finished dressing her. I remember standing and crying as she marched down the aisle on Steve's arm. My minister and others had to know I was drunk, and I deliberately stayed away from the photographer.

When I got home one of my church members said, "Honey, I know you are tired so you go on and lie down and I will help make the people comfortable." She knew I was drunk. Everyone at church knew I drank too much. I had been drinking and going to church for many years and it was impossible to remain forever hidden. I was ashamed that people were talking, but I *couldn't* stay sober.

One Easter Sunday I wanted to go to church, even though I had been up Saturday night drinking. I attempted to dress for church and tried to straighten my hair, while my hands shook like a leaf on a tree. So I poured a small drink to steady my hands, then another. Soon I was able to steady the comb and finish doing my hair. Steve said, "Why don't you stay home? You are in no shape to go to church."

"I've got to go. This is Easter Sunday, the day that Jesus rose from the dead. The least I can do is go to church today," I said. That was my true feelings although I was drinking. I dressed and went on to church.

As always, the church was packed on Easter. I finally spotted a single seat about four rows from the front and fifth seat in the row. There was hardly standing room. The choir was singing "Was You There When They Crucified My Lord?" I love that song and felt very emotional as I joined in singing. I closed my eyes and sang every verse and every chorus along with the choir. When they finished, I opened my eyes and saw a visible ring around me. People had gotten up and moved away from me. I looked around me and saw a lady whisper to her seat mate, "She's drunk." I had gargled with mouthwash, but I couldn't brush my teeth because the toothbrush gagged me and would make me vomit. I even ate some toothpaste to kill my breath but nothing kills the odor of alcohol, expecially from the night before mixed with four shots before going to church. I was so ashamed I got up and stood in the back until the service ended. As soon as they said "Amen," I almost ran out because I didn't want to talk to anyone.

I remember saying to myself, "God is no longer my Master. This bottle is. God is going to punish me because the Bible said, 'Thou shall have no other God before me,' " I felt so ashamed and guilted. I was living a Hell on earth and didn't know what to do or where to turn. God knows I had tried to control my drinking in every way. I only wanted to drink a few just to have a nice time. What was wrong with me? I didn't tell Steve what had happened, but someone did. It ended in "I told you so."

Out of control and terrified

I was alone at home one Saturday night. Steve had gone out with the boys. My sons had gone to a dance just a few blocks from the house. My boys knew I was alone and sipping when they left. I no longer went out with girl friends or anyplace drinking without my husband. He felt that I was chasing after him. But the truth was that I was afraid. He didn't know that I had lost complete control of my drinking, and most times didn't know what I was saying or doing. I was terrified and didn't know exactly of what.

My boys called and said, "Sis, get dressed. Put on your black suit with the white fur collar. We're at the Cave and the old folks are in front. We're in the back. We'll walk down and get you so you won't be lonely." I heard them singing before they reached the house. They were real clowns and said, "May we have the pleasure of taking you out for a spot of tea, my lady?" So we left for a night of fun.

I was drinking double, double whiskey and Coke. The barmaid sat two extra drinks in front of me which I hadn't ordered. "The man down the bar sent them to you." She pointed to a very young man, not much older than my daughter. When I saw who it was, I remembered that someone had told me he was a drug addict. It was alright for me to be a drunk but I wanted no part of an addict. I refused the drinks and the man got angry with me. He insulted me by calling me obscene names. I got up and told the barmaid, "I'm going home." I told the lady to go and tell my boys I was on my way home. I left, and evidently the man was thrown out at the same time. He tried following me, still calling me names. My boys had now come out of the dance to walk me home and they heard him. Everything happened so fast. They grabbed the man and beat the devil out of him. They were young, healthy track and football players and the man was no match for them. I was scared to death. And again I felt remorseful. Why didn't I stay at home? Then this wouldn't have happened! I had no business out with my children. Suppose one of them had gotten hurt or in trouble? I went on home and finished getting drunk, while I explained the whole thing to Steve.

Now, Lord, I can just live!

My boys were in their senior year and it was time for graduation. They were all excited over the tailored suits and new hi-fi for graduation presents. We had consented to them having the party at the house. (That was the only time I didn't have to break mop and broom handles across their butts to get some work done around the house!) They had brand new Stacy Adams shoes that they bought while washing dishes at the Jewish Hospital after school.

Graduation day came, and I saw my last babies finish high school. My son Ed was valedictorian of his class. My Spike graduated with honors, besides being a great athlete. I had told them all their lives that they must work to further their own education because financially I just didn't have the money for college.

Spike immediately signed up for the Marines and was stationed at Camp Pendleton in San Diego. Ed decided to try for college and work. I promised to help as much as I could. He finished the first semester, and I paid for the second. Believe it or not, but he sneaked and signed himself into the Marines so he could be with his brother.

Both the boys ended up at camp. They called me one night and said, "We are so damn glad to be back together."

I thought to myself, "Thank you God for helping me raise my children. It was tough but we made it! My daughter is married and I had no trouble with her. Her husband said she was a nineteen-year-old virgin! My boys had no police records. It was rough but God helped me to see it through. Now, Lord, I can just live!"

As sad as a funeral

About a month later, Mom called long distance from Dad's church, "Sis, this is Mother. You better come at once. Your daddy had a stroke in the pulpit!" I was in the yard drinking and dancing when I received the call. I was wearing black and white plaid shorts and a black blouse and was drunk as a skunk. I pulled a bag out of the closet, put on nylons and sling pumps, pulled a skirt over the shorts and grabbed a coat. I grabbed two dresses, still in the cleaner's bag, took off for the terminal station and jumped on the train within an hour. I had an all-night ride to Athens, Alabama. I slept off most of my drunk and woke up with time enough to wash and dress again. Mom and a couple of Dad's members met me. Mom was so upset and I was scared to ask if Dad was dead. She said, "He has been asking for you all night."

We went to see my dad. He was asking for me but he didn't know it. Dad had a blank look on his face, and saliva was running out the side of his mouth. He had had a stroke and the doctor said there would be brain damage. He would have other strokes, but he could live for years, they told me.

Dad did get better but not well. So he retired, after fifty years as a CME minister.

To see Dad or any of our ministers retire is as sad as a funeral to me. Dad talked of the hymn, "Go Preach My Gospel Said the Lord," both when he had started fifty years ago and when he retired. Mentally, Dad never stopped pastoring.

He and Mom settled in the house in Rossmoyne. They were on social security and had saved their money, so they were no financial burden to their children.

Dad saw me drunk and almost had another stroke. He balled his fist up and if I hadn't left, I'm sure he would have hit me. We all had been in the basement drinking and everyone left by the side door. They said "Come on, Sis."

"No, I want to tell my dad 'bye!"

"No, don't go up there, you are too drunk! Come on and get into the car."

"Hell no! Leave me alone."

I pulled away, fell up the steps and stumbled right into

Dad. He said, "This is my house, and you and everyone
else is going to respect it. So help me, Sister, I'll pull my
belt off and whip you like a *five-year-old!*"

I left, and Steve and everyone else jumped on me. I
didn't need any lip from anyone! I had already torn my
ass and didn't want to hear their mouth! I went on and got
my hidden bottle out of the clothes hamper, poured me a
couple of big drinks and got so drunk I didn't give a damn
what they were saying.

Dad was invited to preach at our church one Sunday. I
had promised and should have shown up there. I had the
greatest intentions of attending the services but had gone
over the river and stayed out all night. As the driver
passed the church, I mumbled in my drunk tongue, "My
daddy preach there — did I tell you my dad is a preacher?
I am a preacher's *daughter!* My dad *taught me* to love
God. I know *I* am a Christian! I went to Sunday School. I
love my church."

"Aw shut up Sis, Goddamn!" my husband yelled.
"Every time a nigger gets drunk, he wants to start talking
about God. We are all going to Hell, shit!"

I didn't get to church. Instead we all went to my house
and partied all day. As usual I went to bed early Sunday
so I could work on Monday morning.

Losing my 'cools'

Lately I had started to be so jumpy. I was afraid of my
own shadow. Noises bothered me even when I wasn't
drinking. It bothered me when I couldn't remember what
happened the night before.

No one likes to look bad to their in-laws, especially the
older people, but I had become obvious. For example, my
mother-in-law came one Sunday evening to a fish dinner,
and she asked, "Why don't I smell the fish? I've had my
mouth watering all the week waiting for my fish!" I was
half drunk when she got there and asked, "What fish?"

My husband said, "You know that you invited my mother to dinner when we were over there last week." Thank God I had fish in the box, but so help me I still didn't remember asking her to dinner.

I was becoming so sick from alcoholism that I was losing my cools and didn't know it. I could, in many cases, stop staggering and look a person in the eyes but I didn't see them. Steve's family eventually knew that I drank too much. And the pathetic part is I *hated* every bit of it. I *hated* myself for drinking. I drank like the men in his family and more than some of the men. I felt so bad everytime they saw me drunk that I had to drink to get drunk to forget it. I was going around in circles, just like a squirrel in a cage. But I told myself, "I am at home and if they don't like what I do, they don't have to come around me."

Steve often told me, "Sis, you drink too damn much."

I said, "Listen who is talking? You drink, too."

"I am a man. It's different," he replied.

"Well," I said, "I am a woman and I go to work every day just as you do. And furthermore, I buy my booze — I don't ask anybody for anything."

The phone rang late one evening. My husband answered it. He hung up and told me, "My daughter is at the terminal and wants me to come and pick her up." We both went to pick her up. In addition to her surprise visit, another lady was with her. His daughter was now twenty-one years old and with her was her seventeen-year-old half sister. We all spoke and introduced ourselves.

I asked, "Why didn't you call and tell us you were coming? We could have been out of town or something."

We were busy getting the room ready, and I helped them to unpack. Steve looked sort of embarrassed, and soon left saying, "I'll be back after while."

We continued to unpack. Oh NO! The overblouse did not hide her condition from a side view. That was why I wasn't told she was coming. I finally got the ladies settled, and in the privacy of our bedroom I told Steve, "Irene is pregnant and I believe her mother sent her here to have that baby."

He talked with them the next day and she admitted her pregnancy. They said their mother and stepfather had moved to Detroit and left them in D.C. Irene said her boyfriend had gotten into trouble and was in prison. She had brought her sister along to take care of her.

Two female devils

Now I had to live with those ladies all day, every day! I had a resentment that is hard to explain. I had been completely ignored in their deciding to come and stay with us. Nobody gave me the chance to say whether I wanted to be bothered with them or not. Here were these ladies and I had to keep them in my home against my will. To add insult to injury, I had to work and help support them.

One day they told my husband that I was next door in bed with a man! He cursed me out about that. I told him it wasn't true. "Why don't you put those grown women in a place of their own?" My God, how blind could a man be! I tried to accept them but I was too filled with resentments. I knew they were phony. I constantly confronted Steve about getting them an apartment. I even went to his mother and sister and asked *them* to talk to him.

But he didn't listen. He only came back and gave me more hell for talking to them; he said, "I told you my kid can stay here as well as yours."

I said, "But Steve, we are not dealing with kids. These are grown women and they have been around. I am here all day and you should hear the things they tell me. Mildred said she was sent to a reform school for hitting another kid in the head with a bat and they think it's *funny*. They told the boy next door to use voodoo on a girl. I am afraid of them."

"I don't want to hear a damn thing you have to say," was his constant answer. His mind was completely closed. I stayed upset the entire summer of 1960. I drank more and more. I had to drink, I was so nervous. I was drinking to the extent that I was no longer aggressive but I was becoming passive, with no fight left. I didn't know what to strike at, so I was trapped.

One day Mildred was sitting at the kitchen table while I was trying to prepare dinner. I was cooking greens, neck bones and rice, a menu to stretch our grocery money. She said, "Why do you cook greens and all that cheap food? Cook some steaks or something."

I was loaded and said, "Why don't you get up off your lazy eighteen-year-old ass and get a job and buy steaks?"

Irene chimed in, "She doesn't have to work! My daddy will take care of us!"

"Your daddy don't have a damn thing but what we accumulated together!" I stopped dinner, went upstairs to the bedroom, closed the door and stayed there. When Steve came home he came storming up the stairs with those women trailing him. His daughter was crying like an innocent baby. These ladies should have been Academy Award winners — they both could really act.

From that day on I no longer had *resentments* towards those women — I *hated* them. I drank more and stayed in my room, coming out only when I had to. They had the run of the house, and anything they did was alright with Steve. They wouldn't go to the store for a loaf of bread. When the phone bill came, it was over a hundred dollars, thanks to them calling all over the United States. I asked them why were they making all those calls that we couldn't afford to pay. And Irene answered, "Go on, woman. Pay the bill." I felt like slapping her down that flight of stairs, but instead I went next door to the bootleg house and got drunk. I was drinking much more daily, something I had never done before. But drinking was the only way I could cope with the very sight and presence of them. I was upset twenty-four hours a day.

I went to the clothes hamper, got my bottle and went to my room to drink and think. When Steve came in, I tried *one more time* to talk to him. "They're breaking up our home. I can't stand much more of this. You've *got* to get them out of our house or we can't live together."

"Then get your black ass out," he said. So, there we were! He was talking loud so they could hear him, so now they knew! All the trouble was too much — I was losing weight because I could no longer eat. I was living off beer, wine, whiskey and cigarettes. I was drinking myself to death trying to keep my nerves together.

I thought maybe he'd come to his senses if I could hold out until she had the baby. I wanted him to just put his arms around me and say, "I love you." He actually treated his dogs more kindly than he did me. We no longer had sex, all we did was walk around the house unhappy. I had been drinking almost every day for a month and was nervous and sick, both physically and mentally.

Mildred said to me, "Why don't you fix your hair like my mother?" I didn't answer her. Later Irene said, "Why do you fix your meat that way? Why don't you cook your roast like my mother?" I turned from the stove and said, "Why don't both of you D.C. whores go *home* to your mamma? I didn't send for you!" But they didn't give up. Irene said, "My grandmother taught me about voodoo and how to fix a nigger."

I tried to control myself but months of resentments, hate, humiliation, and frustration came to the surface and erupted like a volcano. I grabbed a knife from the kitchen sink and swung at Irene's belly, "You are one bitch that will not have to go the hospital. I am going to give you a cesarean right here."

She screamed and grabbed a paring knife. I cut at Mildred, screaming, "Come on, kill me! You are killing me anyway — but I'm taking one of you with me!"

I just wanted to see them bleed. I didn't care about the promise I'd made not to hurt a human being. In my sick and confused mind, they were not human but two female devils. I didn't care if I was killed as long as I could take at least one of those lying women with me. Somebody walked in, saw what was happening, and started screaming for Steve. His nephew and another friend caught my arm. I begged them to "let me take those two with me." They all left that night, but Steve had them back the next day and they all looked at me in a defying manner.

Tranquilizers, sleeping pills and booze

No one talked around the house; it was like a morgue. I walked to the store, bought a pint of dry sherry, took it to the bedroom and just sat and drank. This nightmare had to end some place. I was drinking and trying to think. Those women, my husband and his family, only thought of me as a drunk. No one seemed to care how I felt, and they all thought it was me causing trouble.

The next day I went to the doctor and told him I was having "domestic problems." He wrote a prescription for tranquilizers to settle my nerves and told me to take three a day. "Do you drink, Chaney?" he asked. "Yes I drink a couple of beers *sometimes* on the weekend." I took the tranquilizers three times a day and continued drinking beer, wine and whiskey. I was no longer able to function. Any noise was torture to my raw nerves. I would almost have a heart attack when my husband walked in the house because I couldn't stand his verbal beatings any longer. I could see hate for me in the way he looked at me.

I lasted about one week with the booze and pills and then I couldn't sleep anymore. No matter how much I drank, the pills were not helping me. I was only skin and bones, down to about ninety-one pounds. I went back to the doctor and he gave me sleeping pills to help me rest. I'm not familiar with drugs but they were tiny yellow capsules and the first one I took did knock me out so I was able to get a good night's rest. Within a week's time I started hearing voices. Even as I write now, I can still feel the pain. I went to the bathroom every night, threw up clear water and went back to bed. Then I'd get up, take a tranquilizer, go back to bed and vomit again. Now I was living off tranquilizers, sleeping pills, booze, cigarettes and water.

One night I was thirsty and went downstairs to get a drink of water. I had to pass the kitchen table to reach the refrigerator. Those two women were sitting at the table when I walked in. I froze in one spot — they had horns and great big fiery eyes and tails, and were grinning at me. *They were two devils.* I went to the bathroom sink and gagged. Someone called the life squad because I couldn't stop vomiting. I was given oxygen all the way to the hospital and after I got there. They worked on me until I was out of danger.

Going down, down

My doctor gave strict orders and said he would put me in an institution if I went back into that house. Steve handled it lightly, saying there was nothing wrong with me. Irene had gone into labor and Steve had the nerve to call me in my sick bed and ask me to sign so he could get the money to pay her hospital bill. He said Mildred had gone back home, because he said he found out "she is a liar and a troublemaker."

My house seemed so strange when I came back. As I checked my closet and dressers, I noticed that some of my clothes, linen, records and wigs were gone. Mildred had taken them. I spoke to Irene and she said, "Hi, Sis." I saw it was a strain for her to be civil, but she was trying. I spoke, "Hello Irene, let me see the baby." It was a cute little girl.

Steve and I were trying again. We went next door to the bootleg house to celebrate. I ended up drunk and vomited all over the bedroom, enroute to the bathroom. It was disgusting, especially since it was my first night back with my husband. Fortunately, he was drunk also and had fallen to sleep. I stumbled around the room and finally got the mess cleaned up. I wanted so much for us to work at saving our marriage. There had been so much heartache and so many troubles for the last months.

I went next door to the bootleg house and got drunk that Sunday. That Monday I was at work hung over and feeling very sorry for myself. I went and sat on the back steps and cried. Although I had returned, Steve wasn't keeping his promise.

Something was wrong and I knew what it was when I saw the makeup on his undershirt. I now had woman trouble along with my other problems. I took my bottle of whiskey to the kitchen with me and fumed and drank, while I prepared dinner, slamming pots and pans. By the time Steve got home, I was high as a kite. He walked in and said, "Hi!" I said, "Hi your ass!" I told him, "I know you're playing around and how would you like it if I stayed out with other men? That's another reason why our home has fallen apart."

He knew I was drunk. I saw him waiting until I went to sleep. I left the bedroom and went downstairs to sleep. He came down and checked on me. Carefully he walked back upstairs and dialed the phone. They didn't know I was on the extension, listening in. He thought I had passed out. So I surprised the hell out of them when I hollered, "Get off my damn phone!" I heard Steve slam the receiver back on the hook and run downstairs at full speed. I had another reason for getting blind drunk that night, and the next day my head and stomach ached until it was torture. I threw up black blood which scared me because I had thrown up dark blood before when I visited my brother in New York. That time I drank myself into Harlem Hospital with the same headaches and stomach cramps. That Friday I stayed at Mom and Dad's to help her out. When I went back home, I opened a pint of whiskey and started drinking again. As usual, Steve didn't come home that Saturday night. When he walked in Sunday morning at nine o'clock, I felt no hurt. He gave me a defiant look and I asked, "Do you want me to fix you some breakfast?" He said, "No, I don't want you to do a damn thing for me." I didn't answer. I dressed and went to church, came back home and drank all Sunday evening.

I was hung over again that Monday at work. My stomach felt like butterflies were fluttering inside. I made several trips to the bathroom and threw up. The supervisor asked, "Chaney, are you still having domestic problems?" She thought that was the only trouble, but she didn't know that alcohol was equally my problem. I knew that I drank too much, but all my friends drank, so what was wrong with me drinking?

I was able to talk with Steve, and we decided to sell our home. We saw the real estate broker who was to sell it for us. As usual, a number of possible buyers came to look, and it took months to find the right one. I didn't tell Steve, but I planned to split, alone, as soon as the house was sold. I confidentially asked the realtor to look for a very small house for me. I was beginning to feel like a human being again since I was making plans. When I returned from looking at a house, Steve asked, "Where have you been for two hours?" I answered, "Maybe the same place you are every Saturday night." I didn't even look around at him. He said, "You are talking mighty smart lately. You better start crying again if you know what is best for you." I slammed out the back, and sat next door getting drunk for three hours.

When I got home he had called one of his close friends to talk some sense in me. I soon cursed them both out. Steve went upstairs, threatening to pull a gun and shoot me. I left and took a cab to my mother's, but only stayed at Mom's a few days, until things cooled off a bit.

The realtor called and took me to see a very small one-bedroom cottage with a small front porch, a large kitchen and a large back yard. It cost $7,000. The down payment was $1,000 and payments would be sixty-five dollars a month. It needed some small repairs, but it was just what I wanted. I told him if he would give me a few days, I would give him the down payment. I went to my parents and asked them to loan me some money until our house was sold. I had saved some of my checks and also had taken an extra job at the country club that would provide me summer employment. Since I was not divorced, I bought the little cottage in my brother Nelson's name. I had my house three months before I left Steve — mentally I'd already quit on New Year's Eve when he said, "Our marriage will get worse — because I'm going to treat you worse." So it was just a matter of getting my shit together before bailing out.

One day Steve was doing something at the stove and I was sitting at the kitchen table drinking whiskey and Coke. He turned and asked, "Why do you keep looking at me so funny? Ever since you came back home I've been watching how you stare at me. What the hell you keep doing that for?"

I calmly asked, "Do you want a lie or do you really want the truth?"

"I want the truth."

"Well, the truth is, Steve, I *can't stand you. The very sight of you makes me sick.* In my eyesight you are nothing." I kept talking and my cup was running over. "And another thing, you stood here in front of your nephew and said that I refused to have sex with you one night. Just how low can you be to discuss our sex life with the men in your family?? Well let me tell you something, Mr. Big and Mighty, I would rather be screwed by a rattlesnake's tail than you."

He looked at me like I had really gone crazy and all he said was, "Alright now, you better watch yourself." I was so steamed up — I was crying and slammed out the front door to sit alone on the porch, but I felt like I had cleansed my very soul after telling him off. A couple of weeks later we had a buyer for our house.

Moving out — and into chronic alcoholism

I told the movers to come Saturday night instead of Monday. While he spent the night with his girl friend, I moved all night until 4:00 a.m., drinking and stuffing things in boxes and bags. I kept praying that he wouldn't come home. This was one night I didn't want him home. Finally the truck was loaded with my things. I looked around, did my final checking, locked the door and walked out of a fourteen-year relationship.

I felt nothing but relief. It no longer mattered to me who was right or wrong, it was only a matter of survival.

I was just like a person balanced on one foot at the edge of a very high cliff. I had reached the chronic stage of drinking and didn't know it, the stage where I could only get worse if I continued to drink. I didn't know anything about alcoholism. Years later I learned that at this phase an alcoholic has only three places to end up if he or she continues drinking — jail, hospital, or dead. I had already been hospitalized twice; by the Grace of God I had missed the jail. So, ignorant of my insidious disease, I continued to drink and went down, down.

I held my extra job at the country club during the summer months, while school was closed.

I worked in the checkroom and stayed loaded. I was now drinking some on weekdays, too, which was a change from my pattern of weekend drinking. All the rich people would slip me drinks and big tips for taking good care of their expensive furs and jackets. When all the help left work, we were floating. Also, the waiters saw that I kept a glass during working hours. I wouldn't get really drunk while working, but I wasn't feeling any pain.

One waiter, in particular, kept me in drinks and hung

around the checkroom every chance he got. His name was Grant, and he told me that his regular job was teaching school. He waited on tables part-time. He was divorced and had a small son who was with his ex-wife. I told him of my recent separation. One night he invited me to go to a movie. I told the other locker room maid about him and his approach and asked if she'd go down and get my lunch so I could avoid seeing him. I just wasn't interested in anyone. It was so good to be able to go home and not be called M.F. or bitch. There was no one to say, "Don't you think you've had enough to drink?" I could and was drinking all I wanted every weekend and my off-days. I would spend days at Mom's helping her with Dad, who was getting more senile.

Grant waited until I got off one evening and drove up as I walked to the bus stop. "Chaney, I've been waiting an hour. Come on and I'll drive you home."

I could hardly refuse so I said, "O.K., and thank you."

We talked, mostly about the job, as we rode home. He had a bottle in the glove compartment and we both had a drink. I didn't ask him in, so we sat in front of my house and had a couple more drinks.

He asked, "Will you go out with me on Friday?"

"What time?" I asked. "I don't get off until 7:00, but I can take a change of clothes."

I went on into the house and ran a hot bath, with my glass setting by the tub. Afterwards I drank myself into a stupor.

Grant picked me up on Friday. He was well dressed in a dark suit and tie. I wore a tan lace sheath dress, tan and brown shoes with matching bag, and tan gloves. All the club members and help commented on how nice I looked. I felt light-hearted and free. We really enjoyed Jackie Wilson doing his thing. Grant made absolutely no advances and took me to my door, where we said goodnight.

I went out again with him the next week. He invited me

to come for dinner with some friends in his apartment. We were sitting in the car, mixing drinks of whiskey and Coke. We were both high. I was more so, because I had drunk more than he — I'd excused myself while we were out and sneaked a few extras from the flask in my purse. (I was very seldom without my flask, just in case.)

He said again, "You can even trust me to stop with a sweet brotherly kiss!" Finally he said, "Let me see you to your door and I'll see you when I pick you up for dinner."

The dinner was great! Chicken and dressing, green beans, candied potatoes and ice cream for dessert. He had a variety of booze and the box was loaded with beer.

I said to his friend, "Grant seems to be prepared for twenty people instead of two couples."

He replied, "He always keeps a houseful of booze whether anyone is coming or not."

My alcoholic mind said, "My! My! My! You don't say!" (To me, that was the same as a man pulling his thing out in a whorehouse when business is bad.)

Grant didn't like going to joints. He drank either at home or at parties, and I didn't insist on him taking me out. (I wasn't ready to run into Steve yet.)

After dinner we put on records and mixed drink after drink. As the hours wore on, we danced closer and closer. Grant whispered, "You know, my guests could go home anytime they are ready." We both understood that I would not leave. We were man and woman together and wanted to be alone. Finally his friends did say goodnight. One friend stopped to ask, "Can I drop Chaney off at her house?" "Mind your own business," Grant replied. We all laughed as they went out the door.

While Grant went to check things out in the bedroom, I quickly poured a big drink and gulped it down. Then I called sweetly to ask if he wanted me to make us a drink. We sipped and talked for a while and finally floated into bed. We knew that this was it, and we would be seeing each other for a long time. The next morning he was gone when I woke up. I was hung over and glad he wasn't there because I threw up and had diarrhea. I managed to get a bath and put on makeup before he returned. Later I noticed that he didn't drink in the morning, and thought, "You've got to watch yourself, Chaney." Grant had gone out to have an extra door key made for me. So we were steadies.

Nothing to do, with a houseful of booze

When school opened I no longer worked at the country club. He returned to teaching during the day, and waited tables at night. He didn't quit work until about 12:30 a.m. I got off at 4:00 p.m. so I had plenty of time on my hands. Sometimes I waited at his apartment and drank myself blind on weekends. Sometimes he stayed at my house. Finally he suggested, "Why don't I leave three or four fifths of booze at your house, so I can have plenty when I'm here, and you can have something to sip on if you want it?"

"Yes, why don't you?" I said. What a situation for a chronic alcoholic to be in! (I thought it was the most *rewarding* thing that could ever happen to me.) He could drink daily and stop whenever he wanted to. I seldom drank with him when he came home because I had to get up early for work. On weekends I would drink before he got off, sleep, and wake up to join him to drink some more. This was my pattern all that winter.

Just before school was out again, I told him, "Grant, I'm to start work in May so that I can have my summer job at the country club."

He said, "Make out a list and add up the total amount of money you need. Let me know, and I'll take care of you until your job opens. By this time next year we will be married anyway, if you hurry and get your divorce."

So I stayed home for the summer. This was dangerous for me, because I had nothing to do and a houseful of booze. I went no place except to Mom's and church on Sunday. We didn't go to clubs since he didn't like going. I wasn't a cheat, I still liked one man at a time.

I started drinking during the week, but heavy on the weekends. It wasn't long before I was so conspicuous that Grant had noticed. He said, "I don't like to see you drink to the extent of getting drunk." My head was smoking and I said, "Now don't you start preaching at me, *please!*"

We started arguing because of my drinking. I got my bath one night and it was so hot I decided to stretch out on the couch for a few minutes. I was drunk and must have passed out when I laid down. When I woke up, Grant was standing over me shaking his head in disgust. I didn't have a stitch on, my hair was in rollers and I was still too drunk to get up. I just laid there, grinning like an opossum and feeling shitty. He didn't say a word to me, just went to his bedroom, closed the door and went to bed.

The next day he said, "I am only going to buy one fifth of whiskey, on the weekend *only*. So we will have to make that last." I said, "Alright." I was too ashamed to argue.

True to his word, he reduced the supply of liquor to one fifth between us on the weekend. One little ole funky fifth for Friday, Saturday and Sunday. I thought, "This just may be the answer to my drinking problems."

He came in that Friday night with the bottle and mixed us a drink. I could feel that glow from the first drink spread all over my body as it diffused through my blood stream. We sipped on our drinks and he mixed one more, put the bottle in the closet and said, "Now that is enough for tonight. Tomorrow night we can have a few more drinks and Sunday we will finish that bottle. That's plenty for you to drink."

I said, "Yes, it's plenty" — but he didn't know the hell I was going through. I sat there holding that watered-down drink, scared to drink it and scared not to. I had to have more because I had started drinking. We got up and went to bed. He was tired and soon fell asleep.

I was afraid to open the squeaky closet door for the bottle, but I couldn't sleep — my mind was channeled in one direction. I got up and put my coat on over my gown. It was very cold, but I walked four blocks to a bootleg house at Rockdale and Reading Road and bought a pint of whiskey to go. I stopped at a wine bar, bought a Coke, and walked back to Grant's apartment drinking out of the whiskey and Coke bottles. I had killed about a quarter of the pint and was high as a Georgia pine.

When I got home he was still sleeping peacefully and I breathed a sigh of relief. I felt like a mastermind, pulling such a smart trick on him. I thought, "Now watch your ole fifth. I'll drink with you, *plus* my treasure." (I was actually obsessed with drinking. It was torture to see him set that bottle in the closet and forbid me to drink. To an alcoholic, that is the same as putting a fix in front of a dope addict and saying, "Stop shooting up." The only difference is one addict drinks his dope and the other mainlines. I was hooked.)

I didn't see Grant was trying to do me a favor, I saw him as just being smart and trying to run my life. I drank as he slept and resented him rationing my booze. I hid my bottle and went to bed. He felt ten feet tall because he was controlling my drinks, and I played the game with him until he left for work. Later I walked back to the liquor store, bought me a pint and took it to the apartment. When he came home that night, I had it sitting on the dresser.

"Where did this whiskey come from?" he asked.

"I bought it." I said.

"I told you, Chaney, that all we needed was one fifth for the weekend!"

"I know what you said and *yours* is still in the closet. I don't have to kiss anybody's butt for anything."

He looked at me, defeated, and said, "No, you don't

have to beg me and if you really want it I will buy it." So
he started keeping his usual supply of liquor in both our
houses again.

Only sorry until the next time

He took me to Cleveland for a football game. We checked
into a hotel for the weekend. There was a bar downstairs,
and we took two fifths with us. He ordered a small tub of
beer on ice and set-ups. For weeks we had planned to see
this game, but I got drunk and stayed so drunk the whole
weekend that we couldn't go to the game. His fun was
spoiled because he stayed with me. He knew me well
enough by now to know that I would head straight for the
bar downstairs where the action was. I was never a person
who enjoyed drinking alone. I wanted someone around,
even if that person was asleep.

I felt very guilty and remorseful after spoiling our
weekend. He had lost time from work to show me some
fun, and I had goofed again. It seemed that I messed up
every plan, and God knows I didn't want to. As soon as I
started drinking, I was no longer dependable — *I hated
myself* for being this way, yet I continued.

He told me, "I am not going to ever take you on a
vacation again."

I said, "I am sorry."

"I've heard that before. You are only sorry until the
next time," he replied.

I couldn't say anything because I really felt the same. I
knew there would be a next time and I didn't know what
would happen, except that I would get drunk again.

Grant told me two weeks in advance that we were going
to have two couples for dinner in his apartment. They
taught at the same school with him. He asked, "Chaney
will you help me prepare the food? And promise me you
will not get drunk?"

I said *yes* and really meant it this time.

I stayed at his house and helped to get everything in order. We had a few mixed drinks while doing the finishing touches. He said, "I'll drive you home to get dressed and you take a cab back." He drove me home and kissed my cheek, "You really worked hard to help me. Dress real pretty so I can show off my wife-to-be."

I had my clothes all laid out on the bed. I had bought a pretty light blue dress with a wide belt and full skirt. I poured me a big drink before I started my bath and drank it down, trying to get my nerves together to face those teachers. After all, I was a high school drop-out. I wondered if they would hold conversations that were way over my head. I poured another drink and thought, "No, Chaney, you know that you can talk to anyone without any problem." The phone rang so I mixed another drink while talking. I finished that one and hung the phone up. I made another so I could do my nails or maybe I should get my bath first? Did I put my clean undies out? I better go and see what time it is. Oh it is almost time for me to be there, I can't be late. I better be sure and call a cab on time. I must not be late.

I got out of the cab and dropped my purse, spilling all its contents. I bent over to gather my belongings and fell. I went to Grant's apartment and rang the bell; he opened the door with a big broad grin, saying, "Here she is, everyone!" His voice simply died out. I stood there — I didn't get a bath, I didn't comb my hair, I didn't change clothes. I had slipped on my worst house shoes and was as drunk as a fiddler's bitch. I stumbled to his guests. "Hello, I am Grant's finance or I mean fiance. I am so glad to meet you, you are all welcome anytime. I hope you enjoys your dinner. Now Grant fried the chicken, but I cooked the dessert, yuk, yuk." I made a complete fool out of myself.

Grant grabbed me by the arm, took me to the bedroom and whispered, "Damn you, Chaney! Stay in here and don't come out." He closed the door and went back to his guests. I couldn't have cared less! Let him stay in there with his precious friends! I don't give a damn! I was very, very happy in the bedroom. Why? There were two whole fifths of booze in the closet. I have no idea how long I stayed in the bedroom nor how much I drank. I was in a complete memory blackout.

When I came to my senses, I was getting out of Grant's car at my house. He was saying, "Come on." He unlocked my door with his key, and we entered the kitchen. He said, "Here, I want to give you your key. I love you Chaney, but you drink entirely too much. I have a position where I can't have a drunk for a wife. You just wouldn't fit in. I can't stand being embarrassed like I was today. Sorry things had to end this way. I hope someday you will straighten up." He turned and walked out the door.

I fell across the bed and woke up vomiting all over my new dress and the covers. I was hung over all the next day. I realized what had happened, even though I had trouble putting all the pieces together. I really did it this time. Grant had really walked out on me, and it was my fault. How could I face everyone who knew we were to be married? Again I leaned on my crutch for support, and opened one of the bottles, poured a drink and cried (and drank all day).

The next day was a repeat performance. As I said, I usually didn't drink daily, but for a whole week I drank heavily. I cried and worried and drank, feeling like a complete failure in every department. When I tried to stop drinking, my whole body positively vibrated. I couldn't hold anything steady, and kept vomiting and gagging. I sat there in my lonely little cottage for days.

Part Four

The Long Way Back

My own skid row to sobriety

Setting the stage for dying

On Saturday night I prayed, "God, you know I can't face this night and I can't face another day. I can't stop drinking and I can't live drinking. So forgive me for what I am going to do." I got up and changed my bed, cleaned all ashtrays and dishes, dusted the furniture. I took a good warm bath and used my best perfume. I put on makeup and combed my hair. I put on my new red gown. I had heard somewhere that red didn't show blood so plainly. I'll stay in the kitchen because they can mop the tile floor. I took the white tablecloth off because it would show blood. I was drinking and setting the stage, only it was not for acting — it was for real. Finally everything was in order and I sat my bottle to my left and my gun to my right on the kitchen table.

I sat there and prayed, "God forgive me for everything I've done wrong. But I can't stand another day." I poured another drink to get the nerve to pull the trigger. If I held the gun to my temple I wouldn't feel pain. I was not afraid, I felt a relief to know that I no longer had to face life's problems. It would soon be over. I finished the drink and had my hand on the gun.

I thought of AA. I don't know why. I had no idea what they did to help anyone. I said out loud, "Alright." I thought, "I'll call, but I know they are not going to do a damn thing. I can come on back home and finish what I started."

I poured another drink and dialed information for the phone number. I called, and some man answered, "Hello, 405 Oak Street, may I help you please?"

I had gone through the whole ritual of preparing for my own self-destruction without shedding a tear. But the voice on the phone caused the flood gates to open and I started crying hysterically, until I couldn't talk. He kept saying, "That's O.K., lady, I am still here. That's O.K., take it easy. Where are you? What is your name and phone number?"

I stopped crying and answered, "I am at home, my name is Chaney and my phone number is . . . " I burst into tears again, "I don't want to drink and be bad, but I can't stop, I am going to kill myself."

"No, why don't you let me come and talk with you, or can you get someone to bring you here?"

I said, "I think so."

"I will hang up while you see if someone can bring you. If you don't call me right back, I will call you or come to your home."

"No, I'll get someone." As sick as I was, I didn't want him to come and get me because I still had booze and wanted to drink enough to get nerve enough to go to AA (to get sober). Does it sound screwed up? Well, that is exactly what I was.

I called my daughter and said, "Vivian, please, I want to go to AA for help, please, for God's sake." I was crying so hard I never hung up the phone. It was still in my hand when she walked in.

We changed roles the minute she saw the condition I was in. She rushed to me, cuddled me as I had done for her when she was a child, and spoke to me like I was a little child. I dressed well in a navy blue suit and light blue gloves. She combed my hair again and put my shoes on for me. I poured another drink and she didn't try to stop me. She only said, "Hurry and finish your drink, and come on."

AA and 'C'

I had no idea what they would do at AA, but I thought they were going to give me drinks until I tapered off. Why I thought this, I don't know. But I wanted to have the extra drinks in me before they started me tapering off.

I don't remember if my daughter moved the gun, I don't remember the ride to AA. I blacked out. The next thing I knew I was in a hall and there was a roomful of people, all White people. A man was standing at the podium saying, "Good evening, ladies and gentlemen, welcome."

A man looked up and saw me. He got up, gently put his arm around my waist and led me to the snack room. He gave me coffee and some other people joined him in helping me. I still don't remember where my daughter was. All I can remember is those strange White people fussing over me. I knew they couldn't be for real. They were saying things like, "Take it easy, Chaney, we love you." I became defensive and turned to the man who first helped me and said, "Go on and leave me alone. You don't give a damn about me. You're just getting paid to be nice to me." I pulled away and became very hostile and said, "All you White people don't care about *me* because I'm Colored!" In my sick and confused mind I was facing those mean White people in Selma, Alabama. They were my enemies, not my friends. I remember thinking, "Where is the rope for hanging?"

They didn't argue with me, but I heard someone whisper to a lady, "Why don't you call 'C' and see if you can get her. I think she can help." I have no idea how long I sat there drinking coffee and crying my heart out with my head down. I saw a Black hand and felt an arm around my shoulder. I slowly raised my head and looked into the eyes of a Black lady. I burst into another flood of tears and hugged her waist while she cuddled me like a child. She was an usher at my church and not an alcoholic but an Al-Anon member whose husband had a drinking problem. (Al-Anon is a group for the family of the alcoholic, who gather together to learn how to cope with the problem drinker.) Later I learned that they called her because I wasn't identifying with the White people. I needed a Black image to help me feel comfortable. As soon as I saw her I felt that she really cared and wanted to help me. I felt that we two Blacks understood each other, and had something in common, so I did identify and I did settle down.

She said, "I'm going to take you to the hospital, Chaney." I was given literature to take home. I don't remember if my daughter drove us or if we traveled in a cab or if we went directly to the hospital. When I came to my senses, I was back in my apartment and "C" was still with me. She babysat me that night, holding my head while I vomited and cleaning me like I was a baby. I kept saying, " 'C', pray for me, I am so ashamed, don't tell the church people about me, please. I don't want them to know I am like this. Please don't tell anyone. I don't want people talking about me. I am so sick and tired of being sick and tired. I just can't go on like this."

She said, "You are going to be alright, Chaney, you asked for help. Very seldom can a person stop drinking alone when they have reached your stage in drinking. I promise you that I will not tell anyone about you. Me and all those people want to help you, not talk about you. You are not bad but you are very sick. If you want to get well, you will have to stop drinking."

She asked, "Do you have anything in the house? I will not pour it out, but if you are sincere you will pour it down the drain yourself. Remember, Chaney, you can't have the first drink. You have had your last drink. You can stop drinking and you will never have to go through this again if you don't want to. But if you want to continue living in hell, all you have to do is take just one drink and start all over again." She didn't say another word but just sat there and looked at me.

I slowly got up went to the dresser and took the pint of whiskey out. I was shaking and, my God, I needed a drink. I had to have just one to settle my screaming nerves. It had been hours since I had a drink, I just had to have one. I walked to the kitchen sink and shook so until the glasses rattled as I reached for a glass. I opened the bottle and tilted the bottle to pour me one and screamed, "NO!" I burst into tears while I leaned over the sink and balanced on my left elbow and holding my forehead cupped in my left hand. As I sobbed and shook my head from side to side, I was pouring every drop of that full pint of misery down the drain.

"C" had not uttered a sound, she had not moved until I poured the whiskey out. Then she quickly came to me and put her arms around me and led me to the bed. I said, "Please help me, I am so scared and sick, I can't make it here alone. I am scared to stay all night in this house." She said, "But you are not alone, I am with you." I was so sick and scared and said, "I am going to do whatever you tell me. I hope I can make it through the night."

There WAS a Power in that room

I don't know who wrote a very popular song which reminds me of my first night of trying to stop drinking each time I hear it. It doesn't move me sexually, but the words have a special meaning to me and move me in another manner. These few lines I want to share.

"Help me make it through the night
Yesterday is dead and gone
Tomorrow is out of sight
But tonight I need a friend
It's so sad to be alone
Help me make it through the night"

She stayed with me, while I vomited and cried, walked the floor, tried to sleep and couldn't.

She kept saying, "We are going to make it, just keep trying."

I said, "We belong to the same church and we both believe in God. Will you pray with me and ask God to give me strength?" We prayed and I remembered what my dad had often quoted from the Bible, "Wherever two or more are gathered in My name, I am there also." I couldn't remember if God or Jesus had said those words, but the important part is I truly believed those words. I believed that there *was* a Power in that room as we prayed. I believed there was a Power greater than me who could help me overcome my obsession. I believed! I believed from that moment on that I could resist the first drink.

I told "C," "You can go on home now. I can make it and I am not going to drink."

"Well, I would like to pick you up for an AA meeting this evening. Will you go? I'll be here at seven."

She was on time and I was dressed. It had taken me hours to dress. I still hadn't eaten and was sick and weak. My entire body was shaking. Even my voice had a nervous tremor in it. I could have gotten booze only half a block away. But I didn't go for it. We rode the bus to Newport, Kentucky, to a church. There were about twenty-five white people in the room. "C" introduced me to several and told them I was new. They were all as friendly as the other group of people and said, "Welcome, Chaney, we're glad to have you join us. You are going to get better every day that you don't drink."

There really was hope for me

That was the very first time I had ever heard anyone say they were alcoholic. To me, that was shock number one — since society had me believing alcoholics were degenerates. Shock number two was equally as baffling because the speaker standing before us saying, "I am an alcoholic," was a priest. I plainly remember him looking right into my surprised eyes, "I guess some of you wonder how could a man of God become an alcoholic? Well, I am going to toss the same question at you. How did you become an alcoholic? I am first a human being, a person, and then I became a priest!" When "C" and I left, I felt that there really was hope for me. I didn't feel so alone with my problem, and I didn't feel so low and dirty anymore — I was not some kind of monster.

After "C" said goodnight to me, I sat there and prayed God would help me to stay sober today. After a couple of hours had passed, I was so awful sick I was sweating until my gown stuck to me. I tried to pour a cup of coffee and scalded my hand twice. My stomach and head hurt, and it felt like bugs were crawling up my arms. I was so sick. My God, I needed just one little drink to settle my nerves. But "C" and the priest had said, "No matter how tough things get, *do not take that first drink.*" I positively walked the floor most of the night. It had been almost twenty-four hours since I had a drink and my alcoholic body was screaming for that drug. At one time I started dressing to go around the corner to the bar for just one double. Instead I prayed, "Please God, what is the line to the hymn Dad used to sing — oh yes, 'Jesus knows our every weakness, so take it to the Lord in Prayer.' "

I was never so happy to see daylight before in my whole life. When I looked in the mirror at myself, I looked like someone who had just had major surgery. My eyes were swollen and red with dark rings around them.

The phone rang early. It was "C". She asked, "How do you feel this morning?"

"I feel awful, I hardly slept last night."

"Did you take a drink yet?"

"No, but I need one."

"You make yourself a cup of coffee and try to eat something. When did you last eat?"

"I think it was about three days ago. I can't keep anything down, not even water."

She said, "If you have ice cream, eat that. I will be there

to pick you up at seven-thirty for beginners meeting at AA tonight."

"Alright, I'll be ready and thank you," I said weakly.

365 one-foot pieces

We went into an upstairs room where a man sat at a desk. Around the walls were chairs and sofas. There were about ten of us and some were shaking as bad as I. I couldn't stop crying and was feeling terrible about it, until I looked across the room to see another lady shaking and crying too. The man at the desk told us his first name and said, "I am an alcoholic and I know how you new people feel, because I once was new also. But I haven't found it necessary to take a drink for X number of years. And I stay away from the *first drink, one day at a time.*"

I forced myself to stop crying because I wanted to hear what he was saying. It was hard to believe that he had ever been as sick as I. He looked so healthy and peaceful. I don't remember all that he said, but one statement stuck. He said, "On my job I am a pipe fitter and if my boss asked me to move a 365-pound pipe across the street, I would tell him it was impossible because it was too heavy. But if I could cut it into 365 one-foot pieces, then I could take one piece at a time until the entire pipe was moved. Sometimes it will get rough and you will have to pray or ask for help to get through one hour or *five minutes.* Get phone numbers and call someone. Reach for the phone, not the drink."

I was given more literature and asked to come back that Wednesday.

I continued to shake all that Monday night, slept for a short while, and jumped up wet with sweat again. Tuesday morning I was able to eat a soft-boiled egg and a glass of milk which cramped my empty stomach, but did stay down. I was so nervous I felt like I was losing my mind. I picked up the phone to call Grant and decided not to.

Not insane — I am an alcoholic!

The AA literature was lying on the kitchen table and I started reading just to occupy myself. I scanned several pamphlets. There were twenty questions prepared by Johns Hopkins Hospital with a headline which asked *Are You An Alcoholic?* I remember I answered out loud, "I don't know."

I really didn't know how to determine what an alcoholic was — I just figured that I drank too much. So I started reading and checking off answers to those questions — there were all kinds of questions about how alcohol was affecting the person's life, if it caused difficulty in sleeping, if it was jeopardizing the job, if I drank alone, if I turned to a lower class of people as drinking companions, if I felt remorse, if my sense of ambition decreased since I started drinking, if drinking was affecting my reputation, if I ever had a complete loss of memory, if a physician had ever treated me for drinking, if it was affecting my home life — that was the *only* exam I ever made A+ on!

When I finished I hollered out loud, "Thank God, I know what is wrong with me! I am not going insane, I am an alcoholic!" For all these years I had been asking and praying, "Dear God, what is wrong? Why did you make me different than everyone else?"

So now my illness had been revealed. When I went back on Wednesday, I talked to "B" and told him what I had discovered from the Twenty Questions. I said to a lady, "I am not sitting in the back. I'm going to sit up front and find out how you people are staying sober." (I was fighting a racial battle mentally, but no one accommodated me. All they showed me was kindness and concern. I finally had to give up and admit that these people were only trying to help me and they understood where I was coming from.)

I attended meetings and didn't take that first drink. I did get better daily, just as they had said I would. They told me to stay out of joints and not to hang out with my old drinking buddies. I did whatever they suggested. "C" had left me in their care, and they all were helping me. I didn't have to fight to be accepted because I was Black, as I thought from the first night. To them I was just another sick alcoholic who needed help.

They don't want to lose their floor mat

About one week later Grant stopped by my house, I was sitting at the table drinking coffee and eating a sandwich. I didn't tell him about me going to AA. He asked, "How have you been?" and said that he had brought me a bottle.

I said, "O.K. Put it on the dresser." I silently prayed for God to give me strength. I wasn't ready to tell him I was on the Program, and I was afraid to have that bottle near me. I didn't know how to handle this situation and no one was there with the answer.

I walked to the bedroom, and saw the bottle staring at me, like a monster from outer space. I grabbed it, opened the drawer and pushed it way back, under some clothes. I leaned against the drawer after it was closed and looked in the mirror. Sweat was pouring down my forehead. I remembered what the man had said, "Sometimes you may have to pray for five minutes' strength." So far I had managed not to open the bottle — I had kept the *plug in the jug* as I had been told.

Grant left, and returned a few days later with another bottle.

When he was leaving I said, "Wait a minute," and went to the dresser drawer, took out the bottle, picked up the new bottle and said, "Here, take both these bottles with you. I don't drink anymore."

I told him that I didn't want to drink and had joined AA and the people there were going to help me stay sober if I didn't take the first drink.

He looked at me with a sarcastic smile and said, "Those

ex-winos can't do a damn thing — you're not going to stop drinking — so why don't you just forget it! Go on and have a taste."

I was really surprised at his reaction — he had given me hell for drinking, he was the one who had seen me at my worst and walked out on me for drinking.

As soon as he left, I called one of my new sober friends and explained everything. She said, "Chaney, sometimes the very people who give us hell for drinking too much are going to be the first to resent us getting sober. They no longer have anyone to dominate and push around. They hate to see us stand on our own feet. Some people don't want us to stay sober because they lose their floor mat. But no matter, don't you take that first drink." I felt better after talking with her. I was beginning to understand why she called me a new *baby*, because there was so much I didn't know, and so much to learn.

Filling my time, not my glass

She asked me one night, "Chaney — you say that you are lonely? Isn't there anything very special in your life that you wanted to do before the bottle took over?" I told her, "Yes, I've always wanted to finish high school." She insisted on taking me to register immediately. She said that I had to fill that void — too much time was very dangerous for an alcoholic. So I registered at Hughes High School.

Grant kept showing up to visit me. Finally he saw that I was serious, so he stopped bringing me booze but continued to drink in my presence. He'd said I couldn't and wouldn't stay sober, but I was making a liar out of him. *I was making it!*

I told him I was going back to school within a few weeks. He said, "That's good, because I still want to marry you *now that you're not drinking.*" So we were engaged again. School opened, and I went back to school after all those years.

My job opened the same day and I returned to work. A few weeks later a couple of the ladies noticed a difference in me at work and said, "Chaney, we don't hear you talking about the fun you have on weekends, anymore!"

"No, I don't go out very much — I'm helping a very young girl who has a drinking problem. I promised her I wouldn't drink if she wouldn't. So I'm not drinking in order to help her." (I had rehearsed that story perfectly before going back to work. I didn't feel that they would understand if I said I was an alcoholic. I wasn't ready to be uncovered, and I didn't feel that my supervisor would understand my problem.)

I really got hung up in school. I had always loved school from childhood. I worked forty hours a week and went to school five nights. My weekends were spent cleaning house, going to church on Sunday, and doing my homework. I studied hard because I was so anxious to learn. My mind couldn't retain very well in the beginning, and I burst into tears one night in class.

I had a very understanding elderly teacher who immediately asked the class to take a break. He asked me, "Chaney, do you have a problem that you care to discuss with me?"

I found myself saying, "I guess I'm just nervous. I have a drinking problem, but I no longer drink. But sometimes everything seems to get on my nerves and I get so confused. I study so hard and when I make a low grade it upsets me." I was encouraged after we talked.

Grant and I got married and again I worked at homemaking. He still taught school daily and waited tables at night. I would get home from work just in time to say goodbye to him. We both were as busy as bees. That first year went by fast.

Some marriage miseries

I noticed that he was getting home later as the months

passed — he had been grading papers on weekends while I studied. But now he was paying someone else to grade his students' work. He spoke very negatively about his concern for his students, and began to become withdrawn.

One day a man rang the bell and asked to see him. I told him my husband wasn't home. He looked so surprised and said, "Your husband? I didn't know Grant was married." I found out the man had known Grant for two years. He said that my husband had told him and others that I was only his housekeeper. Naturally, I confronted Grant with this when he came home, and he blew up. He accused me of checking on him. I explained that the man came to our house. He got angry and stopped speaking to me. Finally he returned to normal, and we made up — but he still stayed out.

Our next major round happened when he walked in one day and said, "A real estate man will be here for you to sign some papers. We decided that since I am your husband, I should manage your property and it should be sold."

I said, "You and *him* decided?"

"Yes, and you should draw out your retirement also."

By that time my temper had shot up ten stories high, and I said, "O.K., I tell you what, you go and get the real estate man and bring him here so both of you can kiss my _____. Don't you think because you are a little chicken shit teacher, that you are dealing with a fool! I have been cuttin' this ole ugly world for years, and you don't decide a damn thing about my property without talking with me first!"

I thought he had been acting bad enough, but from that day on he *really* did his thing. He started sleeping in the guest room, deliberately avoiding me. He would turn sideways, to keep from touching me, if we were passing through the same door. If I entered the kitchen and he was cooking, he turned the stove off and went in his room. In the guest room he kept his private salt and pepper shaker, mustard, bread, etc. I don't mean this set-up lasted for days or weeks but for months.

I saw him leave the motel near the school where he taught. He worked hard at making me blow my stack — but I didn't drink. I continued to go to work and to school.

Graduating, ten feet tall

Finally, through all this mental torture, I was getting ready for graduation. I sent invitations to all my friends and relatives. They had planned on a party for me at the neighborhood house. I felt like I was a Ph.D. on the night I received my high school diploma! My elation even showed in my graduation photo — it turned out the best picture I've ever made. One of my teachers (the one who had befriended me) gave me a lovely jade necklace. Everything was so beautiful, but Grant didn't come. I lost all respect for him that night. He said, "What do you want me to do, jump up and down just because you finished high school?"

I registered for college at the University of Cincinnati. A friend, who was a teacher, went with me. I had one hundred and twenty-five dollars given to me for graduation and used it to pay for the two courses I was taking. Again I dug in to learn. I felt ten feet tall. Here I was! Sitting in the classroom at one of the greatest universities in the United States and just a few years back I was a high school dropout, and a drunk! Ego trip? YES! I felt good and very proud of myself. I completed my courses in December.

My dad had another stroke and Mom called me to come right away. I didn't have a car, and asked Grant to take me. He said, "I'm tired of that sick old man." So I took a cab and went alone. But I was as hot as a peppered pudding, and mentally raised hell all the way to Mom's. I

decided to never again ask him to take me any place. As
soon as I could, I got a friend to help me pick out a car for
myself and teach me how to drive. I was only interested in
getting to Mom's and church, but the main thing is, I
learned.

Grant still locked himself in the guest room at night. I
had mixed emotions about him. I wanted a good husband
and he was acting so shitty. In my mind he was as a
roomer, or just someone who came and went. It just
didn't matter to me anymore, or at least I didn't think so.

One day as I walked home I became extremely dizzy
without any warning. I almost staggered into the path of
an oncoming car. I hardly made it home and had to crawl
up the steps. I couldn't understand it because I had been
sober over three years. I went to the doctor who told me I
would have to be hospitalized for tests. I was losing at
least a pound a day and was getting weaker. I told Grant
that the doctor said I had to go to the hospital right away
to see what was wrong with me. He responded, "I'm not
going to have a sick woman on my hands."

I looked at him from my bed and I couldn't control the
tears. I laid there, all alone with my thoughts and said, I
am not going through this again. I pulled myself up,
crawled down to the basement and got my bags. I put
most of my clothes in sheets and tied them up. I didn't
explain, I just didn't care. After I left I only made one
more trip back to the house to get my furniture and forgot
the whole thing.

I really feel that the marriage vows should be changed a
bit so that me and many others can stop lying. It is awful
to promise to stay with someone 'til DEATH DO YOU
PART; if you stay with some of these bastards, death
soon *will* part you because they will worry you or beat
you to death. That part of the vows should be changed to,
"WILL YOU STAY WITH THIS MAN OR WOMAN
FOR AS LONG AS YOU CAN STAND THEM, OR AS
LONG AS YOU'RE HAPPY?" To me that would be more

realistic. People can't seem to obey *God's* Ten Command-
ments, so to promise to obey *man's* is a lie. Pick up any
newspaper and compare the number of marriage licenses
to divorces and you will see what I mean.

I do take marriage serious and work hard at it. But I
flatly refuse to stay with any man who will mistreat me
TILL DEATH DO US PART. To hell with him! Nothing
will make me stay — not even if he's filthy rich, with a
gold thing and silver balls! If I'm not treated right and
fair, I'll bail out. And if I lay off-the-wall trips on a man,
he should split. We both can get someone else. Love
affairs and marriages are like the junkman — what some
people don't want and throw away makes other people
happy and able to survive. JUST KEEP ON PUSHING,
shake the dust off your feet and don't look back.

I never have felt any regret or hurt over having left
Grant. In fact, it is hard for me to remember that he was
my husband. I felt ashamed to face the ladies at work, and
to let them know that I had had two broken marriages
within four and one-half years. But I squared my shoulders that Monday when I returned to work and said,
"Well, ladies, I know you are going to gossip, so here it is.
Grant and I separated. So, go on and talk!" (I hated myself
because I started crying.)

A back-street affair

I stayed at Mom's waiting for my first-floor apartment.
The tenants had thirty days before they would move.

Mom and I were sitting at the kitchen table talking one
Sunday afternoon when the doorbell rang. I opened the
door and saw Jay standing there, grinning from ear to ear
as big as you please! I was really glad to see him. It had
been years since we had seen each other. After all those
years I felt different toward Jay. I didn't feel that he was
just a guy that I had gone out with. He sensed this and
said, "Hey, Sugar, come here and let me see how you

feel." He held me tight for the first time in years. I took him downstairs to speak to Mom and Dad. Mom remembered him and was also happy to see him. She said, "Jay, it looks like my child is having so much husband problems." He said, "Well, don't you worry, Mom, I am going to see about her."

It sounded so good to hear a man say that, after my battles with Steve and Grant, that I guess I was ripe for picking. I wanted love and understanding from a male companion. It had been months since I shared a bed with any man, since Grant had gone on his sex strike, and my old ideas about a cheating wife hadn't changed.

Jay asked if I would like to go a swimming party. As soon as we walked in the door, he fixed us a drink just like old times. I said, "Oh, I forgot to tell you, I haven't had a drink for over three years." He poured my drink into his glass and fixed me a coke. The odor of whiskey almost made me throw up, because it brought back the memory of all the years I was so sick, The music was blaring, and Jay and I danced over and over to the sound of Ray Charles' song, "Together Again."

I called Mom and told her I was spending the night "with a girl friend." Jay and I split for the motel. We didn't think of right or wrong. (I, who did not and would not have an affair while living with my husband, was now entering an affair with a married man.) To clear my guilty conscience, I said, "Other women went with my husbands, so what?" So I continued to go out with Jay every weekend.

Finally my first-floor apartment was available and I moved into its five rooms — two bedrooms, living room, kitchen, and combination dining-room and den and bathroom. It was a beautiful apartment, and Jay helped me work long hours to get it in order. When we finished, we decided to have some friends in for a celebration. They were mostly his friends, since I had been out of circulation for so long. We had fun dancing and eating fried chicken, potato salad, cole slaw, cornbread and chitlings. Jay had bought plenty to drink. He was positively showing off all his work he had done.

I was very happy with the arrangement of our "back-street affair." He was with me every weekend and called me daily. We had a go-between who could call us at our homes if we needed each other during the week. He made a good salary and helped me if I hit a bad spot, yet I knew he was married and had a family. (I was going against my norms, and deep-down inside it bothered me.)

His friends started dropping in on weekends, since they knew he'd be there. Every Friday he'd buy his usual one-half gallon of whiskey, and case of beer. I hated the smell of whiskey but one day when I was shopping, I decided to get a bottle of gin "just in case" someone stopped by who "liked gin." So I stashed it in the living room closet.

We all had fun and balled all Friday night and most of Saturday. One of the ladies asked me about my separation, and I started talking about Steve and Grant. They all sat there while I repeated some of my bad experiences. Although I don't know why, I became emotional for the first time in months. The lady was so sympathetic and said, "Oh, you poor thing, how could you take all that! Here, take a cold beer and quiet your nerves."

After three and one-half years of sobriety, I DRANK THAT BOTTLE OF BEER.

Sick thinking, sick drinking

Now I had been told that the disease of alcoholism progresses whether you drink or don't drink, and that if I ever took the first drink, I would get drunk again. But the people at AA had lied. Because I *did* drink that beer and I didn't get drunk. So the next weekend, I drank two bottles of beer and stopped. The third weekend I drank two bottles of "nice cold beer" and sneaked two shots of gin from the hidden bottle in the closet, and I still didn't get drunk. I thought to myself, "Now I know how to control my drinking!" The fourth weekend I drank two bottles of beer and lost count on the gin. I looked at that gin bottle the next morning and said, "OH NO!" That *empty* bottle seemed to stare at me and say, "OH YES!" My God, I had gotten drunk again after three and one-half years of being sober. I thought "Those people at AA was right." I *did get drunk* from the "first drink," although it took me four weeks to get there. I felt a terrible disappointment in myself. And what a hangover!

Jay said, "Oh, it's O.K., Sugar, but I don't want to see you get sick again. Just drink enough to be social." So I got drunk that day in order to forget the night before. My sick thinking was that I might as well go on and drink now that I'd already screwed up, that I had already blown my beautiful years of sobriety.

My usual pattern of weekend drinking started all over again. Jay saw that I was back in full bloom again, so he bought his whiskey and my gin every weekend. Noisy parties and toasts continued from Friday evening to Sunday evening.

About six weeks after I first got drunk again, I woke up one Saturday feeling violently ill, and vomiting. My stomach was sore to the touch. I didn't drink the rest of the weekend because I was too sick and in too much pain. That Monday I went to the doctor, still lying about how much I was drinking. He gave me medication for my upset stomach and that helped. But the next weekend I was at it again in the noisy smoke-filled joints with Jay and the crowd. So long as I drank, I didn't feel guilty about being with a married man. "If the lady couldn't keep her man, that was her tough luck." But during the week when I was not drinking, my conscience said, "Chaney, you are wrong, wrong, wrong." So each weekend when Jay came to me, I drank, partly to feel more comfortable with my guilt.

Mom called and said Dad had another stroke and was

very sick again. When I went to see him, he couldn't talk. Mucus formed in his throat which had to be drawn out with a machine. He could no longer cough and the doctor was afraid he would choke to death if he stayed at home. That was a sad occasion. We didn't want Dad to leave home but we had no choice, since we were not trained to use the machine.

It was a very sad, cold day in November, 1966, when I packed his things and took him to the nursing home. When I turned to leave, I felt like I was deserting my daddy. He looked so pitiful to me. He was helpless, and I was leaving him in the hands of complete strangers. I did what I had to do — and I got drunk. I cried and drank, and some of my drinking companions cried with me. (At least, Dad was too senile to realize I was back on the bottle again.) I went to see him straight from work daily and exchanged his dirty clothing for his clean clothes which I had washed the night before. Somebody in our family had to wash the clothes because we couldn't afford the extra laundry charges.

Facing reality was hell

Mom was no longer young either. Now she was alone and lonely. She often called, crying, to ask me to come and spend the night with her. I was running myself down, holding a forty-hour job, going to see Dad and taking care of his clothes, seeing about Mom; and also, I was drinking again on weekends. For the first time in my life, I wished I had not been the only girl in the family. Nelson agreed to move into Mom's home, and we moved Mom into my house with me. Now that she was in the house with me, I was saved from so much running. Mom had known that I was drinking again, but I had managed to keep her from seeing me drunk. But now that she was so close, I could no longer stay hidden.

I will never forget the Saturday when I fell *up the stairs* and crawled into her kitchen. When she turned and saw the condition I was in, she burst into tears and said, "Lord, I can't stand any more. Sister, you are drunk, I thought you had stopped getting drunk. I am burdened enough, without you getting drunk. Just go back downstairs!"

I started crying and feeling sorry for myself, passing the buck. "Look at her," I felt. "She's picking on me again." So I staggered back downstairs, crying, and left Mom in tears.

The sad, painful part was that I had to wake up the next day and realize what I had done to Mom. Facing reality was hell. I had to take a few drinks to face her again. This time I slowly climbed those steps to her apartment. She was sitting at the table eating her breakfast and looking so lonely and sad. I stood there a few minutes while my heart bled for her. I ran and fell on my knees and buried my head in her lap and said, "I am so sorry. God knows I don't mean to hurt you." She cried with me — but the next weekend I was drunk again.

I learned how to eat my cake and keep it too by parking my car around the corner and putting a note on my door saying I was "out." I would drink real quiet in my apartment while Mom thought I was gone. (Who was I hurting and fooling? Chaney.)

One day the nurse called me at work and asked me to come quickly because my Dad had gotten worse, and they couldn't move him to the hospital until I got there. I drove like a madwoman to the nursing home where the ambulance was waiting to transfer him to General Hospital. He had had another stroke and was needles and tubes from head to foot. All he could do was lie there. After two weeks the doctor told me we would have to move him back to the nursing home because they could no longer help him. I became hysterical when the doctor tried to tell me, "Your father is over eighty years old, and he has had one stroke too many. The only thing that is separating him from death is that his heart is still beating — he won't regain consciousness again." My Aunt Katie stood there in shock.

That night I got drunk again. My brothers came to stay with Mom. Jay took me over to his friends to spend the night in an attempt to take my mind off my Dad. Jay had gone to the hospital with me and saw how sick he was.

Your daddy is dead

About a week later on a Monday morning I woke up about four o'clock and just sat on the side of the bed. I was not too hung over, but it seemed like so much was happening that I just felt depressed. It was time for me to leave, but I continued to sit on the couch, smoking cigarettes. The telephone shocked me when it rang. I said, "Hello," and heard a voice say, "Hello, Chaney, this is Doctor Kress. Daddy Allen passed at five o'clock this morning. He didn't suffer. He just slept away."

I didn't think so much about myself, but how was I going to tell Mom? Fifty-six years of marriage and eleven children. I had to think — I went to the closet for a couple of drinks to steady my nerves, before I climbed those stairs, feet feeling as heavy as lead. Mom was up and sitting in her easy chair. She looked up and saw me and said, "Oh Lord, your daddy is dead, ain't he?" She absolutely went in shock that day, April 10, 1967.

I made all the funeral arrangements, and continued to drink, but I didn't get drunk. Mom could not attend the funeral service. She just sat. She stopped fixing her food, cleaning house, bathing, or combing her hair. She completely withdrew.

When I buried my dad, part of my heart went into that earth. To me, he had always been the greatest Black man on earth. His death, along with me beginning to drink again, placed me right back on that same high cliff where I balanced on one foot. All I needed was a push to go over.

Now that Mom had withdrawn, I had to take care of
her. I put her in the tub nights after work and bathed her.
I combed her hair and rubbed her body with lotion.
About two months after Dad died, she started having
headaches and pains in her legs. Now my weekly responsibilities included taking her to the doctor for shots and
filling her prescriptions. Every weekend I was still drinking and getting drunk with Jay and the boozers.

Just like a robot

Over the next year I got so I couldn't think clearly
anymore. The memory blackouts were getting worse. I
could cook and clean house and not remember what I had
cooked — or when I had cleaned. I was functioning just
like a robot every weekend. I would get on crying spells,
where I sobbed to Jay, that "I want my daddy back." All
my drinking buddies would come in to my apartment and
ball until wee hours, and I would make the rounds at bars
with the crowd. Every weekend I was getting sicker. I
started having the a.m. dry heaves and shakes. One
morning I woke up and had wet the bed. Another
morning, I found I had laid all night in my own vomit.

In April 1968 I started celebrating my birthday a week
ahead. It was spring holidays at school so I could ball and
not have to go to work — so I balled for a week. When
the weekend came, Jay brought his half-gallon of whiskey
and my half-gallon of gin. I was already on cloud nine
and tore into that gin. I drank until Monday morning,
vomiting in bed. My stomach cramped, and I was wet
with sweat and urine.

When I tried to stand, the floor seemed to come up and
I fell backwards. I tried again to pull myself up by holding
on to furniture and bumped into the dresser. I stumbled
into the coffee table and tore a hole in my leg. Somehow I
made it to the bathroom and vomited blood each time I
gagged. I became so weak that I hung my head and arms

on the toilet stool to rest. My God, I am going to die here, in all this blood and that filthy bed. I heard a knock on my door, but I didn't answer. I heard my brother say, "Mom, her car is outside — but she isn't home."

I laid there hanging over the toilet stool, my face lying where my butt was supposed to be, praying for the strength to get up. Finally I was able to get a face cloth and wash the blood off. It took me hours to clean my bed and change linen. I folded thick towels and wrapped them around the faucet to keep the running water from making noise, while I ran a bath. The smell of the food cooking upstairs almost made me start vomiting again. I thought that now at least I will be clean if I do die. When I got up to get a glass of water, my hands shook so that I couldn't pour it. I turned the water jug up and drank from it and ended up wet all down my front. My God, I can't go on like this. I was doing so well. *Now* look at me. All that day and the next I stayed hidden in the house.

Beginning again

The following evening I bathed and dressed and walked to AA, the first time I had been there in almost *four years!* I didn't know anyone. There were lots of new people.

I was scared and was about to walk out, when a blond man walked to me and said, "Hello, I'm Joe. Come on and let me buy you a cup of coffee, and we can sit and rap for a while." He asked if I would like him to go through beginner's classes with me. I told him how nervous and scared I was and couldn't say that I had been to AA before, so I went through the six classes again.

The statement I heard this time, which stuck in my mind, was "You can't run with your old drinking buddies and stay sober." So I tried to avoid Jay and the crowd and attended meetings. But he wanted to see me badly enough to come several times to pick me up at AA, to join him. (I went along — but I didn't take a drink.) I started sobriety again — one week sober, then two weeks, then six weeks . . .

For some time I had been planning going to California to visit my kids. Now that I was sober, I really started making plans to leave. I bought some new clothes and called the kids to tell them I would be leaving in June. My brothers and their wives were to take care of Mom during my absence. Finally the day came, and I was on my way to the West. I had bought a pint of gin to take with me. "Not that I was going to drink, but just in case" someone *else* would like a drink on the "long three day" bus ride. I enjoyed the ride for the first day and night. The second day I became tired and nervous and that night my feet were swollen. There was no place to take a bath, and I couldn't stretch my legs out. When we stopped in Arizona, I went into the restroom and opened my bottle and took a couple of "sips" so I could tone down enough to sleep. I did not take another drink and made it to California.

Reunion calls for celebration

My children met me and there was a happy reunion. They took me to my son Spike's house. He said, "Sis, I'll be back in a few minutes — I'm going to get a bottle." I told him to look in my makeup kit and get the gin. He made everyone a drink, and asked if I wanted one, or if I was still on the wagon. (The boys still didn't understand the disease of alcoholism.) I said, "I really don't drink, but I *am tired* and want to celebrate with you *kids* — so fix me a small drink." I had a couple of cocktails, but I didn't get drunk.

Then my daughter took me to her house where I was going to stay during my visit. Her kids were so happy to see their grandmother again. My daughter showed me through her house. She said, "Sis, I don't drink, but look at my 'little bar.'" What she had were about six small bottles, each with a different brand of booze. She had it set up real cute and was very proud of her collection, more for the looks than the contents. I admired it with her.

I said, "Vivian, all I want is a hot bath. And then let me stretch out in a bed." I cleaned up and went to bed and she left for work. (She was a nurse and worked the three to eleven shift at night.)

I slept until late the next day because I was so exhausted. That night my Edward and Spike brought friends to meet me. They were so happy to have their mother with them. They even brought a camera and made pictures of all three of them and me clowning around and having fun in the photo. But, they also brought a bottle! And I had a couple of drinks with them. Every day the boys came and brought a bottle. That weekend they took me out to a club and I had a few drinks.

Hooked, terrified

After a week in San Diego, I was hooked again — but I didn't want Vivian to know that I was back in the same shape as about five years ago, when she first took me to AA. So I couldn't ask *her* to go and get me a bottle. And I knew how proud she was of her "little bar," so I didn't want to bother it. I kept praying that she would hurry and go to work, so I could find a way to get my drug. I had no car, was too far from the liquor store to walk, and didn't know where one was anyway. When she left, I had to open one of her prize bottles — I just had to have one drink until I could find a way to get my own bottle. I had to think of some way.

My daughter's girl friend lived across the street. I went over, knocked on her door and asked, "Will you please drive me to the store? I am coming down with a cold and would like to get a bottle of gin to make me a toddy; I already took a couple of aspirins." She said, "You probably caught cold on that bus. I don't have the car — my husband has it and he went fishing." I thought, "Oh, now what!"

But she said, "Come on in. My husband has a bottle of gin, and I will fix you a drink." As she took out two glasses and mixed us a drink, she said, "I see you watching me to see how much I put in your drink. Don't worry — I'm not going to make it too strong! Vivian will *kill* me if she comes home and finds I have made her mother *drunk!*" We both laughed. She didn't know that I was watching her because she wasn't making it strong *enough.*

I sat there while she talked and didn't hear a word she was saying because I was dying inside while I had to sip on that watered-down drink.

Her kids were playing outside, and one of them started crying. She said, "Excuse me, while I go and see about these blasted kids." As soon as she got out the door, I moved like lightning and grabbed that bottle and poured a *real drink* into my glass. I went to the faucet and replaced the amount with water.

In a few minutes she returned, but I had made it. She asked, "Would you like me to freshen up your drink?" So she added more booze, ice and soda. *Now* I had a drink that I could feel! She fixed me another when I had finished that, and I floated across the street, high and happy again.

My Eddie came the next day and took me to *his* house, where he had a couple of bottles and quite a few friends. Everyone ended up with a few drinks before eating, (and they were all satisfied). When I saw the *last* of those bottles empty, I panicked. I sat there looking around, as though a miracle would happen. And it did! I saw a couple of bottles in a glass case, prize bottles that my son had brought from overseas somewhere. I filled a big glass with booze and hid it in the bathroom, which I visited often. Soon I became obviously drunk. Some lady said, "Eddie, your mom is getting high. She can't drink much, can she?" He said, "No, she is chicken." What they didn't know was each time I went in the bathroom, I was reinforcing the booze in me!

The next day we all went to Tijuana to do sightseeing. The kids pointed out different things to me and did everything possible to see that I had a nice, enjoyable vacation. But the main thing that attracted MY attention in Tijuana was a half-gallon of gin for "only three dollars and seventy-five cents." I bought one to take back to Ohio "to my brother Lee." And another to "keep at my daughter's just in case" that someone stopped by. I was only fooling them, but not myself. I knew I was making sure I had my own supply while I was in San Diego. I was making sure that I wouldn't run out again.

My children took me out that night to a very nice club. They introduced me to their friends, and we had cocktails. The waitress came around about every thirty minutes to serve those watered-down drinks. It was torture to wait that long for a drink. (A real boozer can't wait a half-hour between drinks.) From my past experiences, I was very familiar with clubs, and I came prepared with a secret bottle in my purse. Between drinks I went to the ladies' room and drank from my bottle. For a chaser I cupped my hands and drank water from the faucet. So again, all my kids and their friends thought I was a pantywaist who got high from "a couple of cocktails." I managed not to get falling down drunk, but I was absolutely hooked again and I knew it. I was terrified, yet I *just couldn't stop.*

My visit was up within a few days, so I was packing to leave. I wasn't drinking and it was during the week. I had already finished one of the half-gallons of gin, with the help of my sons and their friends. But I still had the other which I carefully packed in an athletic bag. I made the long trip back to Ohio without opening it. I gave Mom her souvenir and gave Lee the half-gallon of gin. Henry was there too, and we all made drinks. This time I joined in, even though the weekend wasn't here yet.

We decided to go out for a while to a joint. Quite a few young people were at the joint, all dancing and having fun. In my mind, I was still in California having fun with my children. So I got up and started dancing too, making an ass out of myself. There is no fool like an old fool! I thought I was looking sexy but I was only looking silly. I was aware of this — yet my gin said "go." I kept drinking as fast as the drinks came, and had a bottle in my purse for when they didn't come fast enough.

I woke up the next morning, fully dressed in a wet bed, then drank a beer to try to settle my stomach before I went upstairs to Mom. When she saw me, she said, "You need to rest a couple of days from that long ride. You don't look well."

I went back downstairs and called Jay to tell him that I was home. He seemed to go with my drinking, just like peaches and cream! Soon he was there, carrying the usual supply. That night I got drunk again and woke up the next morning, sick and hung over again, only worse.

The last drunk

Before I'd really sobered up, a male friend called and asked me to go to a formal dance with him. I told him I would. So I stopped drinking for a few days, so I'd feel good by the evening of the dance and did all the little things ladies do for formal affairs. I already had my dress, but I wanted some new accessories and a new hairpiece. By Saturday I was feeling much better. All I had in my house was a half pint of gin, half of which I drank while dressing. I poured the remains in my flask to take with me.

Again — I was still snowing myself with the phony idea that alcoholics don't dress well or look good. So I dressed very carefully in my gold formal with matching black and gold bag and shoes. I even wore my mink stole!! Which proved obviously I wasn't an alcoholic! I was proud of how my friend looked in his black tux, too. He was six feet one, and real black — and that black and white outfit made him even more attractive than usual. Mom said, "Ain't no flies on you two Negroes! You look *good*."

By the time the dance was over at two-thirty in the morning, we had drunk about four rounds of those watered-down drinks. And I had finished the flask in my purse. I *had* to have something more to drink, and I knew my home supply was gone. Saturday night — no liquor stores open till Monday — a desperate situation for an alcoholic. So I suggested a nice bootleg joint. He wanted to go to a place which let him run a tab, although he explained that it wasn't too nice and I wouldn't like it there. "I don't give a damn," I said. So we went. My stomach and nerves were jumping, I needed another drink. I had started, and had to *finish*. All I could think of was another drink.

We walked into the dimly lit room with people sitting all around on sofas, chairs and stools. My friend told me to sit in a chair in the front room. He came back with a pitcher of gin, two glasses and a glass of soda pop. We finished that one, and he brought another. And that's all I remember until the sunlight woke me up the next morning.

I was not in the front room, but in another room, sitting in a big, greasy, nasty, stuffed chair. My friend was asleep slumped on the end of a sofa next to me. Next to him snored some dirty lady, sitting up with her hair in rollers, and thongs on her dirty, crusty feet. Her dress was short, her legs were parted and she had on no panties. No one seemed to notice. Four guys were shooting craps on a table covered with a blanket. A wino lay on the floor in a corner, and every time he coughed, he spit up red stinking wine.

I looked around at the bare wood floor and the dirty ragged furniture. My God, what am I doing here with these people? And in this place? How much lower is it

possible to fall for a drink? I could hardly look at that
vomiting drunk and that nasty wet lady. I tried to raise
myself from the chair to wake my friend. I had to get out
of that dump! As I looked down, I moaned. I had vomited
gin and soda all down the front of my beautiful gold
formal dress. And somehow burnt two holes in it. I had
dragged my mink right through that stinking vomit. (And
I had the nerve to think I was better than the other people
in that room!) I was ashamed to wake my friend and let
him see me in this shape, to see me get up, all wet behind.
I covered myself as well as I could and asked the house
man for a drink. I paid him and looked at the dingy glass.
There was lipstick on it. I took my handkerchief and
wiped it before drinking. I had to get my nerves together
and try to stop shaking, so I could get out of there before
my friend woke up.

I ordered a half-pint to go and asked the house man to
call me a cab. He asked, "Don't you want your friend to
take you home?"

"No. Will you please call me a cab. Here is a dime for
the phone call!" I shouted, which made me feel better than
the "common drunk." The house man yelled back that he
didn't want my lousy dime. When the cab came, I took
my dirty wet self home. I carefully looked to see if the
neighbors were up and sneaked in past Mom and my
brothers. I balled my dress up, threw it in the garbage and
tried to clean my stole the best I could, until I could get it
into the cleaners. I took my bath, and was barely dressed
when Jay came in with a bottle and a couple of friends.

We balled all Sunday morning and left for a picnic later
in the day. There were tubs of iced beer, sodas, wines,
gin, whiskey, vodka, Scotch. For a couple of days I had
been drinking hard — not even "recovered" from my
"vacation," but I drank at the picnic like it was going out
of style. I was drinking because I *had to*. I knew I *should*
stop and knew what I was doing to myself, but *couldn't*
put that bottle down.

When it started raining, all thirty-five or forty of us moved under the picnic shelter. I had to go to the bathroom, which was quite a long way, especially during the rain and me being drunk. I staggered around the shelter until I found a post, pulled my slacks down, and peed! Too drunk to notice if they saw me or not — and until this day, I still don't know! I just wanted to drink — more and more. All my self-respect was totally gone.

When the picnic was over, one couple invited everyone to their house. Jay's friend said, "Better take Sis home. She is about to pass out drunk." Jay agreed, but I argued. They took me home anyway and Jay covered me on the couch before they left. I was mad at him and her. Who did she think she was? Telling him I was *drunk* and to put me to bed! I got up and called a cab and went on to join the others. I stopped and bought some beer because I didn't want the people to think I was coming just to beg for drinks, I could pay *my* way!

I was not there long before I started getting very sick. I tried to ask where the bathroom was, but when I opened my mouth to speak, vomit absolutely shot out all over the carpet. I ran wildly to where I thought the bathroom was, but it was the kitchen. I threw up in there also.

The host grabbed my arm and violently pushed me to the toilet stool, where I finished vomiting. He and his wife were very angry at me. I remember him saying, "You drunken bitch, you should have stayed at home. I don't appreciate you messing up my house, and I have to clean this shit up."

He drew his hand back in a slapping position. I immediately picked up a heavy ashtray, and we were getting ready for battle. One of the guests, a friend of us both, said, "Come on Sis, I'll take you home." I left, but all the way home I kept calling him a sack of M.F.'s. In my sick mind, *he* had done wrong, not me. And that was all I remembered until I woke up in my bed the next morning, with my clothes and shoes still on.

The terror of drums and voices

Many times before I had been sick from drinking, but *never ever* as I was that morning. I was wet from my neck all the way down. When I turned my head, I saw the pillow was *soaked* with blood. I was even more terrified when I started vomiting blood. I pulled myself up and had diarrhea. Shit was running down my legs from under my slacks.

I turned and looked in the corner of the ceiling to see who was calling me. Someone was calling me, and I answered, "Wait, I've got to go to the bathroom." But the voice called me again. "Chaney, Chaney, Chaney." And others joined in and kept calling my name. Finally they started chanting my name and beating drums to a rhythmic beat. I covered my ears with both hands to drown out the sound, but it didn't help any. I stumbled toward the bathroom and made it as far as the den, when I saw who was calling me. There they were — about fifty little men about two inches tall, fully dressed in Salvation Army uniforms. Each of them was carrying a drum. And every time they called "Chaney, Chaney," they beat their drums and marched and kept perfect time. Each time they beat their drums they looked up, right into my eyes, and smiled. I didn't want to hurt them, so I held onto the furniture and walked carefully around them.

I was dying. I made it to the bathroom and tried pulling off my dirty slacks. More blood was running down my legs. I thought I was bleeding to death. I remember turning the faucet on, but instead the water turned into the head of a black snake which slowly oozed out of the faucet. He kept getting longer and his head got larger and larger, as he came closer and closer to me. I started screaming. He had wrapped around my feet and was holding my body as tight as a vice, with the head as large as a dinner plate staring me right in the eye. I screamed and screamed — but no one heard me or came to help me.

I tried to free myself. The drums got louder, and bugs were beginning to crawl on the walls. I kept struggling to free myself, but I couldn't. Those drums felt as if they were all hitting me in the head with hammers. I wanted to call out to Mom and my brothers for help — yet I didn't want my family to see the condition I had put myself in. I was too ashamed. I, who wanted to make them *proud* of the only girl in the family.

The next morning I was too weak to stand. I laid my head on the toilet stool, too weak to even raise my head up. If someone had flushed the toilet, my head would have gone down the drain. My urine and bowels seemed to be under control.

I crawled over and pulled the dirty linen off the bed, and pushed it into the hamper. I put the bloody pillow under the bed. I didn't want my family to see it. I was staying hidden and was *dying alone.* I used every ounce of strength and will power to spread a clean sheet and blanket on the bed. I was washed down in perspiration, which I tried to wipe off. When I raised the towel to my face, it was still covered with "bugs." I tried to shake them off the towel, but they jumped on my arms and in my hair. The little men called me louder and faster and beat their drums to a faster beat.

My mind flashed back to my Sunday School days. I started remembering some of the verses Dad had read from the Bible. The verses seemed to be going around, and around, and around . . . MAN'S EXTREMITY IS GOD'S OPPORTUNITY . . . COME HE THAT IS BURDENED AND HEAVY LADEN AND I WILL GIVE YOU REST . . . WHATEVER YOU ASK IN MY NAME I WILL GIVE YOU. IF A CHILD ASK HIS FATHER FOR BREAD HE WILL NOT GIVE HIM STONES.

I remember falling down on my knees and praying to my God: *"Dear God,* you said we all are your children. I know I have done many wrongs. I have asked you to help me before, and returned to the same things. But here I am again, asking you to help me. I can't go any further. I am coming to you with a heavy heart. I am so tired. Please take me in your arms and rock me to sleep, just one half hour. Please, God, reach your hand out and pull me up just one more time. And I will spend the rest of my life helping any alcoholic who suffers. This I ask in your name, AMEN."

I got up and laid down in bed. Again I said, *"Please God."*

When I woke up and looked at the clock, I saw I had slept for two and one-half hours! The bed was not wet. My stomach still hurt, but I was able to make it to the stool without having an accident. I could still hear the drums but not so loud anymore. I still heard voices but I didn't see the army of little men. I was shaking from head to foot, as though my very bones were being disconnected. My lips were trembling, and I could not stop biting them.

Dear God, make this the LAST drink

My head had cleared enough for me to know that I was going into D.T.'s and convulsions. Without medical aid there was only one thing for me to do. I knew I had one can of Budweiser left in the refrigerator. I staggered to the kitchen, holding onto the walls and made it. I took the beer out. My hands shook so that I could hardly open it, but I did. Before I turned that drink up to my shaking mouth, I prayed "Dear GOD make this the LAST drink!" I spilled some, but got most of it down. It was enough to quiet the nerves and calm most of the shaking. Now I didn't need the beer left in the can, so I walked to the kitchen sink and *poured it down the drain.*

This was the summer of 1968, and Blacks all over the nation were singing I'M BLACK AND I'M PROUD — and listening to the one and only James Brown sing I'M BLACK AND I'M PROUD. And on that summer day I turned the radio on, to drown out the sound of the drums.

And there it was again. "I'M BLACK AND I'M PROUD, say it loud, I'm Black and I'm Proud, I'M BLACK AND I'M PROUD." *On and on* the song went. Hearing that song mocked me and made me feel again I was a disgrace to my people. I quickly snapped the radio off and moaned out loud, "Stop singing that song. I'M BLACK AND I'M *DRUNK!* I don't feel *proud.* I'm nothing but a drunken bitch. I am *Black,* but I am not proud."

I had reached MY bottom. I had reached MY skid row.

Part Five

RECOVERY

Helping Others Like Me

Listening to the winners

When I went back to AA I started to listen. I mean *really listen.* I was told that I had to take the cotton out of my ears and stuff it in my mouth and shut up and listen to the winners. The winners were the people staying sober and not *playing* in and out of the Program.

I want to share a very important mistake that I made. When I first called for help, I was sick and I needed and wanted help, but I did not enter the Program to get *sober for myself.* I wanted to get Grant back. And when he said I was not going to stop drinking, I stayed sober to *show him* that I could. The result was, when we separated and I no longer had to *show him,* I got drunk. That was not a good enough reason to attempt sobriety.

So I learned, as I listened, that I must stay sober for myself *only,* not husband, wife, children, parents or boss. No one but Chaney. Stay sober for the first person who is hurt by the first drink — and become a bit selfish. I am an important person in this world. *I am somebody!* I had to learn by listening, reading and watching everything I could find on alcoholism anywhere, anytime, any information I could gather and study. I had to work at *learning* how to stay sober.

I had told my sponsor about my affair with Jay.

She said, "Stay away from drinking people."

I told her, "I want to start being honest. I feel so guilty when I am not drinking. I know I am wrong."

She replied, "Guilt is something you don't need. In order to cope with guilt you are going to drink — I am going to be frank with you, Chaney. Keep that guy and you will keep drinking. Leave him and the crowd alone and you can stay sober. Now it is up to you which way you want to go."

Soon I told Jay that I was going to AA and had stopped drinking. He didn't knock it, but he started pulling away from me. I started going out to dinner and movies with my new *sober* friends. He began to realize that I was serious and no longer wanted to continue our "back-street affair." We remained friends with the understanding that he and I went our separate ways. I felt clean and free once I was out of that affair and I didn't have to carry any guilt or drink to forget.

I attended meetings regularly. I had found some hope with my new friends and now was just beginning to think of what was best for *myself.* My brains were no longer foggy from booze and I was beginning to realize why I had failed to stay sober before. Now I was really listening to the winners!

I pretended not to be home when drinking buddies rang my doorbell. I closed the door in my brothers' faces when they showed up with bottles.

Mom asked me on cold snowy night, "Are you going to another meeting? Why don't you stay here and watch T.V. with me?" I answered, "Mom, I don't want to hurt your feelings, but I am the same person you told that you wished I had never been born and you hated to look at me drunk. You said a drunk woman looks like a wet dog. Do you want me to spend nights watching T.V. and keeping you company and drinking? Or do you want me to go to meetings and stay sober?"

She said, "No! My Lord! Honey, don't drink, go on to your meeting." So I was learning to step on anyone's toes who got in my way of staying sober. I was learning and listening.

I started going back to church and it felt good not to be hung over. I was sure most members knew of my past drinking. Even though I didn't publicize that I was on the Program, many people saw the change and told me how well I was looking. I was gaining weight; my skin was clearing up. The rings under my eyes were disappearing. Now when I served Holy Communion, I felt good and clean. The Program was helping me grow and gain more self-confidence. They taught me that I was never *bad*, but *sick* and I was getting well.

Of course, there were a few in every crowd, even in church. One Sunday, a group of ladies were talking about a member who was getting married for the second time; she had divorced her first husband of many years. As soon as I got near them, one lady who had been married to one husband for twenty-five years said, "A woman can have many men, but only *one* husband. That is what the Bible said, and that is what I say." She looked right at me and there was no doubt she meant it as a personal dig. I ignored her, but she had hit home. I talked to my friends about this and they told me to not hold resentments. If anything bothered me, I should *talk about it.*

Again, to my readers, this is so very important: They told me, "You can't unscramble an egg! If you started cooking and intended to fix an egg straight up and scrambled it instead, there is nothing you can do about it! You can stand there and stare in that frying pan for the rest of your life. But all the King's horses and all the King's men cannot put that egg back together again. So what can you do? You can eat that scrambled bastard, or you can clean the frying pan and start all over again. If you are careful and keep your mind on every *Step* and what you are doing, you will end up with an egg straight up.

"So that is the way it is with we alcoholics. All we can do is start all over again to straighten up our *scrambled life.*" I've never forgotten this example of dealing with past mistakes in life, and I often remember it when talking to others who kick themselves for the "past mistakes." I listened and learned when they told me not to hold resentments, not to blow up, but to deal with any problem, big or small, if it really bothered me. But NOT to deal with it violently.

Helping others, helping ME

One Sunday at eleven o'clock service, a man walked in, obviously drunk. He staggered up to the altar and quietly knelt. Then he got up and staggered out without a word. My God, I could identify! I felt for him right in my gut. I knew the Hell he was in.

When service was over, everyone was talking about "him." One lady said, "What a disgrace! I am so glad *I* am a child of God." I looked her straight in the eyes and as arrogant as I could, I said, "And he is too." I walked away while her mouth hung open. I was remembering all the times their tongues were flapping about *me* when I was in the Hell on earth.

But I still went to church. And I felt ten feet tall the first time the usher told me to go outside, because someone wanted to see me. When I got out, there was one of my sober friends who said, "Chaney, there is a very sick Black lady who needs your help. We have tried, but I think she can relate to you better." I worked all that Sunday, and it was night before I left the hospital with that lady. She was very sick and had no place to stay. I took her home with me, put her to bed and kept watch over her all night. That was the first time I tried to help a fellow alcoholic.

From then on, I was often called from church, home, or wherever I was to help.

One lady said to me one Sunday, "Honey, don't forget your church comes first."

I said, "Too many of *us* Christians are quick to criticize

a drunk or drug addict or anyone else who does something wrong. I feel, to be Christ-like *is* to help — so I will see you *after* I take care of this drunk."

Without realizing it, I was changing my *self*-centered attitude and was thinking of *others*. The people I helped called me when they were depressed. They called *me* instead of drinking. I was needed; and before I realized it I had been sober for a *year*!

I'll never forget how elated I was as I prepared for my very first talk at AA. I felt reborn. I felt that if I had made it for a year, maybe there was hope of me staying sober forever! I kept reminding myself to "work the program one day at a time," and it worked. I remembered what the pipe fitter had told me years ago about cutting that heavy pipe into 365 pieces! It was such a special occasion that I even bought a new dress for the evening.

Mom said, "Baby, I want to go too, I am so proud of you." So I dressed Mom and helped put her in the car.

I was scared stiff to talk to all those people at the Saturday night meeting. I wrote an outline of twenty-four lines that I wanted to remember. As I write now, I am still holding that little dirty ragged sheet of paper.

I hardly recognized my own voice. For the first time I was *really* saying, "My name is Chaney and I am an alcoholic." After a few minutes of nervousness, my stomach settled down. I talked about my experiences "on the way, on top, and at the bottom." When I finished talking, I felt good inside. Washed and clean.

I became as addicted to the AA program as I had been to drug alcohol. It became my way of life. It was never too cold or too hot for me to go to a meeting. It didn't matter if the people there were rich, poor, Black, White, or purple with yellow stripes. I was contented and at peace with myself and my Higher Power. And I could finally go to work on Mondays *not hung over*. I had spent my weekends doing things that I felt proud of. Also, I was able to talk about church activities like the other ladies.

Although I couldn't tell them of the hours I spent working with alcoholics because I didn't think they'd understand, I knew and felt good inside. I loved *Chaney* again. I was listening and growing.

The serenity to accept

Mom had gotten worse and now she could hardly walk. The doctor said she didn't "want to." I was doing all I could to motivate her, but to no avail. So I still cleaned her upstairs apartment and took care of her. My brother Lee was living in my basement apartment, and he helped with her as he had with my dad. My job at the school was tiring, but I liked it and all the people I worked with. My house payment and all my bills were paid one month in advance. Mom's illness was the only particular problem I had.

I was learning to live and breathe by the Serenity Prayer (written by Reinhold Niebuhr and adopted by AA people.)

GOD GRANT ME THE
SERENITY TO ACCEPT THE THINGS
I CANNOT CHANGE;
COURAGE TO CHANGE THE THINGS I CAN;
AND *WISDOM* TO KNOW THE DIFFERENCE —
Living one day at a time;
Enjoying one moment at a time,
Accepting hardships
As the Pathway to Peace;
Taking, as He did, this sinful world
As it is, not as I would have it;
Trusting that He will make all things
Right if I surrender to His will;
That I may be reasonably happy in this
Life and supremely happy with Him,
Forever in the next. AMEN.

The first five lines which I learned early in the program

were the reason I was able to accept Mom's illness in her old age. I couldn't change it and had the wisdom to know that I couldn't. But I can say that I was "reasonably" happy. I had a good regularly paying job, a nice home, my own car, three closets of good clothes and a few dollars in the bank. My health had improved, and I was feeling great. I was active in church, staying sober and enjoying my new sober life.

One evening I had gone to a meeting and afterwards some of us had gone out for dinner. We had joked and just had a good time until midnight when I said goodnight to all and went home. I checked on Mom and she was asleep, so I undressed and went to bed. I remember saying out loud, "Thank God, another day sober. It has been a year and three months since I had a drink. Thank *you!*" And I drifted off to sleep.

I dreamt someone was telling me to move, move. "Where?" I asked. I sat straight up in bed, and looked at the clock. It was 2:30 a.m. I thought what a crazy dream! I'm doing alright for myself here in good ole Cincy . . . I think! I went on back to bed and was soon asleep.

The next day the dream was still with me. I told a couple of friends about it. As the days passed, I tried to shine it on, but the thought wouldn't leave me. I thought, "I couldn't leave Cincinnati *anyway* — Mom is sick and Lee is living here. I couldn't possibly put him out. He and his kids are doing well now, I *have to* stay here and keep my house so they will be near, and I can see about them. What a crazy dream, *anyway.*"

Just a few weeks later I came home from work. Smoke met me in the face. I stood there, too scared to move. Then I ran up the stairs, two at a time, praying. I knew Mom couldn't walk down the stairs. Thank God, she was not burned, although the house was full of smoke and black soot.

After she had put her lunch on the stove to warm, she had fallen in the bedroom and couldn't get up again. The food had burned itself out and was still on the stove. Although Mom couldn't get up, she had managed to pull the phone off the table to dial the operator. She told them the house was on fire, and she couldn't get out. When the firemen came and couldn't see the smoke and couldn't hear her from the closed second floor, they left and marked up a false alarm. Mom laid on the floor for hours! The only thing that saved her life was that she was able to breathe fresh air from the crack under the door, or she would have died. I was terrified and hysterical. I managed to help her get up and into bed.

From that day on, I was terrified whenever I left the house. I didn't know what to do, because I had to work. I asked about a nurse, but I couldn't afford the fee. I couldn't find anyone to care for her during the day. The doctor told me, "You should put your mom in a nursing home. It is too dangerous to leave her all day."

"No! I'll work something out."

I called Vivian in San Diego and told her how sick Mom was. She said, "Why don't you come out here and I can help you." I listed all the reasons I couldn't, and we dropped the subject.

A few weeks later Mom had a stroke and was hospitalized. It was an even heavier job for me to work and go to the hospital every night. Yet I felt better knowing she was not alone. Her right leg was crippled, but the nurses and doctors made her walk with a walker. She seemed to be doing better.

One day Lee said, "Mom seems to be much better," and sat there quietly for about five minutes. "Sis, if Mom wasn't sick and you hadn't so much on you, I'd move to California."

"You would *what?*" I asked. (I shouted!) "Are you for real, Lee?"

"Yes, I want to leave Cincinnati. I'm tired of this town." I remembered my stupid dream of a couple months back and said, "Let's talk about this. If you're serious, let's start making plans."

So by the time Mom came home from the hospital, we had made plans to move to San Diego, California. That was in December, and Lee left in January. I put my home up for sale and felt upset when three deals in a row fell through. I became nervous from all the disappointments. I was trying to sell furniture and the house stayed full of people picking over my stuff nights and every weekend. I was going up the wall.

I went to one meeting where my sponsor looked at me and said, "Chaney, you shouldn't get too tired, even too hungry, or upset. You're overtaxing yourself and it's dangerous for you."

I said, "But, I don't know what to do. I've already sent money to my daughter and paid rent for three months out *there!* Everytime I think the deal is closed on my house, somebody's credit is bad. I would like to wait here until it is sold."

She asked, "Didn't you say that you have enough money to move with? One thing, remember you can get drunk from all this pressure. Or you can put that damn house in your attorney's hands and let him sell it and get the hell out of Cincinnati. *That is Changing The Things You Can.*" (She was a *tough* sponsor!! She didn't pet me, always came to the *point!)*

Well, Lord! Here I go!

I wanted to stay sober so I *listened* to the winner. And I did just what she told me to do. I told my attorney to let the refrigerators, stoves, beds, and anything else that I didn't sell from the four apartments go *with* the house. I called the airport to make our reservations, and one week later Mom and I were on our way. Mabel, a lifetime friend, helped me lift Mom into the car and drove us to the airport. Mom had to be lifted onto the plane. She could barely walk and was getting sicker. She had been terrified taking her first plane ride, but she said, "I am not scared anymore. This is the only time I will remember flying anyway. When I fly again, it will be when you bring my body back to bury me with your daddy."

Three days after we got to San Diego, the moving van came with our belongings. I kept busy for a while getting Mom's place straight. Lee moved in with Vivian, and Mom had her own nice little garage apartment right in Vivian's yard. It was good now that I had help. My daughter still worked nights so someone could be with Mom during the day. Everything looked like it was working out fine.

I called AA as soon as I got to San Diego and found I could go to meetings within walking distance of my apartment, which made me happy since I had sold my car. But life doesn't always go as planned. Mother had another stroke one week after we moved and was not able to even turn over. I had no other choice but to put her in a convalescent home. For a few weeks she worried, but she soon adjusted and was satisfied. I told the nurse when I took her to the home, "I am not pawning her off to walk off and forget her. Every day you will see me or some member of our family. Anything she wants, you get it for her. She is not being thrown away." I felt guilty.

I had given up a twelve-room home and was now living in a one-bedroom apartment. It was a very nice place, and I thought I would use my retirement pay from my school job and my savings to help pay the rent until they ran out. I was no longer snowed under with material things. Now that I no longer had so many responsibilities, all I needed was a job. The only one I could find was making sandwiches at a restaurant four hours a day, five days a week, for two dollars an hour. My take-home pay was thirty-seven dollars a week. Each Friday when I got paid, I went to the bank and cashed my check and drew out enough money to live off that week.

Believe it or not, but I was not the least bit worried!

Somewhere, somehow, I knew things were going to be alright. The dream was no longer crazy. I felt that my Higher Power was trying to tell me something. If anyone had told me six months earlier that I would be moved to San Diego, I would have thought them stone nuts. Yet here I was. I felt there was a reason and I didn't know or question anything.

I remember and often speak of the prayer I prayed just before Mom and I left for the airport. I said, "Well Lord! Here I go! Maybe I am making the worst mistake in my life. I'm giving up everything. This is the one and only time I've ever really and truly walked out on *faith*. Now I am putting my life in your hand. And if it turns out to be a mess, it's going to be your fault!" I didn't realize that I was doing exactly what I should — *LET GO AND LET GOD*.

I was trying to help myself. I wasn't satisfied with my little job, yet I wasn't worried. I went downtown and took a typing course, but I was not interested and dropped out. I completed a bank teller's certificate course, but couldn't find a job because I didn't have experience. It was trying, yet I never felt discouraged. I felt no regrets for leaving Ohio.

Talking at an AA meeting one night, I said, "I am only bringing home thirty-seven dollars a week and I'm just as happy as if I had *good sense!* I am just as happy as a sissy in an all-boys camp. Somehow I know everything is going to be *alright.*" My Higher Power was still with me.

The next day a lady called me on the phone and said, "Me and my husband enjoyed your talk last night. He wants to know if you would like to learn silk screening. He will teach you and pay you sixty-five dollars a week while you are learning. You can make over a hundred dollars a week after you learn."

I said, "Wow! When do I start?"

A week later I was on a new job. Now I didn't have to use my savings, but I still had to conserve. My rent was

120 dollars a month plus gas and electric and phone and food and carfare. I was on a tight budget, but I could manage.

Transportation was another problem. I lived sixteen miles from my work and five miles from the closest bus stop. My supervisor, who was a fellow alcoholic, made it possible for me to work by suggesting that I take the bus to his house and then ride with him to work. Sometimes his wife invited me to dinner. They were great people and so very good to me. I worked religiously at learning the trade and within a few weeks I was actually silk screening. I enjoyed printing things like the decals for the helmets of professional football teams, and I still have the Chargers' "lightning bolts" on my flower pots!

After work I'd take the bus to see Mom and stay with her until after visiting hours.

My supervisor and his wife took me to see about a crypt. I picked my casket and paid down on the crypt and casket. I told them, "Should anything happen to me, I don't want the kids to have any problems. So I will get these things done now."

After about a month I was tired of depending on my supervisor for transportation, so I asked him and his son to help me pick an economy car. They spent all day one Saturday, and I settled for a brand-new Pinto. I couldn't afford a car payment from my salary, so I drew $2,000 out of my savings, paid $1,700 down and got my insurance and licenses. Now I didn't have to depend on him, and I could get to more AA meetings where I had friends, the only people who really understood me. (My children and my brother love me but they don't understand an alcoholic the way another alcoholic does.)

No longer spilling the wine

I looked up the address of my CME Church and joined. I was immediately put on the Stewardess Board to serve Communion, just like I had back in Cincinnati. How good it felt that I no longer had to spill the wine because I was shaking from a hangover! I did tell the minister and church members that I was divorced — but not that I'd been divorced three times. I also told the minister that I once had a drinking problem.

I knew I had built-in safety for staying away from the bottle as long as I stayed near all my new sober friends. They accepted me and continually invited me to dinner and took me to out-of-town meetings; I was never lonely. In fact, I had to refuse some of their invitations.

I had only one brief bad experience a couple of months after I moved to San Diego, when I was introduced to a retired Navy man who drank. I told him that I had a "drinking problem" and I would get sick if I took a drink. One night in his apartment, one of the ladies asked, "Why don't you fix Chaney a drink?"

He said, "She *claims* that she can't drink." I didn't say anything. He turned to me and said, "I am going to fix you a drink. And the way I mix it, I guarantee you will not even taste it."

I picked up my coat and started putting it on as I replied, "You haven't heard a word I said. I'm not PAYING to attend AA meetings. I didn't tell you the *taste* of alcohol was my problem! I said it made me *sick*. Go on and tell all your friends I am an alcoholic, I don't give a damn! You can make *your drink* anyway you want. When you finish mixing it, take a douche with it, you M.F.!!" I walked out and refused to see him again.

Actually, I had no business with him and his drinking friends anyway. I saw that our relationship was going to get me back into trouble. In time, I learned how to find out *early* whether my dates were drinkers! If they said, "Yes!" I'd say, " 'Bye." Everyone may not have to go to this extreme, but I *do*.

A need to talk SOUL

I was enjoying life. My kids and grandchildren were

regularly visiting me or inviting me to their homes. The only thing that bothered me about AA was there were practically no Black people. I am not a racist, but I wanted to mix with my own race and I wanted to talk SOUL. I had heard of a couple of Brothers who were "on the Program" but had not met them.

Finally, one night I met a Brother named Tate, but not at a regular meeting. I had gone with a carload of White friends to a prison honor camp, where they were having an AA banquet. As soon as the opportunity presented itself, I cornered him and asked, "Say, Brother, where in the hell are the Brothers and Sisters here in San Diego? I've been here for months, and every meeting I go to is lily White! I want to see some SOULS!! When I saw you come in, it was just like a child seeing Santa Claus."

He said, "To be honest with you, there are only a couple of Sisters who recently joined, and me and four or five other Brothers. We go to the Imperial Group over at the Catholic Church. Also, we are meeting at my house to see what we can do to get a rehabilitation house for Blacks in our neighborhood. I'll come and pick you up for the next meeting."

He kept his promise and I went to the meeting where for a change there were about eight of us Blacks and three Whites. A couple of days later, he took me to a meeting at his home where they were discussing future plans for the Rehab House. Tate's wife was a lovely person who made me feel right at home. They had two sweet boys, as fat and healthy as little butterballs. One of the Brothers talked all through our meeting as we discussed the possibilities, and I liked him. When Tate was taking me home I asked, "Who was that guy talking?" He said, "That's my friend Curtis. It was his and my idea to start seeing what we could to do start a Rehab House in the ghetto. I think he got his shit together."

An AA dance was coming up that all the groups were planning to attend. I had no date, so I asked one of my male church members to go with me. He and I had gone to the movies and out to dinner several times, just as friends — absolutely nothing personal. I told him, "I've already bought the tickets, but I don't want to go alone. And I just don't know anyone single in this town." About three hours before the dance, Tate called and said, "Hey Sister, I've found you a date for the dance tonight."

I asked, "Who?"

"You remember the Brother that you saw at my pad, Curtis? He doesn't have a date either," he said.

"Isn't he married?" I asked.

"No, he's just like you, he ain't got nobody either."

I said, "I sure do appreciate what you did, but I've already got a date — so I will see you all at the dance. Tell him to ask me some other time."

We all met at the dance. There were at least 300 people — and about *six* Blacks. We had a good time. I danced several times with Curtis and others.

Curtis called the next week and asked if I would go to the ball game with him. I said, "I don't want you to think I am rejecting you, but I am so tired. I worked ten hours today and had to go see poor Mom who was so restless and irritable; I'm exhausted."

A couple of days later he called and asked me out to dinner. I said, "I can't go now because I just put on a pot of food. It should be ready about six o'clock, so why don't you come and have dinner with me?" He said, "Alright, I'll be there about seven o'clock."

We enjoyed talking and we spoke the same language. We really had our own private *meeting* and enjoyed each other's company. He left with the understanding that we would see each other again. A few days later, we went to the ball game. Soon we were going to meetings together and joining the others for dinner. It became known to everyone, *Curtis and Chaney!* We both felt that our Higher Power put us together. I told him, "I had to come west to find the best."

Curtis was a good and honest working man who had been in the labor union for years. He saw me struggling to live off my small salary, and eventually he said, "Why don't I just move on in and take your responsibilities?"

I said, "It is O.K. with me! Go to the house and get your things."

"They are already out in the car," he replied.

We both looked at each other and cracked up. He wanted to get married right away, but I said, "No, Curtis, I am so tired of marrying and divorcing. I've made all my future plans, even my crypt and casket. I hope we can get along, but just in case that we don't, we will not have to go through divorce court." He didn't argue with me, but just continued to be cool. I felt so good inside when I drove home from work, knowing my man was waiting. I had been alone, it seemed, for years. And it was good to have a companion.

Learning to be a counselor

One evening when I came in, Curtis said, "A program for alcoholics is opening in the Black neighborhood. They will be needing counselors. Would you like to try for a job? Or do you like silk screening better? I am going to be chairman of the policy advisory board."

I told him I didn't know one thing about counseling. And, too, I only finished high school, plus a couple of college courses. He said, "I'm not sure of all the qualifications, but I know you can handle the job, as much as you run your mouth!" As it turned out, I qualified and accepted the job.

I felt so bad to tell my supervisor at the silk screening shop that now I wanted to leave. I felt awful. But I realized that the minority alcoholics needed help, and this was going to be the first and only alcoholic program in the whole country for the minorities. I *had* to say, "Yes, I will try."

I was hired, and three days later I was sent to University of California, Santa Cruz, to start my training as an alcoholic counselor. Although I had lived the life of an alcoholic, I still had to learn how to *convey* my experiences to the public and how to reach clients. We were driven like slaves from 7:30 a.m. to as late as 11:00 p.m., five-and-a-half days a week. It was hard!

Many speakers from business, from colleges and from other alcoholic programs came in. Our instructors were integrated staff. Future counselors from as far away as Alaska came to the training. Among the things we were taught was how to deal with different ethnic groups.

The main and most important point was I was torn apart and was forced to look and learn who *Chaney* was. I was surprised to find how little I really knew about myself. For example, they were videotaping our role-playing, and I was the counselor. When I looked and saw myself on TV, I went into an act. I leaned back in my chair, stuck my chest out and really acted as a *professional* counselor "should." I talked real proper and used a few big words. I was *looking good, baby*, and really performed for my instructors and my class. My instructors were looking at me with wide-eyed surprise. By the time I finished, I was on a real ego trip, and looked at my peers and instructors for their compliments.

One Sister from Los Angeles said, "Chaney, you sure was trying to talk like White folks, wasn't you?" And all my classmates chimed in, "Sure was. Wow!"

My feathers fell — they didn't like my counseling technique. I looked at my five instructors and they were shaking their heads. One of them verbally attacked me by saying, "Chaney, that was nothing but a phony pile of shit you just did! If I came to you as a client and you talked to me in that manner, you would immediately turn me off. You were being phony, you sounded phony and you *was* phony."

I was embarrassed and in tears. They all tore me apart

and said how awful I had performed. They were laughing at me and making fun. I said, "I don't like to be put on the *hot seat* like that. To hell with all of you! That's why I am here is to learn. If I already knew counseling, I would have your instructors' jobs. And I don't like everyone pointing and laughing and talking about me like I am a monkey in a damn cage."

The instructor who had attacked me started smiling and nodding his head and said, "*Now* you sound like Chaney! I am a Brother and I talk and act like a Brother. You are a Sister and you do the same. I want to tell you something about yourself, Chaney. You are a *born* natural. Your personality is magnetic — people love you. They can and will feel that you care. Always speak and act natural, no matter who or where you are and you will be able to reach most anyone. You don't know your own strength."

He said, "I want you to role-play the same thing again. Only this time be Chaney." When I finished, they all cheered. All the Souls were saying, "Right on, Sister!"

So from that day on, I don't change my style of talking for anyone. I enjoy being myself. And if anyone don't like it, that's "tough titty!"

Another day when we were role-playing, one of my White instructors played my client. He started by saying, "I am here because I am an alcoholic and need help." I touched his arm and said, "Just settle down and trust me, I am going to do all I can to help." Without any warning, he drew his arm away from me and said, "But I don't want no *nigger* to help me."

I forgot we were role-playing and blew up. "Well you blue-eyed S.O.B., go back out there and drink your damn self to death! The sooner the better!" I cooled off when I saw him smiling.

He asked, "Is that the way you would react if a White client said that to you? Here is where you must learn how to handle this situation, if it ever happens. And you are likely to run into these type of people, but you shouldn't blow up. A good way is to say, 'It is obvious that you have two problems. Now first we will deal with the drinking and maybe your dislike for me will clear up later.' "

We were also taught community organizing and family counseling. We were given many handout sheets to keep for reference. Every three months thereafter we attended one three-day session held at different college campuses throughout California. I felt much more confident when I returned to my office. My past drinking loaded me with experience, and the training reinforced me.

Now all I needed were the lady clients I was hired to work with! I had to build my own case load since it was a brand new program, so I had to beat the bushes for clients. I visited many agencies and told them of the Center and the services we provided. I went on radio stations and made tapes, I appeared on TV several times. Soon I really had a caseload of ladies. They were calling for appointments and information, and coming in for counseling. A typical day included working eight hours, going to some homes and picking the ladies up and taking them to AA meetings in the evening.

I soon found out that many wanted help and seemed very relaxed with me, but they simply would not take to AA. Many said, "I've tried AA, and I just don't like it." Yet some clients who attended AA for the first time just love the Program and would not return to the Center! (*Different strokes for different folks!*)

Still, I had the problem of how to help the clients who would not go to AA meetings. Some said they did not like the "God part" and didn't even believe in God or *any* Higher Power. One man said, "When I have a pocketful of money *that* is my Higher Power." We were not selling "religion," but sobriety! I would worry and pray all the time, *which way do I start?* I asked other counselors for ideas, I tried getting the clients together on Friday nights for rap sessions, but soon we ran out of conversations, and it became dull. I tried some Transactional Analysis but soon learned that many minority people do not dig it. I needed to find a way to translate my own experience — and my experiences working with clients — into something everybody could understand. I had to develop my own education class as I went along. It took almost a year.

There's only one reason for drinking

Over a period of time from talking to clients, I have heard people give all kinds of "reasons" for their drinking. The biggest reason I've heard over and over, is "I drink because I don't have anything else to do." This is a reason I've heard from minority people especially — but there are other reasons too. Some said, "I wouldn't drink if my wife/husband stayed off my back." Many people say they dig the taste of booze. Many use alcohol as a relaxer. Others drink to get high, while many drink as an escape from unpleasant situations. Many depend on alcohol as a sexual stimulus. Some use booze as a pain-killer. (This is often stated by some of the little old ladies and men with arthritis.) Many say they no longer feel *shy* when they are drinking.

Several painters have told me that alcohol keeps their lungs clear from paint fumes. Many ladies state that alcohol is good for them while in change of life, because the booze "thins" their blood. Some men said they drink while working out-of-doors because it keeps them warm. Several entertainers tell me that they use booze as a stimulus, and to keep their nerves together.

These are only a few of the reasons I've heard — the alcoholic can give many, many more. Also, these reasons are only excuses — the only reason a person drinks is because *they turn it up and swallow it.*

I am now fully aware that we Americans are living in a drinking society. We are brainwashed to drink. Our society gives us *permission* to drink.

A mixed-up society

The alcoholic should avoid drinking places and drinking people. Yet, if you decide to spend a quiet evening at home watching television, the first thing you see is an advertisement of a big, cold, long-stem glass of beer! In most movies the characters are drinking.

Try taking a nice relaxing drive to get your mind off drinking! Every few miles you'll see great big neon signs advertising some brand of alcohol! If someone dies, alcohol is served at the wake. If there is a wedding, alcohol is served abundantly. When we are sad we drink. When we are happy we drink!

Our society says, "drink, drink, drink." So we drink. Then our government gets the tax dollars from the sale of booze. If we are caught drunk from the drug alcohol advertised by society, we go to *jail.* And society collects more money from us through attorney fees and fines, for drunk driving and other alcohol-related crimes. Society positively recycles the alcoholic's dollars. Isn't this a mixed-up society? Although no one obviously *forces* us to drink, we are not able to get away from alcohol completely. It is all around us.

It is simple to stay away from the first drink, but it is not *easy.* You have to constantly remind yourself that *I can't have it, I am an ALCOHOLIC.* One drink is too much for me, but ten will not be *enough.*

Give and take — and tolerance

Most alcoholics have some kind of *childish* personality. They seem to pamper themselves. They want to have things *their way.* And when he/she *can't* (or you rattle their cage), usual they will *fix you,* by *getting drunk at you!* Many people get angry or upset with their spouse and slam out the door, head for the nearest bar to appease their feelings — only to end up calling hours later for the spouse to bail them out of jail. But *they fixed them!* Once the alcoholic becomes *aware* of acting as a spoiled brat, he or she starts to grow up. We begin to realize that things will not *always go our way.* Life is give and take.

The alcoholic who is to stay sober must learn *TOLER-ANCE.* I've learned to keep my mind open as well as my ears. I continue to listen to all the information I can find on the disease of alcoholism. I've heard several doctors say that brain damage starts with the first drinks. One can of beer or a glass of wine or a shot of hard booze begins destroying our nervous system and brain cells. Many poor souls walk the streets, mumbling to themselves. What they are actually doing is drinking themselves into insanity.

I was at the point where I had to admit *complete defeat.* I couldn't go any further with alcohol. My body could no longer function with this drug. I was *poisoned* physically and mentally. I knew I had reached my *bottom* and was as low as I could possibly go.

Getting honest

There was only one thing for me to do after I knew I was defeated. I had *had* it, Baby, no lie! I had reached the end of my "drinking journey." It was time to get *honest* with myself. I had to go back to AA for help. Only *this* time — I had to really *be* honest. I had been "half-stepping." But when I asked for help in 1968, I was no longer playing games with me or others. I honestly desired help for Chaney *and Chaney only.* There was no doubt, no reservations, no more B.S.! I had been playing the dishonest alcoholic game for years. I had *sneaked the drinks, told the lies,* made false *promises,* and thought I was being *smart.* But I was the fool. I had only snowed myself. So I had to start being honest with the first person I hurt when I took the first drink — ME. If you are to get sober and *stay sober,* you need to do the same. Honesty is the key to open the door to sobriety!

Some believe that alcoholism is an illness and the alcoholic *can be helped.* The illness can be arrested by *no drinking,* but cannot be "cured." Once an alcoholic, always an alcoholic. My body will always be allergic to alcohol. The disease of alcoholism progresses in a person whether they drink or don't drink. Everyone is not, and will not be, as fortunate as me. I got another chance at life, but so many people *don't.* You may be one who *does* get another chance to stay sober. There is hope for you. *But you must come out of hiding.*

There is no such thing as the alcoholic who can *taper off.* I had to *stop* drinking in order to stay sober. There is no way to taper off, since we have learned that the *first* (not the *last*) drink is the cause of getting *drunk.* I was told that an alcoholic is anyone who is no longer responsible for his or her actions and who loses control after the first drink. So it stands to reason that one can't taper off. I have heard many people say that they or Aunt Fanny or someone else they know used to be an alcoholic. But now they have tapered off and become a social drinker. *Rarely!* Once an alcoholic, always an alcoholic. *There is no such thing as a half-alcoholic!* Either you are in trouble or you are not. It is just like being half-pregnant.

Thinking drunk / thinking sober

When I stopped drinking, I started thinking for *myself.* My brains were no longer trying to function under the influence of alcohol. I slowly started making decisions and was able to carry them out. I no longer walked head on into *affairs* as I did with Jay. I was able to think and realize that there are worse things than being alone. For example I was thinking for *myself* when I walked out of

the Navy Chief's apartment after he tried to give me a
drink, thinking for myself because I avoided drinking
companions.

As long as you *think drunk*, you will stay drunk. When
you learn to *think sober*, you can stay sober. At this point
I would like to share with you what I mean by thinking
drunk/sober. These are reality statements that go through
CHANGE when we want to *stay* sober.

Thinking Drunk

1.
The street people and hustlers
have it made. (Baloney!)

2.
Booze gave me *courage* to face
uncomfortable situations, and
things that I felt was wrong.

3.
Anyone who doesn't drink is a
square, and don't know how
much fun they are missing.
(Fun??)

4.
Give kids booze and they will not
get hooked on it when they are
older. It's O.K. for them to drink
at home.

5.
Booze is a sexual stimulus.
(Bullshit!)

6.
We are supposed to drink and
have "fun" on weekends. It's not
alcoholism if I drink just on
weekends.

7.
As long as one drinks and doesn't
use "drugs" it's O.K. (What??)

Thinking Sober

1.
The street people and hustlers
live in a world of *fantasy* and
dishonesty!!

2.
If I feel something is wrong, I
don't do it. I no longer need false
courage.

3.
Living a sober life is *rewarding.* I
can enjoy more of what is around
me.

4.
Giving kids booze is dangerous. I
have worked with a kid who was
a 12-year-old alcoholic. His
parents started him drinking at
home at age six.

5.
Many alcoholics experience a
sexual *decline.*

6.
The weekend alcoholic can also
get into trouble. (Re-read my
story!)

7.
Alcohol *is also a drug* and gets
one into trouble and sick.

8.
When I drink I don't harm anyone but myself. (This has *got to go!!*)

8.
I first harm myself and *then* hurt everyone *around me,* family, employer. Also I endanger anyone who is *in my way* while I'm driving.

9.
Drinking helps me to "cope" with my problems. (This one makes me *sick!!*)

9.
Drinking *magnifies problems.* No one ever *drank a problem away.* Drinking *causes* many problems.

10.
A beer drinker can't be an "alcoholic." Only wine drinkers and the ones who drink hard stuff.

10.
Alcohol is alcohol! One can become addicted on beer, wine, cheap booze or top-shelf Scotch. It doesn't matter what we drink, but what *happens when we drink.*

11.
Hell! I want to *drink!* I want to do my drinking while I am *young.*

11.
"Young" people destroy themselves every day. There is no *set amount* I've got to "put away while I'm young."

12.
I can drive *better* with a few drinks or drunk than I can sober. (Oh, I hear that one often!)

12.
It only takes one drink to start damaging the part of the brain that causes one to think and make judgments. While driving, the head should stay clear to make split-second decisions.

13.
My parties were only successful when my friends were sent home *drunk.* (What was I calling "successful"??)

13.
Now I have parties where no booze is served, and we all have good, clean sober fun. I do not want my friends to leave drunk and drive, *endangering their lives* and others. Also, I do not want them to have an a.m. hangover or get arrested for drunk driving. (Now I *really* care about my friends.)

14.
Alcohol keeps you warm.

14.
When you are cold and drunk,
you just don't feel it. But many
people freeze on skid row *every
winter.*

15.
You have to drink a.m. to be an
"alcoholic."

15.
An alcoholic can get just as
drunk p.m. as a.m. When you
are drunk you are drunk.

16.
Alcoholics are daily drinkers.
Otherwise it's O.K.

16.
Alcoholics can be daily drinkers,
weekend or *periodic* drinkers.

17.
Alcoholics are the people on skid
row. Not a "better" person —
like *me!* (Huh??)

17.
The lowest percentage of
alcoholics are on skid row (3 to 5
percent). The highest percentage
are *business people, doctors,* and
upper middle class people. The
skid row people have the biggest
arrest record because they are
caught. Upper class pay their
way out, or have a bar at home.

18.
All alcoholics neglect their kids,
and are mostly dirty people.

18.
Some alcoholics *over-do* for their
kids out of *guilt.* They can
function and seem quite normal
and work hard to *prove* they are
"not alcoholics."

19.
I can stop drinking any time I
want to! (Not after addiction
takes over!!)

19.
All alcoholics stop sometime —
from sickness, jail, or to prove to
themselves they can. But the
point is not to start by not taking
that first drink.

20.
I *couldn't* be a common drunk
because I dress well. I don't fit
the image!!

20.
Jezebel dressed well also. A
drunk is a drunk no matter what
is *worn.*

21.
I couldn't be an alcoholic because I don't *beg* drinks.

21.
The alcoholic doesn't necessarily have to beg drinks. One can buy enough to kill themselves, and the seller will say smilingly, "keep coming back." He should add "fool." He gets richer, the alcoholic gets sicker.

22.
I'm O.K. because I work five days a week and am able to buy my own booze.

22.
Many working alcoholics seem quite normal. The boss and people around them never suspect they have a drinking problem. Weekenders can stay hidden for years!

23.
I wouldn't drink so much if my family stopped nagging me about my drinking.

23.
It is only a cop-out to say the family — or anyone or anything — causes one to drink. A person drinks because they turn it up and swallow it. No one holds a gun and forces us to drink.

24.
When I hide my bottles, I am putting something over on my family.

24.
I hid my bottle because I didn't want anyone to see how much I was drinking. Also, I didn't want to run out of booze (a sign one is becoming an alcoholic).

25.
I don't take anything from anyone! (We take any damn thing the world lays on us!!)

25.
Aggressiveness is alright if used the right way, but this world is give and take. We all have to take unpleasant remarks sometimes, and we can't fight our way out of everything violently.

26.
Everyone picks on me. (Me! Me! Me! Me! Me! Me!)

26.
Who am I to think that I am so important that everyone is concerned about *me?* So what if people talk, they talked about Jesus Christ.

27.
People talk about me, saying negative things!

28.
God made me a drunk and a bad person, yet he made others sober and good. Why did he make me different? (Must have been a bad day for Him!)

29.
God has forsaken me.

30.
Alcoholics come from a low background (like a prostituting mother and drunk father).

31.
If anyone disagrees or criticizes me, I hold resentments and pout. I think of some way to fix or get even with them.

32.
I live the life I love and love the life I live. (Usually said from a bar stool by some drunk fool!!)

33.
I must be a damn fool to do such crazy things when I drink.

34.
I was alright until I took that *last drink*.

27.
If a person lives, people will *say things.* We make our reputation.

28.
I no longer blame God. He did make me different than some people who can take a few drinks and stop. I am an alcoholic but not *bad,* just sick. He also made me capable of change.

29.
God did not forsake me. He never left me, but I left Him.

30.
Alcoholics come from *all* backgrounds, good and bad, rich and poor and any race, color or creed. Alcohol respects no one, young or old.

31.
I realize now that everyone doesn't *have to* agree with my ideas. Who the hell do I think I am? Resentments will destroy my peace of mind and could cause me to take that first drink.

32.
This was a lie and just a street phrase. It is not the *real me* at all. I do not love a drunk life.

33.
I am not a damn fool, although I acted like one. I was a sick person from excessive drinking.

34.
I was alright until I took the *first drink* that led me to the last drink.

35.
I can run my *own* life and don't need anyone telling me how to live my life. (Me! Me! Me!)

35.
I ran my own life and made a mess of it. I do need God and people to help me. People who need people are the luckiest people in the world. (I live in a world of *OTHERS.*)

36.
I don't need anybody. People are no good anyway. They are all out to *get you.*

36.
I need people and there are many who sincerely care and want to help others. They want nothing in return. People have something better to do than devote their lives to "getting me."

37.
All men are no good. All women are no good.

37.
Because I had unhappy experiences with a few men is no reason to blame *all men.* There are some *great men* still around. And great women!

38.
I don't give a damn what people think of me. (As I drink and drink to stop *caring.*)

38.
I *do* care what people think of me. What blew my mind was the loss of *respect.*

39.
Let us get drunk and *be somebody.* (Hot *Dog!!*)

39.
A drunk may be something but not really somebody. Booze can reduce us to a lower animal. When we are sober, we can become somebody better.

40.
I get a kick out of drinking! (A kick in my brain cells!!)

40.
Only the first few. Then wake up with a *hangover, shakes,* and *sick.*

41.
I look forward to weekends to drink and have fun.

41.
I did not have *fun.* A sick alcoholic lies. They had fun and can't even remember what happened.

42.
I can handle my booze.

42.
This was another lie. I did not
handle booze, it *handled me.*

43.
There is no happiness in this
world. I hate to see daylight
come and I hate nights.

43.
The world is beautiful. I love to
see the sunrise in the mornings
and open the blinds to welcome
it. Nights are beautiful.

44.
I want enough money to fill my
bar with different brands of
liquor so all my drinking friends
can drink all they want. That's
living good.

44.
Since I no longer waste money on
booze, I now can afford the
liquor-filled bar. Guess what? I
don't want *either.*

45.
I like the joints and drinking
crowds — and to ball all the
weekend.

45.
I don't want the joints' noise and
smoke-filled rooms. I enjoy my
peaceful weekends with my
husband, and we are happy
together.

46.
I am so ashamed of what I said
and did last night.

46.
I no longer suffer the remorse
and guilt. *I know what I do each
night.* I am not ashamed
anymore.

47.
God is punishing me for doing
wrong, and I deserve it.

47.
God is a loving God. He did not
make me drink. It was available.
I punished myself.

48.
I am going to be an old drunk
woman stumbling down the
street.

48.
I am going to grow into an old
sober lady.

49.
I worked and can buy my booze.
Free drinks save my money.
(What about my life??)

49.
I do not channel my mind onto
alcohol anymore. It is not
important. Or the center of my
world.

50.
All White people are no good
and hate all Black people. They
don't want to help us, only use us
for their personal gain.

50.
It was White people who helped
me. I was wrong to judge all
White people because of my bad
experiences in Alabama. There is
good and bad in all races. Who
am I to judge? All the White
people in Selma, Alabama were
not nigger-haters, just as all
Black people are not bad.

51.
Alcohol and lemon is good to
sweat the cold out (home remedy
often used by Blacks).

51.
Alcohol is taken into the body. It
doesn't matter if it is mixed with
tea or pee. Many times I got
drunk and caught more cold.

52.
It is alright to run with the
drinking people and hang out in
joints. (What business do we
have there??)

52.
Now that I am sober I have new
friends — not drinking buddies. I
do not go to joints and associate
with the drinkers. It's dangerous
for me. It is not good for my
sober thinking nor for the people
I try to help. It is like a minister
caught coming out of a whore
house, zipping up his pants and
saying, "I only went in to pray
for the prostitutes." Who would
believe him? Who would believe
me if I still went to the drinking
environment?

53.
I am better than the women who
have to do *anything* just to get
their booze. I turn my nose up at
them, because I have a job and
can pay for my drinks. Those
women are CHEAP.

53.
I am no better than the lady who
hustles drinks in bars. If I had
continued to drink and become
disabled or lost my job, I would
have been one of those ladies.
Once I took the first drink I
would have continued. The
woman is to be pitied who uses
her body only for drug alcohol.
But she is *hooked*, not *bad*. For
me it was just a *matter of time*.

54.
Alcohol helps me to sleep
soundly.

54.
Alcohol may help in the
beginning but once I became
hooked, *insomnia* set in and I
couldn't sleep.

55.
A few drinks cannot cause me
any brain damage.

55.
Brain damage starts with the first
drink. (*All* brains — not just
some brains!!)

56.
I have enough "will power" to
stop drinking anytime I want to.

56.
The alcoholic is a very sick
person who has an insidious
disease. Will power alone will
not cure the illness.

57.
Only a head shrink can help me.

57.
The psychiatrist can help some
people. But I was helped by
another alcoholic.

58.
AA will help me to taper off
drinking.

58.
AA told me to STOP drinking.
There is no such thing as the
chronic alcoholic tapering off.
Why? Because the first drink is
the one that got me drunk.

59.
Alcoholics are weak-willed or
insane people.

59.
Alcoholics are normal people as
long as they don't drink. Booze
changes people!

60.
Any doctor can help me to stop
drinking because he is
sympathetic and understands my
problem.

60.
All the doctors I saw did not
recognize or understand my
drinking problem, did not
counsel me one bit about
alcoholism, did not tell me where
to find help. One doctor said in
1973, "If it was left to me, I
would line all alcoholics up and
shoot them."

61.
Alcoholics cannot hold a job.

61.
Many chronic alcoholics hold jobs daily and seem quite normal. Yet we are slowly dying.

62.
I only drink *because* I have deeper problems.

62.
I never drank a problem in my life. Alcohol *caused me* problems. Alcohol *was* my problem.

63.
I am just a social drinker.

63.
Social drinkers do not drink themselves into a blackout, only problem drinkers do.

64.
It is alright to tell a few fibs to get by or keep from being found out while drinking.

64.
Problem drinkers become habitual liars. We have to lie to cover our tracks. And it's a confusing chaos because we often forget what lie we told.

65.
A man who does not drink is less masculine.

65.
A sober man is a real man. And the world respects a man who knows where he is and where he is headed. Hang in there, sober Brother!!!

66.
I can stop drinking alone. I don't need anyone to help me. I've been making it alone all these years.

66.
Very seldom can the chronic alcoholic stop drinking and stay sober alone. I had to have help from God and people. I didn't learn to drink "alone" — and I'm not going to get well "alone."

67.
I am the only girl and therefore *supposed to* take care of all my sick relatives and their problems.

67.
Robert Frost said the world is full of willing people. Some willing to work, the rest willing to *let them!* I owe *myself* something! I learned to help others *to help themselves.* Relatives *will survive* if I drop dead. I am not supposed to make myself miserable to make others happy.

68.
I am doing alright for myself. I have *nice things* just like the people who do not drink.

68.
I had to change my values from material *things* to *sobriety* (love for *Chaney*). We sleep in one bed at a time, one room at a time, eat one meal at a time, and when we die, nothing is buried with us.

69.
"Whatever comes up, comes out." (I opened my mouth and removed all doubts about being a fool! I say anything I please!!)

69.
I only opened my mouth to change feet. Only a fool speaks *everything* that enters their mind. I think more about what I'm saying!!

70.
Chewing gum, mouthwash, etc., will kill odors of alcohol! And nobody will know I've been drinking.

70.
The odor of alcohol is not restricted to the mouth. As you perspire, it comes out every pore. People *"know."* You are also *acting different*, even if you're smelling alright.

71.
You can drink vodka safely because it has no smell.

71.
Are you kidding? Vodka drinkers smell like a walking distillery also. Just like they've been drinking vodka!!

72.
I love drinking in bars, being a "finger-popping" drunk.

72.
The word "bar" was very appropriate for me. It barred me from honesty, hope and self-respect. The bar offered me only tears, heartaches, hangovers, shame, and hell on earth. I thought I was looking "sexy" but I was looking silly — especially when my elbows kept slipping off the bar!!

73.
It is fun and smart to top the others in telling toasts.

73.
Profanity is nothing to be proud of. The morning after "the night before" I felt cheap. What was I doing to myself?

74.
I will change him/her, and make them see things *my way*.

74.
I cannot change anyone. After all I didn't make them. But I can change myself. For instance — maybe *their way might be worth listening to!*

75.
God give me this man/woman, car, house, money, etc. (I prayed.)

75.
I learned to be careful what I asked or prayed for. We may get it! And it might be the last thing we need.

76.
Pour your own troubles. (Usually said while handing your buddies the bottle.)

76.
That is exactly what I was doing. *Pouring my own troubles.*

77.
I do not neglect my family.

77.
Oh yes, you do. A drunk is not very dependable, among other things.

78.
I only drink with my "extra" money.

78.
Working, family people have no *extra* money. A man once made this statement to me. He had nine children to support and his salary was their only income. His wife and kids were in need of shoes and clothing.

79.
Any man is a *real man* who can *handle his liquor.*

79.
You are no less than a man because you do not drink. A person can learn more, achieve more, *sober.*

80.
A white lie is O.K., just like a little sin.

80.
A lie is a lie, be it white, black, red, or brown. A crime is a crime — from stealing a loaf of bread to Watergating. They are all wrong — and all hurt *me* in the long run. Honesty is less *work!*

81.
I am the man of my house.
(Belch, burp!)

81.
Not when you are drunk. The
bottle is the "man of the house."

82.
All men/women who drink are
chasers.

82.
Not in all cases, especially when
you get hooked. It is just like a
dog chasing a car — when he
catches it, he can't drive it. Do
you dig me?

83.
You can't tell *me* not to drink.
You drink yourself.

83.
Everyone who drinks is not an
alcoholic! Some can drink it or
leave it alone. I know people
who have a drink each morning,
noon and night. They are now
over eighty years old and *have
never been drunk.* So they *can*
tell the problem drinker
something.

84.
Although my children are grown
up, I will *make it up to them for
neglecting them* as a child.

84.
You cannot unscramble an egg.
You can only start living better
today.

85.
The bar is *the place* to find a
good husband or wife.

85.
We hear complaints *later* that the
spouse "hangs out in bars too
much." Look for a mate
somewhere else.

86.
Lord, just help me to stop being
sick and help me out of trouble
(jail, broken home, loss of job)
and I *promise you* I will stop
drinking.

86.
When we are sober we no longer
have to bargain with God. "NO
more *deals!*"

87.
I used to hide my identity and
not even say my real name! The
name "Chaney" is unique —
there aren't too many ladies with
that name. The *nickname* "Sis"
was a protection for me, an *alibi!*
I could lie about my actions by
saying, "It must have been
another 'Sis' — after all there are
lots of people called Sis!"
Everyone would know if
CHANEY did something — but if
"Sis" did — they had to ask,
"Which Sis?"

87.
Now that I am sober, there isn't
any need for alibis — including
ALIBI NAMES. I can feel proud
of what Chaney does.

These changes in the way I *think* have been very important to the change in my life. If I had continued to "think
drunk," I would have *stayed* drunk. Some of these
statements took a long time to change. I wanted to share
them with you because I still hear them often from the
people who come for help.

Finding a Power greater than ourselves

Speaking of God or spiritual needs turns so many people
off. But for the alcoholics who want to remain sober, it is
important that we find *some* power greater than ourselves. What or who that power is isn't important. You
find *your* God as you understand God. Many good people
who just don't believe in God have told me they did not
take to AA because of the "spiritual part" of the Program,
yet these suffering human beings do need help. So as I
work with people, I have learned to say, "This is not a
religious program. You are here, and I am here to help
you with a drinking problem. Just keep your mind and
ears open and listen." I do not tell people that *any one*
thing or program will keep us sober.

1
Start taking one or two hits while socializing with the Brothers and Sisters.

2
Need more booze to get a charge.

3
Head trips begin, can't remember what's going down at work or at the crib.

4
Need a jug to get it together, hiding extra bottle in private stash, feeling guilty and real shitty after getting head bad.

5
Can't deal with the sauce. Get wasted, become a bad S.O.B. and fight.

6
Head trips getting worse, doing more off-the-wall things, blowing the mind and damaging the brain, Baby.

7
Begin to fail sexually. The DO-IT FLUID is keeping you from doing it.

8
Too much money spent on booze at home, hanging out in joints, or on the lots drinking with the bottle gang. Running from town to town. In trouble with the man (law).

9
Become scared of own shadow. Can't find peace of mind but keep trying to find peace from the **Courage Water**. Drinking more and more with anybody and anything. Shaking in the mornings, sick if drinking, sick if not drinking.

SOCIAL DRINKING〉HEADING FOR TROUBLE〉HOOKED〉

Hooked, Baby,
and in deep shit!!!

Roc

SKID ROW

SICKNESS

INSANITY

Got your shit together, Baby, and feel good again!

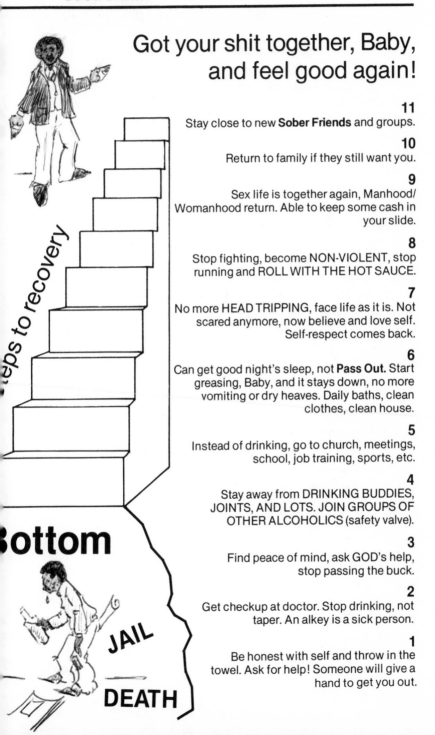

11
Stay close to new **Sober Friends** and groups.

10
Return to family if they still want you.

9
Sex life is together again, Manhood/Womanhood return. Able to keep some cash in your slide.

8
Stop fighting, become NON-VIOLENT, stop running and ROLL WITH THE HOT SAUCE.

7
No more HEAD TRIPPING, face life as it is. Not scared anymore, now believe and love self. Self-respect comes back.

6
Can get good night's sleep, not **Pass Out.** Start greasing, Baby, and it stays down, no more vomiting or dry heaves. Daily baths, clean clothes, clean house.

5
Instead of drinking, go to church, meetings, school, job training, sports, etc.

4
Stay away from DRINKING BUDDIES, JOINTS, AND LOTS. JOIN GROUPS OF OTHER ALCOHOLICS (safety valve).

3
Find peace of mind, ask GOD's help, stop passing the buck.

2
Get checkup at doctor. Stop drinking, not taper. An alkey is a sick person.

1
Be honest with self and throw in the towel. Ask for help! Someone will give a hand to get you out.

Steps to recovery

Bottom

JAIL

DEATH

Some people are staying sober in AA; some people join the church and find Jesus — and stay sober; some Blacks become Muslims and stop drinking; some people make it with psychiatric aid; and other people make it *alone.* The spiritual unrest is the act of drinking, trying to find peace in the bottle. There is no peace morning, noon, or night, because the nervous system is wrecked from excessive drinking. The more I drank to level off, the more upset and nervous I became. As that poison gradually drained from my body, I found peace. I had to really look and face *Chaney,* become aware of my faults and good points. I learned to say, "I'm sorry I was wrong." I couldn't have things my way all the time. I had to grow, I am still growing daily. I no longer pass the buck.

It's important for the recovering alcoholic to join a group to be with *people,* especially a group of people who have the same illness and really understand each others' problem. At some point, I understood that I simply could not drink. I could no longer lean on the alcohol crutch. I had tried it for years and it had proved to be an upper and *downer.*

When I got sober, life's problems continued. I had (and still have) days of depression. I am still a human being. On my bad days and during my trouble periods, I can always turn to my group. I can lean on them for real support and they don't let me down. The song "Lean On Me" provides some helpful philosophy for us . . .

"Into our life we all have pains
We all have sorrows.
Lean on me when you're not strong
And I'll be your friend.
I'll help you carry your load
You won't be alone.
That's all I need, is somebody
    to lean on.
Swallow your pride and you just
    call on me,

> Brother if you need a hand.
> We all need somebody to lean on.
> I just might have a problem that
> You'll understand,
> We all need somebody to lean on.
> Call me if you need a friend,
>   Just call me . . ."

And everybody needs someone *tangible* to lean on some-times. As I continued in an alcoholic group *my hope was renewed!* I said, "If they can make it so can I." They have given me the tools. Now I must do the *work*. My group did help me over many rough spots.

Back in 1972, my mother's doctor decided her right leg should be amputated. I was the one who had to make the decision one day and sign the permission slip. But I was able to do it *sober.* Her life was prolonged for thirteen months. And on November 18, 1973, when she died, I was still sober and was able to go through the sad ordeal. Whenever things got very rough for me during that time, my mind started playing tricks like "maybe one drink will tone you down." But I got through it by leaving my relatives and friends and going to an AA meeting. There I explained my fears, and was not without one of my sober friends from then on. All through the funeral service I kept hearing statements of support like, "Hang in there! Easy does it. Not one day at a time, but just a few more minutes! You can make it. You are not alone, Chaney." With the help of my Higher Power (and sober friends) I survived Mom's death *sober. Drinking will not bring back our loved ones.*

Getting medical help

Sometimes it's important that we get a physical checkup, especially when we are newly sober. Some of us are sicker than others. If you need medical aid, do not hesitate. When I reached my drinking bottom. I was very very sick and had to have both physical and psychiatric aid. My mind was confused from years of excessive drinking. I weighed only ninety-one pounds. I had gout. Surgery had to be done on my feet to correct bone injuries caused by drunken accidents. I had (and still have) ulcers from not eating regularly while I was drinking. During my stay in the hospital, they ran tests and found I was diabetic. I was dead on my feet. I know I would not be alive today if I had neglected getting medical aid.

I repeat: I am not qualified to write from a medical viewpoint because I am not trained in this field — and others working with alcoholics don't necessarily agree with me. However, from *my* experience with alcoholics, we usually seem to have an "addictive personality." *Excess* seems to be the hallmark of the alcoholic. For example, I drank *too much*. I smoke *too much*. Most of the time we worry *too much*, about any and everything. If we love someone, we love too much and are usually too possessive. We do little in moderation! What I am leading up to is a warning: if we are issued medication, we usually abuse tranquilizers, sleeping pills, and pain pills! What have we done but exchanged one drug for another? Please try to follow instructions that your doctor gives you. Do not lie. *Tell* your doctor that you are an alcoholic. And if your doctor doesn't understand the disease, get a new doctor who does. See if you can make it *without any* drugs.

The rewards of being sober

Many people haven't thought about what life might be like *sober* — or WHY BOTHER to *get sober?* It might be important to ask yourself what *you* can do and enjoy, how being sober can be rewarding to *you!* For me there have been many, many rewards. Booze is no longer my master — I only have *one* master, and that is GOD with no other GOD before HIM (namely booze).

I can get up in the morning and face the lady in the mirror with a smile! I can now love Chaney again. I am not ashamed of myself anymore. I have self-respect, and others respect me also. People still talk about me, but now they say nice things. I do not have to lie and cheat to cover my drinking life anymore. I try to be honest with myself and others. When I doubt my honesty, I am not too proud to say, "I am sorry, forgive me." Now I am able (physically too) to give an honest day's work, and feel good all day doing things that I wanted to do before alcohol took over my life. For example, right now I am going to college and writing this book! I realize that I shouldn't be a perfectionist, that I'm not perfect, and I DON'T HAVE TO BE. I just be myself and allow others to be themselves. I still make mistakes and allow others to make mistakes.

I stay closely involved with other dry alcoholics so I feel comfortable while abstaining from drinking. They are my companions. During my depressed moods and when I have problems, I can talk to them, and *not drink*. They are my people and understand me, as I do them.

Since I am sober, it is possible to keep money in my billfold at all times — no longer do I have to squeeze my budget to get a bottle of booze. I can now make future plans and not worry about whether or not I will be drunk! If my plans fail, maybe my Higher Power didn't feel it was what I needed. So I accept my failures and keep on pushing.

Maybe the *biggest* change is that my *life is now based on staying sober and helping others.* "It is better to give than to receive." I now realize the real meaning of that phrase. I live a very simple life and want to keep it simple. *The future seems possible if I am sober.*

I was able to start eating regularly as drug alcohol left my body. No longer was I waking up with hangovers. No longer was my head buried in the toilet stool! No more suffering from dry heaves when I even smelled food. To sit down to eat now and to enjoy a meal is great! This may not seem *important* to a nonalcoholic, but to drunks it is very important *to be able to eat.* There are some alcoholics who can eat like hell, but many are like me — I cannot eat *and* drink. (I was not "about to spoil my booze" with that ole stupid food.) The result is: I have ulcers *today.* Another luxury now is to be able to brush my teeth and tongue without vomiting. That is why many alcoholics' breaths smell like they have been chewing chinches (bed bugs). They would brush if they *could.*

As I got better, I began to sleep normally too. I was no longer drunk and full of alcohol, so I was getting normal and healthy rest. Nonalcoholics think nothing of this. But there is a whole lot of difference between *passing out and coming to* compared to *going to sleep and waking up!* When I was drinking I *came to,* to another morning of vomiting, to another day of remorse, guilt and shame. Now I can *wake up* to a beautiful day. I wake up and brush my teeth, and remember what happened the night before. I can wake up and look in the mirror and look Chaney square in the eyes. Now when I wake up, I keep in mind that I am an alcoholic and I say, "God help me to stay sober *today.*" Each night I don't forget to say, "Thank you for helping me to stay sober *today.*"

I started to lean more on my Higher Power than my "will power." The medical profession has declared alcoholism an illness and a disease, so it stands to reason that will power will not cure a disease. Will power will not cure glaucoma. And how about if a person has a bad case of diarrhea, and someone said, "Why don't you use will power and stop running to the bathroom so much?" Will power doesn't put brakes on their rectum, and they end up as shitty as a bull anyway! So will power *does not* work with alcoholism. And too, the alcoholic has more "will power" than anyone I know or he wouldn't stay drunk all the time. Will power just isn't the cure for an illness. Sober people and a Higher Power helps!

My fears lessened day by day as I stayed sober. I was losing my fear of fear. I didn't hear imaginary voices. I didn't feel that everyone was against me. I was no longer afraid that I could be found out. Another reward of sobriety! As my fears lessened, my self-confidence returned. I began feeling that I could do anything *others could!*

If I made a commitment, I felt confident that I could follow through. I no longer had to feel that I had failed before I started. A long time ago if someone asked me to bake a cake for the bake sale at church, I would say, "Yes, I'll bake one." And deep down inside I would add, "If I don't get drunk." Because I knew if once I got my head bad — forget it. But now when I say, "Yes," I can follow through.

As I stayed sober, realistic thinking returned. Only *more real* than ever before! I no longer lived in that world of fantasy *created by alcohol.* When I was drinking, I enjoyed sitting at the bar looking in the mirror. I could be anyone I wanted to be! I would drink and say to myself, "I look just like Lena Horne!" A few more drinks. "No, I look like Dorothy Dandridge!" I *imagined* that all the guys looked at me with *admiration.* And all the ladies with envy! The sick part of alcoholism is every alcoholic in the joint felt the same way. We were egotistical, sick people. Now as realistic thinking returned and I look in the mirror I say, "Hello Chaney, you ugly devil you! You are very plain outside, but you are beautiful *inside where it counts."* Now that's for real!

As I continued to grow, I realized that I could not run away from all problems. Many alcoholics run all over the country, but the geographical escape isn't always the answer. I am now about three thousand miles from Cincinnati, but California sells pretty good gin and beer too!! I learned to stand still and deal with me and whatever problem arises. Now, some problems I *can* solve and some I can't. But, as I continue to think for myself, I keep in mind — "Accept the things I cannot change, and change the things I can." Not only will an alcoholic run from town to town, but from gal to gal or guy to guy — suffering a spiritual unrest. We learn to stand still and roll with the punches.

Many of us are able to return to family and friends, with no more running away and hiding in the bottle or another town. It is beautiful when the alcoholic's home is saved. An alcoholic who stops drinking and recovers becomes a new person. It is vitally important that the spouse and entire family "hang in" with the sick person if they can — and yet, I've seen the alcoholic "outgrow" the sober spouse. Sometimes they may not be able to live together any longer. Often the sober spouse loses his or her floor mat, because the alcoholic is now changed and won't be pushed around. Sometimes, the alcoholic "tore their ass" so badly while drinking that the families *do not* want him or her back anymore!

Whatever happens, we accept the things we cannot change. I did not return to my broken homes, but that's yesterday's news.I learned not to look back or wallow in self-pity. I kept on pushing. My Higher Power (which I choose to call God) knows me and my heart. He knew that I wanted a good husband; eventually he gave me one. He always gives us what we *need.*

The closest I ever came to turning away from God was when I was with Steve. But now I realize that I would be either in an insane asylum or dead if *that* marriage had survived. (Steve is still drinking, since he "doesn't have a drinking problem." If I had continued drinking with him, I would never have made it.)

And if Grant had not dominated and rejected me for drinking too much, I would not have called AA for help. Constantly, I am learning to accept the things I cannot change. So if you *can* get the family back together, good! If you *can't,* remember you didn't get sober for *them* in the first place! Just take care of Number One by *not drinking.* I honestly would rather *die today sober* than live twenty more years *drunk.*

Just as drug alcohol may cause a sexual decline there may be an increase in sexual interest as this drug is drained from the body. No longer is a man castrating himself by drinking too much. As I work with people, the wives often give the feedback that their sex life is more beautiful than ever. The husbands of the alcoholic woman say the same! Now we all know that sex isn't everything, but it darn sure is important for normal people.

With me I finally reached the point where sex interrupted my drinking pattern. It took "too much time" and I only wanted to continue drinking. Maybe you didn't get that sick. If you are thinking, "I've never gotten *that bad,*" please add the word *"YET"!* Because if you can identify with my story, you are in trouble. And if you continue to drink it could happen. It may seem hard to believe a little bottle of booze about eleven or twelve inches tall (and sitting still) can whip a six-foot man to his knees! Alcohol is powerful and patient. It will wait on you to knock yourself out.

Drinking is very time-consuming and when I quit, I had to find new interests to replace it. Anytime something is taken from a person, it should be replaced with something else. When I stopped drinking there was a vacuum that had to be filled. Going back to school and doing my homework helped to fill that void. Another thing, I never refused to go and help another alcoholic when called. Now that I was thinking *positive,* I started doing constructive things with my life. I set goals and worked to accomplish them.

As I write this book, I've been in college four and a half years already working on my A.A. degree in social science. I *will* have my degree by the spring of 1977. That is one goal which I will accomplish. Another goal was to write this book. I *am* writing and I *will* complete it. So I have replaced fears with new ideals by saying *I am*

Capable! You are Capable too!

Dollars don't bring sobriety

My values in life have changed. I was too hung up on material things. I was keeping up with the Joneses. I felt that I was great *because* I had a job and I *didn't have to beg* and had my own home. I had nice clothes and a car and a few extra dollars in the bank. But I was still a sick drunk. And when I really took a good look at myself and my scrambled life, I *had* nothing.

I have worked with many ladies worth three and four hundred thousand dollars. But they have *nothing* until they learn to stop placing all values on dollars and booze and *place value on sobriety.* For example, one lady worth about four hundred thousand dollars called for help. As I was taking her to the hospital she said, "Chaney, I would give every dollar and everything I own to be able to stay sober and *feel like you are feeling right now.*"

I said, "You can't pay for sobriety with dollars, you'll have to *work* for it. As long as you sit in your penthouse on your rich ass and think you are too *good* and too *cute* to reach out and help even what society calls the lowest drunk, you are going to stay drunk. You are going to have to start saying that your wealth doesn't make you any better than any other drunk. A rich drunk is no different from a poor one. A drunk is a drunk and you are one."

She said, "Who do you think you are talking to *me* like this?" I said, "Oh, I am only one drunk talking to another. Only difference is you are rich and White and I am poor and Black, but we are together." She sadly said, "All my life I have *had to be a lady.*" All the way to the hospital she began to chant, "Screw you, screw you," to every one we passed on the freeway. Even when I was helping to sign her in, she was still saying, "Screw you, screw you," to the receptionist, nurses, and doctors.

Profanity is nothing to be proud of, and I am still

working on that because I'll still drop four-lettered words without thinking. But in this lady's case, she started *coming down to earth!* She got better and walked in the center one day with her little doggie who was wearing a $5,000 diamond collar. She looked at me and smiled and said, "Chaney, screw you." She is now abroad, and I received a letter from her in which she wrote, "I am still sober. My first value now is placed on sobriety. Thanks for using what you called *tough love* on me. It brought me off my pedestal. My peers think I've flipped, but screw them all." She is now placing her own welfare *first!*

Drunks are just like a bucket of crabs

It is so very, very important to stick with new sober friends, *not drinking buddies.* The people I associated with were basically *drinking buddies.* They really didn't give a damn about me. And yours don't give a damn about you either. They are not *friends. A friend will not insist on you drinking something which makes you sick.* With drinking buddies, watch them say, "Oh come on, one little drink can't hurt you. Don't pay attention to anyone who says you can't drink."

You see, misery loves company. Practicing drunks are just like a bucket of crabs. Every time one tries to get out, the others reach up and pull him back. Crabs' legs are made so they can hook on to each other and if they would allow *just one* to make it to the top, then they all could hook their claws to each other and get out of the bucket. Unfortunately, they hold each other back and they all just stay there, imprisoned.

Stay away from drinking buddies

It is important to stay away from *drinking buddies.* If you go to jail for drunk driving, they are not going with you. When you get into trouble they will sit around and talk shit like "Old Joe Blow wasn't *drunk,* the cops *just picked on him."* They are now ready to get into *someone else's car* and drink. Your drinking buddies are not going to contribute to your fines. They are going to drink up their money and not help *you*. (And don't get angry, because if *they* get into trouble you're not going to help them either.) Drinking buddies usually don't help financially, don't have time to visit us in the hospitals and won't come to look at our dead ass either. But they will sit in a bar and cry in their beer and say what great friends you all were — and how they thought so much of you but, "I just can't stand to go look at the body!" The truth is they can't stop drinking long enough to make it! I had to face these facts. I am three thousand miles and five years away from my ole drinking buddies. Not *one* has called to say, "I miss you." But my new *sober friends* call, write, and see me. They don't want anything from me. I don't want anything from them. We just care, and want to stay sober.

Putting away the Blady Mae

To stay sober, I had to learn to control my emotions. It is not smart to always be *so quick* to get somebody *told*. I don't mean to allow people to walk on you. One doesn't get sober *to be a floor mat*. But we learn to be *tolerant*. I had to (and I am still working on this) learn to control my emotions. I no longer react violently, and don't need to carry knives to protect myself by injuring another human being. I don't choose to take life, but to help *save life*. I am *growing!*

I am acting more like an adult than a spoiled brat. For example, one day, I was counseling a lady who came in *hostile* since she was a court-appointed client. I talked with her for about fifteen minutes and saw her getting "wind in her jaws" and rolling her eyes at me. Finally she said, "I wish you would just *shut up talking to me*. I don't like you anyway. In fact, I can't stand you."

I said calmly, "Then you've got a problem, darling. I

will excuse you and you can go home and deal with it, while I take care of my next client." I know that was so different from the other Chaney who would have used a few four-letter words and backed them up with Blady Mae (knife). So I have grown, but I still have a long way to go to overcome my aggressive behavior. We can learn to be less violent.

Looking after personal appearance

When we are drinking, we don't take care of our bodies. We don't take baths or change clothes. Many drunks are today sleeping in doorways and alleys. I had a *shelter*, but I neglected my personal appearance. I was not very "tidy," lying in a wet bed. A sick drunk who stops drinking begins looking at himself or herself. They gain self-respect and start doing something about their personal appearance. A clean person looks better and feels better. Cleanliness is next to Godliness — and helpful for getting next to people too!

Making a decent living

When I no longer wasted my money on booze, I was able to start steps for financial security. Let's face it, it takes money in order to survive in our society. I don't mean making a God out of dollars (as we made a God out of the bottle) but making a decent living. We again can put a few dollars away for a rainy day, being more aware of all these things going on around us. No longer do we drink ourselves into oblivion to escape from life's situations. Being sober, "the alcoholic is given his membership card back into the human race."

If we are fortunate enough to still be employed, our employer's confidence is renewed when we stay sober. He can see a change. I no longer went to work with Monday hangovers and watched the clock. I no longer prayed, "Lord, just help me to make this day and get the *hell out* of here." If we want to be paid, we should do an honest day's work. Many an alcoholic will fall short of his work, looking for hiding places to sleep during working hours (and will get angry if caught). The drunk is the first to raise holy hell if he or she is a few cents short in the pay check. We must start being honest with ourselves. The employer will see the *new you* and trust you again.

No, we aren't fooling our employers! At least every day I get a call from an employer who says, "I would like to know what you have to offer for help to one of my employees. He/she is a good person and a good worker, but lately is falling short in his/her work, or coming to work smelling of alcohol."

My answer usually is, "You are able to call the punches. So let the person know you are aware. Give them the choice of either seeking help or being fired. You will be doing him or her a favor. I suggested that you don't *cover for the alcoholic* because you are only helping him or her to sink further. The problem of alcoholism cannot be dealt with if it's swept under the rug. The alcoholic must realize first that *there is an existing problem* and that he or she can't deal with it alone. Once the alcoholic finds a group, he or she will have people who really care and understand. And these people will be there to lean on whenever we weaken. If we aren't too proud to say, 'Help me.' "

The beauty of seeing sober

Eventually we do start *enjoying sobriety!* I didn't right at the beginning, but I was happy not to feel sick and guilty. I heard and saw the "winners" in AA walking around smiling and asking each other, "How are you enjoying your sobriety?"

"Oh, it's just beautiful!"

I was brand new and still wet behind the ears, so I couldn't see what the *hell* they were so damn happy about! I didn't feel *all that happy!* A little "taste" would have been fine but I was told that I couldn't have it. Yet I didn't want to go back to the bottom of the cliff and hurt some more. But I was too new to really *enjoy* being sober. So don't feel disappointed if you do not feel elated right away. *It takes time,* and you, just like me and every other recovering alcoholic, have to work at it.

It was about a year before I really shared the "old timer's feeling." It rains a lot in Ohio. I remember one day when a hard shower came, immediately followed by the sun coming out again. I was walking out the front steps and saw raindrops on the shrubbery on each side of the porch. They were *big raindrops.* As the sun shined on them, they looked like small green trees sprinkled with diamonds. The green was so *green,* the raindrops were so shiny and beautiful that I couldn't move. I just stood there, staring. I said out loud, "My God, how beautiful!" I looked up and down the street. The dampness on the hillside and the shrubbery in the neighbors' yards looked beautiful. It took a little while for me to start to *SEE* the world as "beautiful" again.

When I was drunk, I couldn't see what was around me. By the time I walked out the door, I couldn't see the shrubbery anyway! I am sure it had been raining on the shrubbery all the while. Now, I try to appreciate every little thing, and take nothing for granted. I am grateful for *everything.*

Those of you who are reading this will have to discover whether you can identify with my story — and whether you too are having a problem with alcohol. There are many ways to have a problem with drinking. I suffered for years before I learned that there were different types of alcoholics. I was strictly a weekend alcoholic. There are some people who are *daily* drinkers, but they are alcoholics too. There are people who are *periodic* alcoholics and they may drink for a couple of weeks and stay drunk. Then they may stop drinking and may not touch another drop for two or three months. Nevertheless, that person is still an alcoholic.

We are alcoholics whether we are weekend alcoholics, periodic alcoholics, or daily drinkers. An alcoholic is a person who is no longer responsible for his or her actions after he or she drinks. An alcoholic is a person who is no longer dependable after he or she drinks. An alcoholic is a person who loses control after he or she drinks.

A non-alcoholic will cash the paycheck, have a drink, go on home, and think nothing about it. But the alcoholic will cash the check and sit right there until he/she spends too much out of that check, or drinks to the point of *drunk*. An alcoholic can get paid on Friday night, cash the check at the bar, and wake up somewhere in some motel with some lady or man without a damn dime left! Meaning that when that alcoholic took that *first* drink he or she lost control.

If you are fortunate and still have your family, sobriety brings a togetherness that you never had before. A recovering alcoholic is grateful, because every little thing is important. So when the home is saved we know just how fortunate we are, because we are certainly used to hearing of broken homes. It is common to hear of from one to six divorces among alcoholics. So as we change, we try to work on self and see where our shortcomings are. Seldom is anyone 100 percent right or 100 percent wrong — drunk or sober, alcoholic or nonalcoholic. Someone said that, "There is a little bit of good in the worst of us and a little bit of bad in the best of us." WE DON'T HAVE TO BE PERFECT — just sober.

It is of vital important for the entire family to understand that sometimes the alcoholic cannot resist the first drink (and counseling and groups do not give enough support and strength right away). Some of us are sicker than others. We may have to resort to Antabuse; this is a drug which, in combination with even a small amount of alcohol, produces nausea and severe discomfort. It is taken daily, but is effective for as long as ten days or more after the last dose. This is effective protection against impulsive drinking, so some alcoholics and their spouses ask for Antabuse. Whatever works for you, *DO IT*. But work at it. Sobriety will not find you. You will have to seek it.

Snowing the psychiatrists

Some people need psychiatric aid, because some of us become very mentally ill from excessive drinking. However, I have seen so many times where the alcoholic will try snowing the psychiatrist! They will tell him what he or she wants to hear! But once the drunk is faced with another drunk, it is hard for them to run their game. All us alcoholics have played most of the same games also. In plain words, you can't bullshit a bullshitter.

The alcoholic often *succeeds* in snowing the psychiatrist. For example, I never told the psychiatrist and the doctors just *how much* I drank. I lied and told them I had a "few" drinks sometimes on weekends. It was a cop-out which let him put all the blame on my childhood. I didn't tell him that guilt from my present life style was eating me alive. My psychiatrist dealt at length with my mother, with how much she loved my brothers, and with how I was a daddy's baby. I went along with him, happy that he put the blame on Mom instead of my drinking. Passing the buck!

When he did discuss alcohol with me a little bit, I didn't understand, because he used words so big I couldn't even find them in the dictionary. I remember thinking, "What the hell is he talking about?" But when I was faced with my problem by a recovered alcoholic, you better believe I knew what they were talking about.

One day, a lady came to my office straight from her psychiatrist. She talked with me for about forty-five minutes and then said, "Chaney you know, I am telling you things that I have not told my psychiatrist. And I have been going to him for a year. I am not about to tell that 'White Man' all my business. I'm not going to tell him that I woke up in a motel with some strange man, and don't know where I picked him up. And I'm not about to talk about my husband to him either. Some White people already think we Blacks are dirt, so I ain't about to low-rate myself and people to him. He'll never write every-thing *I did* on his little pad! But since you are a Sister, let me tell you like it is because I know you understand where I am coming from."

Another lady told me that her psychiatrist had her hospitalized eight times. She even had shock treatments. Yet each time she was drunk within two weeks after she was home. Now she has been sober for four years, and he takes credit for her sobriety. She said he didn't do it. "I never would have made it if I hadn't had someone waiting to help me when I got out. He would work with me twice a month in his office when I was out. Then he went to *his part* of town, and I went back to the ghetto. I was lost and scared and that resulted in me drinking again. I am making it today because my Black people are here to lean on when I need them. I am no longer alone, lost and scared," she told me.

One day a psychiatrist called my office and asked if I would please come help with a client (his patient) who was giving him a hard time. She was screaming, *"Ain't you my head shrink?"* He answered quietly, "Yes, Miss." She said, "Well, *shrink my head, damn you!* I am on the couch!" Oh, she was putting on a show for the people.

I said to her, "Stop acting like a damn fool. Come on and get your drunk ass out of here, disrupting these people." She started crying and said to him, "You can't make me tell you nothin'. Now write that down!" Was she crazy? No! She just wanted attention. And the alcoholic will do anything to get it. We alcoholics have to be careful even when we attempt suicide, because we may hurt ourselves while bullshitting. But at least we get attention.

One of my very wealthy ladies was checked into a drying-out clinic. There she was told to drink *two drinks*, until a bell was rung when she would stop drinking. After a certain period of time she would be retrained and "could return to society as a social drinker." She told me laughingly that they *thought* she had only a "couple" of drinks, but really she had a bottle hidden in her douche bag. Six months later I saw her at her doctor's office where she was bleeding to death (flooding).

Yes, the alcoholic will sometimes snow the psychiatrist and doctor, but seldom can they snow another drunk. If your psychiatrist is not keeping you sober, try another drunk who is now staying sober. If you cannot pray yourself dry through organized religion, try another drunk. The alcoholic has already walked the thousand miles in your shoes and knows what is happening *inside* and *outside* of you.

Special problems of Blacks

Some people may believe that my poverty childhood caused me to become an alcoholic. But to me, that is partially a cop-out because many people have gone through as much (and more) than me and did not turn to drinking. Yet the fact cannot be ignored that Blacks have always been an oppressed people in American society. Out of frustration, many *do* turn to alcohol and/or other drugs to relieve the tension of our oppressed existence.

For example, I have seen Blacks and Whites working side by side doing the same job, yet the Blacks were paid one half the salary received by the Whites. We have been the last hired and the first fired, even though many times we are best qualified.

But drinking isn't the answer to the Black's problem. When you wake up, problems are still there. In many cases more problems have been added. For example, *jail*. I was in court one day with another client, and saw a Black man brought in with chains around his waist. He had pulled an armed robbery while drunk, and stated that he didn't remember what happened. I asked myself, "How long will my people buy alcohol to put them *back* in chains and enslave themselves?"

Naturally, all Blacks object to being controlled by Mr. Charlie — yet many liquor stores are opened in our communities and we continue to support them by drinking our manhood and womanhood away. It is time that we Blacks stop and realize that alcohol was used to control and keep our fore-parents *in their place,* as far back as slavery time. They couldn't make escape plans or any other helpful decisions while drunk, and the slave master knew this. They were all more oppressed than we. They lived under the lash of the whip, half-starved and treated like lower animals. Yet many survived sober, and today we are a great proud Black people. They *ALL did not become alcoholic!*

Many alcoholics were born with a silver spoon in their mouth and never knew any money problems. Yet they are just as alcoholic as I am. So I accept what I have been told: I am allergic to alcohol.

If I eat certain foods which give me an abnormal reaction, I get sick. If I take penicillin, I get an abnormal reaction — I will break out in knots as big as peas. If I take the first drink, there is an abnormal reaction! I immediately get an *uncontrollable compulsion to drink,* more and more until I am wiped out. I accept the fact that I will never be cured. Our medical profession can transplant a heart but cannot cure the alcoholic. Some doctors are alcoholics too.

I am still very fortunate to have the disease of alcoholism, compared to some diseases. I can arrest my illness by *not drinking.* But the cancer patients can't arrest their illness. I am as normal as any other human being as long as I don't drink.

God knows I am sorry for some things in my past, but

my past does not have to make the future impossible! I do not go around with a hung-down head. No lady on this earth is any better than Chaney. I have a problem and I'm doing something about it, one day at a time. Everyone has done something wrong. No one is perfect.

I was at the bottom of that cliff for many years but I am not there today. And I am so grateful, because I realize that *today* is the first day of the rest of my life. The recovering alcoholic can be *reasonably happy*.

Often it seems that I can hear my Dad sing: "Amazing Grace, how sweet the sound that saved a wretch like me! I once was lost, but now I'm found; was blind, but now I see. Through many dangers, toils, and snares, I have already come; 'tis Grace hath brought me safe thus far, and Grace will lead me home."

My book cannot end like a fairy tale that says, "And I lived happy forever after!" I am still working hard at living peaceful and sober *one day at a time*. That is the way we stay sober.

I thank my HIGHER POWER whom I choose to call GOD; I thank Alcoholics Anonymous and people who care about me. *TODAY*, I CAN SAY, "I'M *BLACK* AND I'M *PROUD!*" AND "*I'M BLACK AND I'M SOBER!!!*"
Amen! Amen!! Amen!!!

About the Author

Chaney Allen — author, lecturer, teacher, counselor — has been joyfully sober since 1968, when she made a commitment to God and humanity to spend the rest of her life doing ANYTHING to help ANYBODY suffering from alcoholism. Yes, she DID earn her Associate of Arts degree in social science from the City College of San Diego in 1977, as expected, besides taking courses in counseling at the University of Santa Cruz. Even more important to her than her prized A.A. is her "AA," the education she found in the fellowship of Alcoholics Anonymous. This background, along with her own recovery — with dignity — from the indignities of her own drinking days and her talents for helping others, have made her an authority in her field. She is a founder and member of the California Black Commission on Alcoholism and a founder of the California Women's Commission on Alcoholism. She has been associated since 1971 with the Alcoholism and Counseling Education Center (ACEC), where she has developed techniques for working with minority alcoholics. She helped organize two rehabilitation houses and played a part in establishing a women's detoxification center. The U.S. Navy Rehabilitation Clinic in San Diego calls on her regularly to lecture counselor trainees. She has taken part in dozens of workshops, both as student and teacher, and has appeared on television and in a film, "New Beginnings: Women, Alcohol and Recovery."

As a young woman, Chaney Allen left her native Alabama — her strict upbringing in a CME minister's family and the unhappiness of a teenage marriage — to move to Cincinnati, where she began the destructive pattern of weekend partying and drinking. She has worked in a defense plant, in a beauty shop, at a dry cleaner's, at a country club, in food services, and, after moving to California in 1970, as a silk-screener. In her present vocation, she has at last found a medium for her special vitality.

Chaney Allen now lives in Chula Vista, California, surrounded by a wildly blooming garden and a houseful of healthy plants that respond — just like people do — to her nurturing and warmth.